JUDAISM'S THEOLOGICAL VOICE

Chicago Studies in the History of Judaism
A Series Edited by William Scott Green

JACOB NEUSNER

JUDAISM'S THEOLOGICAL VOICE

The Melody of the Talmud

THE UNIVERSITY OF CHICAGO PRESS • CHICAGO AND LONDON

Jacob Neusner is Distinguished Research Professor of Religious Studies at the University of South Florida and the author of numerous books including, most recently, *Judaism and Story: The Evidence of the Fathers according to Rabbi Nathan.*

The University of Chicago Press, Chicago 60637
The University of Chicago Press, Ltd., London
© 1995 by The University of Chicago
All rights reserved. Published 1995
Printed in the United States of America

04 03 02 01 00 99 98 97 96 95 1 2 3 4 5

ISBN: 0-226-57648-5 (cloth)
      0-226-57649-3 (paper)

Library of Congress Cataloging-in-Publication Data

Neusner, Jacob, 1932–
    Judaism's theological voice : the melody of the Talmud / Jacob
Neusner.
        p.   cm. — (Chicago studies in the history of Judaism)
    Includes index.
    1. Bible. O.T.—Liturgical use. 2. Bible. O.T.—Accents and
accentuation. 3. Cantillation. 4. Talmud—Hermeneutics.
5. Talmud—Study and teaching. 6. Jewish law—Interpretation and
construction. 7. Judaism—Doctrines. I. Title. II. Series.
BM663.N48   1995
296.3—dc20   94-33405
                                                         CIP

For my rabbi
Joel H. Zaiman

Said Rabbah, "Even though our ancestors have left us a scroll of the Torah, it is our religious duty to write one for ourselves, as it is said, 'Now therefore write down this song and teach it to the people of Israel, put it in their mouths, in order that this song may be my witness within the people of Israel" (Deut. 31:19).

Babylonian Talmud tractate Sanhedrin 21B

Contents

Prologue

$\mathcal{H}$oly Israel meets God in the Torah, which is God's self-manifestation to Israel and humanity. The encounter takes place in song, when holy Israel sings the words of the Torah, affirming, "This is the Torah that Moses presented to the children of Israel upon the instruction of the Lord." The moment of the always-sung proclamation frames the occasion of meeting, knowing God as God wishes to be known. From antiquity onward, music carried the words, and, sometimes, melody without words bore meaning too. Holy Israel assembles to sing the Torah in two places: synagogue and yeshiva or center for the study of Torah for God's sake. It follows that the conduct—the singing—of holy Israel in the synagogue and academy or yeshiva in the hour of the giving and the receiving of the Torah marks the moment and the locus at which Israel meets God. In the words and music, gesture and movement, dance and drama and sentiment, attitude, and emotion of that moment, God is made manifest in the congregation of Israel. That is where God has chosen to become known to humanity—so the Torah says, so holy Israel affirms.

Here I set forth those who receive the Torah as God's self-manifestation. I explain the living faith that also is described, analyzed, and, in the context of this world, interpreted in academic writings. I not only describe the logic and rationality of the Torah, the oral part of the Torah in particular. I mean through the explanation to make logical and rational in the mind of the reader the religious world of the Torah as that world sets forth in the Torah how God meets Israel and, through Israel, humanity. I explain for the reader, whether a believer or not, whether a Judaist or not, whether Jewish or not, the orderly, coherent, rigorous and insistent and, to the faithful, compelling truth of the Torah's manifestation of God. Accordingly, in this work, through the medium of engaged description on every page, I engage in sustained advocacy: constructive theology.

What I advocate specifically is that the faith of the Torah is coherent, proportioned, cogent, logical, and rational, within the framework of its premises and its established truths and its givens and its facts. That is why, to begin with, I identify the irreducible truths that in my view the Torah properly studied tells us about God: where and how we know God.

This also explains why I set forth what I conceive to be the future task of constructive theology of the oral part of the Torah, spelling out how the faithful, in studying the Torah, may find a place in the eternal dialogue, the open-ended conversation, made possible between Israel and God by God's self-manifestation in the Torah. I lay out a program of constructive theology for synagogue and academy (or yeshiva), a program natural to the categories and canon: in the written Torah of both, and also in the liturgy—in Siddur, ordinary order of prayers, and Mahzor, order of prayers for the Days of Awe—of the one and in the Talmud of the other.

It is a program, also, that can bear fruit, decades hence, in a systematic theology: a coherent account of everything, all together, all at once. If this book accomplishes its goal, many people will find in that same program a set of interesting questions and productive, even transforming, inquiries. And they will join the work. For theology in Judaism, which is the study of the Torah as a mode of receiving God's giving of the Torah, forms the welcome task of every generation of the faithful, and, each in its way, every generation has fulfilled that task. How Israel found God in the

Torah varies from age to age, but it is the simple fact that, outside of the Torah, holy Israel has never conceived God to have been made manifest.

The governing metaphor of my re-presentation of theological encounter derives from the realm of music. To meet God is like hearing live music: the encounter with God is like the musical moment. That is because performed music always is an event, a happening ephemeral but perfect for its moment, not to be replicated. It is magical, enchanting, and transforming—acutely present in tense and effect. So—the record of the Torah shows—is the moment of encounter with God's presence in the Torah. And that is natural, too, for the meeting with God in song. For the language of revelation—the native category is "the giving of the Torah"—uses the present tense. When in the synagogue the reading of the written part of the Torah is prefaced with a blessing; the obligatory blessing speaks of the eternal action that is continuous and present: ". . . who gives the Torah." The academy or yeshiva receives its part—the oral part—of the Torah as a set of claims about the truth that pertains for all time but especially at this moment of reasoned encounter. The immediacy of the giving of the Torah accounts for the vitality of contention in that setting. So in both loci God gives the Torah to Israel—not gave, but gives. The principal setting for the self-manifestation of God, therefore, is in today's synagogue liturgy and in the contemporary labor of learning in the academy or yeshiva.

The theological voice of Judaism (the worldly word for the faith) in the native categories of the faith, then, is dual: the synagogue's chanting of the Torah in one medium, the written part; the yeshiva's singing of the Torah in the other medium, the oral. That is because in the synagogue the written Torah is declaimed on Mondays, Thursdays, and the Sabbath day. In the yeshiva or study place (not a building but an assembly of sincere disciples) the oral Torah now written down in the Talmud and related documents is energetically analyzed, with dialogue in acute contention. Those are simple, worldly facts, and, in the language of the world, Judaism lives as a religion in those two places. While beyond their walls, in the secular world, the task of holy Israel is to sanctify the secular—" . . . this is the fast I desire . . . to share your bread with the hungry and to take the wretched poor into your home; when you see the naked, to clothe him, and not to ignore your own kin" (Is. 58:6, 7)—it is in the Torah, and only there, that Israel meets God as God is made manifest by God's own word. That is where holy Israel learns to identify the face of God, also, in the world: "in our image, after our likeness."

It follows that the governing facts about the Torah come to us from the vivid activities of synagogue and yeshiva: they tell us what happens in those places when the Torah is received in prayer, proclamation, and learning. That Israel meets God in the Torah in particular when, in a setting of piety and reverence, the Torah is sung tells us that Israel encounters God in song. Israel, therefore, sings its way across the ages to Heaven. That is what it means to allege (in descriptive language) that the theological voice of Judaism sings, or, in the language of faith, in the Torah God sings to Israel.

This book will describe the notes to the music. Specifically, I promise to explain how, just as, while a map is not territory, a map shows us where to go and how to get there, so while the notes are not the music, the notes tell us what to sing to re-create the sound. In that way, as the musician re-presents and, therefore, here and now, in re-creating creates the music, so we, Israel, here and now receive the Torah, which is to say, we meet God in its song as Moses did, as Elijah did, as the prophets did, and as our sages of blessed memory knew God, so in the Torah as their disciples we know God. As the performer realizes (and also interprets) the composer's ideas, so in the song of the Torah, Israel realizes—but in its own voice that minute—God's song.

And on the validity of what I have just said rests the entire picture I shall offer concerning precisely where and how, in the Talmud of Babylonia in particular, we hear one paramount theological melody of the Torah: God's singing. At stake in the end is where we perceive the sound of silence, to be filled by us, with our song too. So the stakes are very high, in fact, the highest.

Upon those two coherent facts—the singing of the Torah in its

two media and loci—I build the structure, and form the generative components, of a theological system for the normative and
cogent belief of Judaism. That is, in this work of constructive theology I portray the picture of God in words and music that the
Torah composes for holy Israel. Because the Torah is always sung,
never merely said or read, it is through the metaphor of music that
I offer an account of how I believe those faithful to the Torah ("Ju-
daists," practitioners of Judaism, in secular language) listen to the
melody of the Torah. Constructive theology moves beyond the descriptive at the outer limit of the Torah. Where the Torah falls
silent before our curiosity, space opens up for us to participate in
the receiving of the Torah. We who receive the Torah as God's
perfect and ultimate self-manifestation in the study of the Torah
may even join in the singing. Our own voices join; the melody of
our minds melds. We hear the Talmud's melody, and we fill the
silence with song. Explaining the meaning of these asseverations
defines the program of this book.

I, therefore, mean to conduct a constructive-theological inquiry
into the meaning of the simple and acknowledged fact of Judaism
that God is made manifest in the Torah. Theology—rigorous
thought about religious truths aimed at forming a systematic and
cogent, philosophically valid structure of propositions—takes its
place in a religious system by providing a reasoned account of
what the faithful in full rationality know about God. That is not
the only way of theological discussion, nor is it, in the world of
Judaism, the principal way. Indeed, to know the difference between what is offered here and what one reads in other kinds of
writing about theology as well as of theological writing, a brief
definition is in order.

Theology may be factually studied as an aspect of the study of a
religion; theology also is set forth as a chapter in the practice of
religion. The former, historical theology, undertakes the description, analysis, and interpretation of theological systems put forth
by a religion. The latter, constructive theology, if it sets forth an
entire theological system, systematic theology means rationally to
explore the faith especially for the edification of the faithful. I find

a suitable definition for the work of constructive theology, undertaken here, in the definition of Ingolf Dalferth:

> [Theology] rationally reflects on questions arising in pre-theological religious experience and the discourse of faith; and it is the rationality of its reflective labor in the process of faith seeking understanding which inseparably links it with philosophy. For philosophy is essentially concerned with argument and the attempt to solve conceptual problems, and conceptual problems face theology in all areas of its reflective labors.[1]

That defines my goal here and explains why I identify for rational reflection the bedrock facts of Judaic faith: the sung theology of synagogue and academy or yeshiva.

Constructive theology consequently is only one quite special kind of theological writing. Scholarly description of theology, analysis of a theological system and how it holds together, historical study of theological systems in the history of Judaism—all of these more academic kinds of study promise interesting results for study about religion.[2] This is not a *discourse* about the religion of Judaism but an *exposition* of the Torah, Judaism's own word for Judaism. I set forth in a sustained and coherent way the systematic theological statement of the Torah (that is, again, Judaism), as I propose to set forth that religion's rationality. Here, therefore, I offer a work not of history or literature or religion but of theology.

The descriptive work already is well advanced, therefore allowing this (for me) fresh initiative. For I already have completed ample studies of the history, literature, and religion of Judaism in its canonical writings—Scripture and the classical documents of the oral part of the Torah as well. In these pages, the facts of history and history of religion, which have occupied me for thirty-five years, give way to the acknowledged truths of theology, and problems of historical description, literary analysis, and religious-

---

1. Ingolf U. Dalferth, *Theology and Philosophy* (Oxford: Basil Blackwell Ltd. 1988), vii.

2. In the acknowledgments at the end, I explain what I plan to do in theological-descriptive work beyond this book.

historical interpretation are set aside in favor of an altogether different intellectual challenge, one I am now ready to meet. What I want to know is the rationality that infuses the truth of faith, not the (mere) facts of history, literature, and religion: the logic of those of us who through the Torah meet God. What faith seeking understanding finds out in the Torah about God is captured in the song I mean in these pages to portray, and, in the end, a few measures of which I even sing: the melody of the Talmud in particular.

The logic of this book, however, does not stand on its own, separate from all my prior, descriptive work. To the contrary, I wrote this book soon after completing a scholarly account, for academic purposes, of the principal medium for the theology of Judaism, which is hermeneutics. That work is *Judaism States Its Theology: The Talmudic Re-Presentation*.[3] I demonstrate that the hermeneutics of the Talmuds, particularly the Talmud of Babylonia (which in this book is called simply "the Talmud"), bears the main weight of the message. Now, once I had reached that conclusion on narrowly descriptive grounds and through analytical procedures, I stepped aside from the labor of systematic historical study. For then it seemed to me entirely natural to cross the line, always clearly marked in my writing, between description, analysis, and interpretation, on the one side, and the exposition of a different logic and rationality.

3. Atlanta: Scholars Press for South Florida Studies in the History of Judaism, 1993.

One

GOD SINGS

$\mathcal{G}$od sings to Israel. The Torah is God's song. In secular, descriptive language, in Judaism, God is made manifest in the Torah, and it is in the Torah that Israel meets God.

Israel's God is a God who sings, neither in the storm nor in the thunder but in the voice that pierces the silence, the thin voice, the urgent voice. The halting, nervous, quavering chirping of the bar or bat mitzvah, the boy or girl at puberty called for the first time to read the Torah to the community assembled for prayer in the synagogue, is the voice that Moses heard from the cleft in the rock. Moses, denied the vision he sought, heard instead the voice to proclaim the name: "I will proclaim before you my name. 'The Lord.'" It is the thin voice of silence that Elijah heard—that same Elijah present at the circumcision of the bar mitzvah, that same Elijah who at the end of time will announce the coming of the Messiah. Through song eternity breaks through into the here and now of time.

I say, "God sings," because, when received with reverence by holy Israel, the Torah always is sung;[1] I call the Torah God's song,

---

1. That in ancient times books ordinarily were sung aloud, not read silently, is a fact not germane to our inquiry. For, speaking within the framework of the

because the Torah is given ("revealed") by God in the act of self-manifestation. So the Torah itself proclaims its own origins in Heaven: "I am the Lord your God . . . ," "The Lord spoke to Moses, saying, Speak to the children of Israel and say to them . . . ," "I will make all my goodness pass before you and will proclaim before you my name, 'The Lord,' and I will be gracious to whom I will be gracious and will show mercy on whom I will show mercy. But you cannot see my face." These and companion proclamations leave no doubt for holy Israel that in the Torah is God: the record of God's call to humanity through holy Israel. Israel receives the Torah to meet God, and in the Torah Israel's encounter with God takes place.

But to take place is to locate in ordinary space an event of utopian potentiality. Where in particular is the locative event of encounter to be found? This act of self-revelation and, therefore, encounter in the Torah takes place before living Israel in two places, synagogue and academy. In both meetings the Torah is not read but sung, and the singing serves to transform secular study into sacred service. Thus—in line with these facts of the faith as practiced every day and everywhere—the theology of Judaism finds its voice in the singing of the Torah. Israel sings God's song on its way across the ages—song without end—through eternity, to Heaven.

Then to describe the theology of Judaism we have to identify its melody. Three propositions consequently form the burden of this chapter.

Israel Receives the Torah Where and When It Is Sung

We return, now, with a clear understanding of what is at stake in these public places. These are the locations in which the Torah takes place. That is so because the Torah is given to holy Israel; so, in the location in which the individual becomes the community,

---

Torah, we may note that those books, when sung, belonged solely to this world, while the Torah—words, some in books, some not—when sung echoes out of eternity. In more secular terms, facts of history play no probative role in the theological inquiry into our meeting with God.

the place in which the quorum forms and words are said in public and, therefore, put up for public disputation and exposition, there and then God calls to Israel. Precisely what happens in these places? How in them does God, speaking in the present tense, give the Torah? All that has been said to this point prepares the way for the final solution to the mystery of how Israel takes place, how the Torah is given, how the gift is received by Israel, when and where God is made manifest—all ways of saying one thing. That thing in secular words is: here is the theology of Judaism, its theological voice.

Israel Meets God in Song

In the Torah, specifically when and where it is sung, Israel meets God. That meeting is in the synagogue and in the academy, where, received with song and dance, blessing and petition, God's pronouncement, that is, the Torah, comes in words and sentences to Israel, God's people. Assembled as all Israel in synagogue or as the particular disciples of the Torah in the academy or yeshiva, God's people hears the sung words: receives and determines to obey, to dance to the compelling rhythms, to sing with the forceful melody. And in the song without end, the never-finished symphony, there is how the covenant with the founders, Abraham and Sarah, Isaac and Rebecca, Jacob and Leah and Rachel, continues: the covenant in the flesh, the covenant in the Torah, wholly one in Israel.

God Sings

The Torah manifests God, and the Torah is sung, so God's self-manifestation takes place in the Torah, which is God's song; the simple point is, in the Torah it is God who does the singing. That proposition, as I said at the outset, I find in the simple fact of the faith as it is lived in the theological verities that govern. I deal with the facts of the faith of Judaism as the religion is practiced. These facts of the living faith form the data for theological construction: in the synagogue the Torah is sung; in the academy, the Torah is sung. In the synagogue and in the academy Israel takes place in the here and now. In the synagogue and in the academy Israel stands at Sinai to receive the Torah. In the synagogue when the Torah is declaimed, the blessing is said, ". . . who gives the Torah." In the academy, when the Torah is studied, the solemn Qaddish for the sages, sanctifying God's name, accompanies the act of learning.

God never talks to Israel, rather he shouts, commands, insists, compels, or whispers, cajoles, pleads: all very operatic. To invoke the world we know: God is not a TV sports announcer on the late night news, saying what happened this afternoon (which everybody knows), but a sports reporter, commenting on the event as it takes place; then, even the instant replay evokes excitement. Prose cannot contain the presence but only poetry; not theology of merely well-worded propositions but sung theology alone suffices. In synagogues we sing all our prayers because we sing the Torah. We do not sing the Torah because we are praying. We sing those prayers in loud voices, because we do not deem it proper to mumble and slur our words when we speak to God. We recite the Torah in the declaimed word, the precise word, because that is the sole right way of pronouncing what God has said. What are we supposed to learn from a simple fact? Do I attach so much consequence to the data that the words of the Torah in the synagogue are not read, not recited, not narrated or acted out or represented in a ritual ("in remembrance") or declaimed in ordinary voice but sung out? Indeed we are, indeed I do. For it is a given in the holy life that when any day we receive the Torah in the synagogue or academy, receiving the Torah takes place just as if it were on the very day on which the words were first sung out. Here is no act of historical memory. It is a proclamation of a present event.

That explains the paradigm I find in synagogue and academy life. In the encounters in both localities it is music—singing out the words—that forms the medium for the message. What conclusions are we supposed to draw from the actualities of the lived faith and its sung theology? I find here the resolution of the paradoxes, the solution of the mysteries that I enumerated above. Here are four more propositions stating the implications of now-established facts of the practiced, living faith, the faith of the Torah in vital, holy Israel.

The Immediacy of Revelation, the Here-and-Now of Song

How do we encounter Sinai at one time in the past and the giving of the Torah in the here-and-now? What chemistry of the present moment unites them so as to surpass the paradox of past and present in one and the same moment? Music comes into being at the moment of performance; written-out notes are not music. Music is intensely present; that is its only used tense. That is why music forms the sole right medium for that message, because God's self-manifestation in the Torah takes place in the immediate and acutely present tense. Music then matches the moment: it is not merely an event remembered out of the long-ago past, a paradigm to be reenacted; nor is the Torah imitated or acted out, as though it is there merely to be recapitulated. To the contrary, these ways of recovering the past are hardly appropriate, since the Torah in the synagogue and academy does not come out of the past but out of the very present, as God is present. Our sages of blessed memory have a way of dismissing the mere facts of history: "So what was, was." The sense in the Talmud is, So what? Facts out of the past bear no consequence for the here-and-now of eternal encounter with God. That is why the Torah is never an inert fact of history. To the Torah, that is, the life of holy Israel, the Torah forms the truth concerning how things are and who is here: the whole in the acutely present, continuing tense.

The Song Is a Very Specific One

Specific words are sung and made to sing in a particular way; it is not singing in general—mere exuberance, an invention of the moment, *la di da, la la, la la*—but a tradition of music matching the circumstance and the sentiment. When we meet God in the singing of the Torah, we encounter not only music but also words. The Torah's song is a very specific one: the words match the sounds. So the Torah tells us much more than that there is a god. It tells us that there is this one and only God, the Lord who speaks to us through the Torah, and who tells us what we are supposed to do and how we are created to live our lives. Why do I insist that that song, that revelation, is specific and propositional, not general with merely the revelation that there is the Presence? To state matters in concrete and secular terms: the way the words are sung is closely prescribed by ancient tradition; the melodies are very old, the conventions of punctilious sound and precise matching of word to music bearing the authority of the ages. Nothing so captures the union of tradition and the present than the fact that the musical modes come from ancient tradition but are recreated in age succeeding age as though made up that morning. I can think of no more accurate a metaphor then for the realization of the Torah in the here-and-now than music; absent the performer, the notes lie dead on the page, black marks on white paper. Performed properly, the notes carry us into the mind of the composer, but they also recreate the mind of the composer in our very presence. Without Israel to sing, there are no words, there is no melody, and the encounter has not taken place and cannot happen. God, Torah, and Israel are one, each essential to the being of the others. Israel contributes the here-and-now, God, eternity, the Torah, the link from there to here and all time to one moment.

Sung Theology

So that is how it is with the sung theology of Judaism: the theological voice of the Torah at that very place, in that very moment, at which the Torah is pronounced. When the words are rightly sung, pronounced with precision, in proper rhythm and vocal pattern, then the Torah's message comes in the words and in the music both. Without song, with the Torah merely read, revelation does not take place; there is no reason then to recite a blessing, as we do to revere the act. For the Torah read, not sung, is a mere book, with inert information. Indeed, it is a document that is danced with. On the festival of the Rejoicing of the Torah, holy Israel takes the Torah from its ark and dances with the Torah, each person in turn, well into the night and the day beyond. The

Torah is the lord of our dance, just as, in time to come, God and the Messiah will be lords of the dance. On the Sabbath when the Torah is read, it is carried through the congregation, accompanied by the singing of psalms of praise and prayer. As music is made physical in dance, so in the rites of proclaiming the Torah Israel responds to the encounter, like Miriam and the women at Sinai, with not only song but also dance.

When with sacred choreography and measured song the Torah is proclaimed, declaimed, then and only then it is Torah— revelation. And that transformation of writing on parchment into the meeting with God cannot serve merely as an act of remembrance; the moment of revelation can never be merely reenacted nor recapitulated but only renewed in the freshness of the song— not new but always renewed, just as music when played realizes its eternal present. It is not played so that we may remember how Mozart made up and played this music, but so that we may encounter this music, this very music, in the here-and-now of the living moment.

God Sings

Come to a synagogue on a Sabbath or a Monday or Thursday, or on a holy day or festival, and you will hear the Torah not read but sung, loud and clear, in ancient chant, melody matching natural sounds of the very words God says. The song of the Torah—I cannot stress too much—ordinarily is sung with great punctiliousness. Where that is not the case, it is a disgrace to the community that receives God in a slovenly way, or not at all. It is solely to hear the Torah declaimed that holy Israel is summoned to the synagogue. Most of the rest of the liturgy may be recited at home, in private, in thick silence. The Torah defines the sole, obligatory public event. This is so not only for what the Torah says in God's behalf but what Israel says in response. Specifically, once the Torah is removed from its holy ark, carried in choreographed parade around the synagogue, the scroll is held up. At that sight of the unfurled columns of the scroll displayed before it, in response the congregation sings back, "This is the Torah that Moses set before the children of Israel at the command of the Lord." Then, and only then, holy Israel has announced itself as present, and the Torah is sung out to the people. So it goes week by week throughout the year: "In the beginning God created the heaven and the earth . . ." through "And there arose not a prophet since in Israel like unto Moses, whom the Lord knew face to face. . . ." So goes the song of the Torah from Genesis through Deuteronomy, song out of the scroll of the Torah. To that, everything else forms massive commentary.

So much for the written part of the Torah, sung as God's song in the synagogue. It is easy to witness or at least to imagine how the written Torah is sung in the synagogue. What about singing the oral part of the Torah in the academy?

Israel Responds in Song

If the written part of the Torah is God's statement in the synagogue, what of that other, oral part of the Torah? For the Torah, for holy Israel, comes in two media: the written, known to the Christian world as "the Old Testament," and the oral, the part unique to holy Israel. This other, orally formulated and orally transmitted component of the one whole Torah of Moses our rabbi, is now preserved in the documents of our sages of blessed memory, in the Mishnah (ca. 200 C.E. [=A.D.]), the statement of the oral Torah as an account of Holy Israel's impalpable existence in the form of a philosophical law code, and then in the Mishnah's principal commentaries and amplifications, the two Talmuds, the one of the Land of Israel (ca. 400 C.E.) and the other of Babylonia (ca. 600 C.E.), and various compilations of amplifications of the Torah produced by the sages represented in the Mishnah and Talmud and called "Midrash," or explanation and extension, of Scripture. These documents all together, form the starting point of the oral part of the Torah, extending upward to Sinai and outward to us. And, for our purposes, what makes the oral part of the Torah equal in importance to the written is, in the careful study of the writings of our sages of blessed memory, through which the Torah, oral and written, joins together and comes to us, we hear God's word and respond to it—and talk back. And the location at which Israel not only hears the Torah proclaimed but joins in the song with words of its own is the yeshiva, or holy academy, where the Torah is studied night and day. And there, too, the theological music takes shape in its own, distinctive melody.

But in the academy the music is less readily imagined, and, in the ordinary circumstance, people not part of the yeshiva world are not likely to find their way to hear the music. The world at large knows the power of sacred music in a holy place, whether sung by the great choirs of the churches, into vast rooms filled with mysterious light, or by the community of Israel, everyone a member of the choir, singing out the words of prayer and Scripture. But the picture of a schoolhouse where people sing their studies finds no obvious analogue in everyday experience. And yet, only when we understand that other kinds of singing—we whom God has made singing out our song to our maker in response to God's song to us—do we truly know God as the Torah, oral as much as written, makes God known to us.

A few words of description will have to suffice to explain how the oral part of the Torah is sung as well. One fact is essential at the outset: that the Talmud and related writings, which form the curriculum of the academy or yeshiva, themselves form parts of the Torah. How they are read and discussed, as much as how the Torah scroll in the synagogue is read and discussed, then tells us about how the Torah is re-presented. Everything that follows rests on the simple fact that just as the written Torah, the Pentateuch, is sung in the synagogue, so the Talmud, the oral Torah, is sung in the yeshiva. That is, the part of the Torah that is studied in the yeshiva is the oral part, written down, finally, in the Talmud of Babylonia (and related writings). How learning is carried on in the academy, then, as much as how the Pentateuch is read in the synagogue, tells us how in Judaism Israel meets God in the Torah. In the walls of the academy deep silence falls only at the moment of prayer at which praying Israel addresses God directly, in the You of The Prayer par excellence.[2] If you stand outside the open window of a yeshiva in Jerusalem or Efrat, you will hear a silence so

---

2. I refer here to the Eighteen Benedictions of obligatory daily worship, and their counterpart for Sabbaths and Festivals, which are recited in solitary silence,

perfect that the sole sound is that of birds chirping—or the falling of a single feather from an angel's wing.

Go to an academy and stand against the wall and listen to the cacophony, as men young and old shout at each other in animated (also ritualized) argument, and you will soon hear the inner rhythm of the shouts and grasp that they are not yelling at one another but singing to one another. In fact, there is a pattern, a sing-song, not an array of civil arguments, calmly put forth for reasoned argument and decision, but an explosion of violent sound, crescendos of phrases, rivers of words, all of them flowing in a powerful current, deeply felt, sincerely meant: the stakes are high. So the men shout at one another, singing to one another, the chant bearing the signals of the sort of argument that is being mounted, the conventions of thought that are being replayed.

But shouting and shrieking mark the location and shape sound all the rest of the time. This one proposes, that one disposes. This one forms a proposition in response to what the Torah (here: the Mishnah, the Talmud, or a later commentator) says, and that one says why what this one says is wrong: here are the flaws. If you are right, then I shall show the absurd consequence that follows. If you maintain thus-and-so, I shall demonstrate the disharmonies that result. Your music is my cacophony, your melody my disharmony. And then you sing back—No, because—or Yes, but—and I sing back: an endless exchange of voices. All the time we are held together in our argument by the shared conviction that what is at stake is truth, not power, nor personalities, nor even the merely formal rituals of an empty academicism such as we may see acted out on an academic stage here or there.

And that is the Talmudic melody: the exchange of powerfully held convictions, formed as rational propositions, set forth by appeal to evidence and argument, in behalf of perfectly secular truth: how things are and how they are supposed to be. Sustained, serious conflict over truth, for stakes exceeding measure, on the

---

each worshipper speaking directly to God. These some call "the amidah," the prayer said standing, and others call "the shemoneh esré, or eighteen benedictions."

part of mature minds, forms holy Israel's response to the Torah, its song within the Torah. For, in Torah study in a yeshiva, arguments takes the form of song, reasoning is reenforced in the upward and the downward movements of the melodic line, and conclusions are drawn in crescendo. Tables are pounded, hands swing about, a choreography not so gentle as the synagogues but as formed and in context also as graceful and expressive. The antiphonal sound of argument carries music for not only debate but dance, with much physicality and many fixed gestures, as much of body as of voice.

True, what you would hear in a yeshiva would be music of an other-than-conventional sort, hot music, not cool music. You need listen only briefly to grasp that the sound is organized, with rhythms, with measures and beats, with upward and downward passages, with hesitations and movement, words spoken largo, allegro, adagio, sostenuto, then agitato—yes, always *agitato*.[3] But it is composed music, not chaos; the alternation of sound and silence such as music requires follows an aesthetic of its own, one that, as we shall see, conveys theological truth in its way as much as words do in theirs.

So if in the synagogue boys and girls chirp, in the academy adults shout. In the synagogue God speaks to Israel. In the Yeshiva Israel talks back to God. To the secular eye, from the educated,

3. I speak on the margins of the yeshiva world, having studied in a classical yeshiva for only one year and then only four hours a day, when I was a student at the Hebrew University of Jerusalem. I took Talmud lessons at Mir Yeshiva, and there formed my impression of how things are in the great hall of the oral Torah. For the purpose of this argument, the simple and ubiquitous facts set forth here suffice. Rich accounts of Yeshiva life show what it means to live in argument over the infinite stakes of God's truth. First place among many fine portraits goes to Chaim Grade, *The Yeshiva* (New York: Menorah Publishing Co., 1967), translated from the Yiddish by Curt Leviant. Grade, through Leviant, speaks not only about but for the life of the Torah as holy Israel lives it. His is the best single account of the many Judaisms, all together and all in one place, in the first half of the twentieth century. Among the world's religions, then and now, Judaisms, as Grade through Leviant lay them out, belong among the most vital and enduring and compelling, for, in context, they made, and make, all the difference to those addressed by them. This I mean to underscore by my emphasis on *agitato*.

academic perspective, the yeshiva is a strange place: it invariably encompasses a large room, full of tables, where bearded men sit chattering at one another, vehemently arguing, banging hands on tables or on books, throwing violent words at one another. That shows they care; the stakes are high. Each brings honor to the other. For argument forms the highest gesture of respect: it means each takes the other seriously. Argument becomes possible only when minds meet, becomes palpable when general agreement leaves space for particular points of contention. And contention for the sake of Heaven forms an act of sanctification, by the intellect, through passion. In the yeshiva people argue about problems that may appear remote from the world in which they make their lives.[4] But they are studying Torah, specifically, the Talmud, together with its commentaries of more than a thousand years, the codes of law that govern proper conduct, the exegeses of words and phrases that make sense of the elliptical text at hand.

What gives the yeshiva the sound of a symphony—Charles Ives is the composer who comes to mind for the occasion, but, in his way, John Cage would have found himself at home—is simple: when this oral part of the Torah is studied, it too is sung, not read, recited in its own singsong, not repeated like any other book. The phrasing of the recitations correspond to measures of music, the recitative of the Mishnah or the questions and answers of the Talmud to melodic lines, the shouting to operatic declamation, the rapid-fire exchanges to duets, trios, quartets. The sound comes in waves, never in unison, rarely in harmony, but yields always a single piece of music. All serious learning in yeshivas takes the form of antiphonal argument: if you say this (voice up), then how about that (voice down). Then bang the table. It is organized sound, shouted theology.

By repeating a line or a sound pattern, or by reprise and development, prose becomes poetry, sound becomes music. Sound that is no longer random carries its own signals; when we know what to expect, or know to expect surprise, we have music. In yeshiva

---

4. This we shall see at great length later in this book when we examine actual Talmud texts.

study the repetitions of lines and the rhythm create the singsong that is song, and if you stood against the wall and listened, you would soon enough pick out the rhythms and the melodies of learning; if you stood in the corridors of a learned society or a faculty, you would hear sound but not music; it would be whispering, mostly, or joking; when stakes are high, people argue; when they take one another seriously, they contend; some shout.

These are the sounds of battle, the clashing of the swords of reason and the cymbals of argument in the Torah. But conflict for the sake of aggression, not God, takes over, and no world of intellect exceeds that of the yeshivas in the venom that can poison argument. If for theology in Christianity men would kill or die, in Judaism they do more than yell and scream, gesticulate and stamp their feet. They isolate, ignore, dismiss, condemn, shun, boycott, and avoid. Blood shed in the Christian theological wars, lives spent in silent isolation from the contentious other in the Judaic theological battles—"This book I will not read because he wrote it, that idea I will not consider because it comes from the proscribed location"—whether God can love the hatred committed in God's name only God can tell us. In the nature of the theological enterprise, love for God's truth competes in effect with hatred for disagreed-with alternatives: heresy for Christianity, schism for the Torah. Not all music echoes out of Heaven; hell has its orchestra too.

That is why to us the natural sounds of the yeshiva prove puzzling and alien. For we are not used to rhythmic speech, sung words, sound patterns that bear meaning. Nor are we accustomed to the verbal violence of the yeshiva song. Sounds natural to us prove ugly to others. To foreigners, we Americans slurp and slide and slur our way through our sentences, we talk through our noses; we do not sing. And, for our part, to our American ears, Swedes and Italians do not sound as if they are talking with one another so much but as if they are singing. The same is so in the Torah academy, though the music is of a very different quality.

So in yeshivas bearded men—and today, at long last, young and mature women as well—spend their days shouting at one another, singing to one another, exchanging melodies—not only thoughts but themes, the way duos or trios or quartets take up a melodic line and, player by player, do with it what they will, the soloists responding one to another, all of them forming a coherent musical statement. And so it is with the massive noise—the organized noise—of the yeshiva. The contrast between yeshiva discourse and conventional academic discourse is captured by the comparison between an exchange of information and an argument; between the speech of a play and the recitative of an opera; between prose and poetry. The only moments of silence in the yeshiva come in the solitude of prayer: then you can hear a feather fall off the wing of an angel. That is where Israel responds to God speaking through the oral part of the Torah, which is the Talmud, also expressed in melody.

These then form my theological propositions and the case to be made in their behalf out of the facts of the life of Judaism today. Here, I contend, out of the life of the vital faith, we identify the location and the moment at which Israel meets God: in the synagogue when the written Torah is declaimed, in the yeshiva (and its counterparts in study halls in synagogues) when the oral Torah forms the centerpiece of sustained argument. Music marks the moment. And that fact of the living faith brings us to a simple question: Why does God choose the way of song, so that the self-manifestation of God in the Torah takes place only when and where the Torah is sung?

To understand the answer, we turn to that puzzle of the meeting with God, a meeting that takes place in two ways or not at all: I with the you of God, we with the you of God. If "we," Israel meet God in the Torah, but I do not, then God is not a "you" and I am not "Israel." If I meet God, but not within the holy Israel, then what standing do I have, in the setting of the Torah that makes the meeting possible only when Israel comes together? The union of "I" and "we" forms the requirement for the Torah to take place, whether in the synagogue or in the yeshiva. God appears to a "me"—I Moses, I Elijah, I Jeremiah, I Isaiah, to name principal cases—but speaks to an "us." God knew Jeremiah in the womb, but calls upon Jeremiah only to speak to Israel all together, the you of Jeremiah shifting over, always, to the you of Israel. No account of how in the Torah we know God can omit the I, and none can conclude with the I. All must speak to the "we" of Israel: God, Torah, and Israel are one. So we come to the question, How is it possible that we are one by one by one individuals, but at an enchanted number form Israel, the quorum, the community? And the answer to that question explains the compelling power of the metaphor of music that I offer in explaining (to use secular language) how in Judaism we know God, or, in the language of the Torah, where and when holy Israel encounters the living God.

The answer to the power of song to form community and bring about communion emerges as soon as we ask the question. In the case of Israel, there is no missing the point. But it is not an obvious point. To begin with, music speaks to the imagination, imposing order by reason of rhythm. Or music through melody and its logic or repetition along what otherwise appears to be random sound evokes response in mind. Israel itself forms an act of imagination: here-and-now related in mind to the ancient Israel of whom and of which the Torah speaks. Sung theology then, serves especially well to realize and express in words the social order of Israel, a community of the faithful, holy and set apart, that is formed in imagination alone.[5]

Since, to the contrary, perceived reality attests solely to the material, physical reality of Israel—an ethnic group, a people, even a state no less—I have to expand on this matter. Precisely why do I claim to see Israel in the setting of synagogue as a fabricated moment of enchantment, and Israel in the setting of the academy as a willful act of transformation? How come I see both then forming an act of vivid imagination, not a mere invocation of simple worldly facts? As a matter of fact, Israel, in the here-and-now,

5. I need hardly elaborate the obvious point that in this world "Israel" stands for "the State of Israel," the Jews for an ethnic group, and Judaism for the ethnic culture of that group. But a moment of reflection will show that in the setting of the Torah "Israel" forms an act of divine imagination, the Torah (not Judaism) an intervention out of eternity into time, and the God who calls to Israel by singing the Torah the one we know not palpably but in the thin voice of silence, in the adumbrations of a voice calling back to us as we hide in the cave, "The Lord, the Lord . . . ." In this context, only the act of imagination governs.

yields only Jews here and there and everywhere, without much in common among themselves except what they declare commonalities. They do not form a community. They do not speak a common language. They do not look alike or talk alike or think alike. No government governs them all, and no one leader speaks for them all, not in politics, not in theology, not in religion. Not only so, but as we move backward through time, to the formation of the Talmud itself, that same inchoate group of people exhibit the same contrasts and yet affirm (all together in much the same way) the same faith.

For Judaism the categories are Israel, the state, or the Jews, the ethnic group; the tradition or the culture or the ethnic way of life; and God takes no place at all. For the Torah, "Israel" is a native category of the sacred, not one formed of mere observation of secular facts of politics or demography; the Torah's Israel is an act of imagination. The Torah's God is the commanding voice out of eternity, the sound that sang, "Let there be . . . ," so that there was. And how to say all this? Music (with dance, with drama, with poetry) forms the appropriate medium of re-creation and representation of this imagined Israel. And that is how it should be: the intangible to convey the impalpable. For consider the case of Judaism: here we deal with a religion lacking conventional institutions, without worldly power. The Jewish people (not the Holy Israel of the faith) in the Exile and in the State of Israel is mostly secular most of the time. The Torah's decisions then come about through consensus; its common patterns of behavior and belief require constant affirmation by individuals; instruments of coercion are few and very local. How does music then serve? It is because it is the way of holding together what is intangible and yet fitting: sound we cannot touch nor yet coerce, yet can hear to resonate on key or off. We cannot coerce music, but music moves us, and not only when we want to be moved.

There is another consideration. It is that where the faith speaks it is because there the chorus sings together. True, as I claim, "Israel" is an act of mind, and in the everyday, Israel, the Jews, form no chorus at all, at least, none that makes music together. And yet Judaism also is a religion that in doctrine reaches decision by consensus—or there is no decision, only endless schism. And Judaism stands on vast and vigorous consensus: God is one, the Torah comes from God, Israel is God's first love—and much else.[6] The Torah, then, stands for a religion that, in the world of prose, corresponds to that of making music by a chorus, sung correctly, on key. It is well to sing the theology: set forth the words and the notes, and assign to the chorus of the faithful the task of making them into music, music sung together by all and all at once. Why do I say so? Because, in the nature of the social condition of Judaism, which is to say, the imaginary Israel that hears God sing in the Torah, that is the only way.

Let me recapitulate this point in more secular language: the theology of Judaism—the right ways of thinking, acting, believing, all of which cohere in the consensus of the faithful—takes the form of not creed demanding assent, nor dogma nor doctrine requiring a statement of the faith. All these are necessary, but none suffices. For none, by itself, can attain authority, impose itself upon all; the reason is already in our hands, the simple fact that God speaks to the individual who studies the Torah, and not only to all Israel assembled to hear the Torah. Music is the medium: all can sing, each one by himself or herself, everyone all together—"Hear, Israel, the Lord, our God, is the one God"—that and many other statements of theological fact we sing together, each in the voice God has given; all say the same words, each finds the right pace; all follow roughly the same notes and melody. But who is there to set the key?

The signal that that is how Judaism speaks—in the consensus of shared song—is: we sing just as we pray, one by one yet all together, each one in so very personal a voice, together; we sing one song, in many voices; we sing all together, saying one set of words

6. I do not mean to obscure the fact that Reform Judaism and Orthodox Judaism disagree, or that the various segregationist Judaisms, all of them called "Orthodox" but each of them dismissing as heretical all of the others, reject all integrationist Judaisms. But both the vast consensus within Orthodox Judaisms, and the equally long list of propositions to which both Orthodox and other-than-Orthodox Judaisms adhere, testify to, if not unity, then consensus on most of the definitive issues.

and following one set of musical notes, forming of the whole nothing so civil as a symphony but something that nonetheless has its distinctive sound. It is right that the Torah should be sung; it is the only way to keep the whole together. The Jews, stubborn individualists, form Israel, one and whole, only because, however diverse belief and behavior, in the end the Torah is sung in one and the same way everywhere. Hear it here, it sounds one way; hear it there, another. Declaimed in Tel Aviv, the vowels are clipped, the consonants exploded; in New Orleans or Atlanta, the vowels drawled, the consonants slurred; in my native New England, the whole sung from not the diaphragm but the nose. The words are the same, the melody is the same, the Israel is one and the same. God alone fully grasps the harmony, fathoms the counterpoint.

To understand what is at stake when and where we meet God, come with me to the place where Judaism lives, which is, the academy and the synagogue, in the hour of prayer, when God is present. Here is where I construct my theology of the encounter with God in the Torah. In the synagogue we pray individually, but all together. Each one, at the moment of petition, is alone. Silence prevails. Yet all say the same words, if not at the same pace or with the same intent, still, at the same moment. Specifically, observe worship in an academy or a synagogue, and you will see, at the most solemn moment of petition, in the recitation of The Prayer itself, the members of the congregation rise together, but each person prays by himself or herself. So speaking to God, all Israel pray by themselves, but pray, too, all together. Then someone repeats it all; but that is the formality; the authentic encounter of prayer, when people talk to God and ask God for what they want, has already taken place. All have spoken by themselves, individually; but they have said the same words, whatever other words they may have chosen to add. And that is how it is with the song. Each sings, but all sing together; each voice registers, but the chorus is heard all together.[7]

---

7. It is not uncommon during the repetition of the prayer for the assembled worshippers to chat with one another and ignore the main event. But, in authentic synagogues and yeshivas, it is unthinkable for conversation to take place dur-

So it is hardly surprising that a religion that treats prayer at its most public as entirely personal and private should find its voice in a chorus and make its statement through consensus. Music is the medium of consensus—or cacophony. And God sings one song, and Israel hears that one song. But each hears with his or her own ears. And when they sing, each sings with his or her own voice, but all sing one song together: that is what happens in the synagogue when the Torah is sung, that is what happens in the academy when the study of Torah evokes song.

How does Israel come into being in song? Many voices join in the song; diverse timbres, keys, quality of sound from sweet to hoarse, perfectly pitched to nearly monotone, join in song. This is not in unison—by definition, people with their many varied voices really cannot sing in unison at all—but it is all together. And why should all Israel not sing the same tune, since it is the Torah's melody, in God's key? Now, as a matter of fact, the Jews, in all their diversity, are not going to sing on the same key, not even on key at all. But the words are the words of the Torah, and the trope the trope of the Torah, and the musical exchanges—the counterpart to the parts to the quartet, changing and trading the melody—are trades of the Torah. Then it is all the same: in unison if not with one another then with God. And in the ears of God, who is to say what is on-key and what is off-key, except by appeal to the Torah that God sings as we sing. To state the simple point: just as ballet is physicalized music, so for Judaism theology is sung thought. That is to say, God's song is truth conveyed not through propositions formed into music, and not through words shaped into works of beauty, feeling, and sensibility, but ideas

---

ing the reading of the Torah. In Reform, most Conservative, and yeshiva-Orthodox synagogues, the reading of the Torah takes place in pure silence. But in integrationist-Orthodox synagogues, such as I have attended, all over Europe and in South Africa and the South Pacific as well, from Madrid to Helsinki, conversation during the reading of the Torah drowns out the voice of the one who sings. In both places, and not a few in between, I preferred at that point to leave rather than witness the disgrace of the Torah by secular Jews in the place of holy Israel. I hasten to add, in the State of Israel liturgical standards are set for the entire world of Judaism, and there matters are as they are supposed to be.

formed rhythmically in their natural sounds, into formations of sense and proposition.

Let us now turn from the facts of the lived faith to the propositions that those facts sustain. What conclusion do I draw from the bedrock facts of lived theology that we have now surveyed and transformed into propositions? Judaism is a religion that forms a union of individual and community; emotion and attitude, fact and truth, belief and behavior, and, therefore, seeks a medium for many voices to say many things all at once. Music is that way: words set to music, rhythmic thought, melodized intellect. Music so uniquely suited to serve as the medium for normative theological doctrine requires us to speak, in particular, of a "theological voice" and of a "talmudic melody." That is because music has the power to allow many voices to speak, each its own line of melody, and all to form a single composition. Only music (with its close friends, poetry, drama, and dance) can do that.

Words speak for this one or for that one, until many adopt them as authoritative: the one, the many, but not both and equally, in the balance, as with music. By contrast, the singular voice that is music has the capacity to sustain this one's voice alongside that one's voice, each enjoying its own integrity, and to form of them all a single chorus. Only music can do that. It is no surprise, then, that the Torah in both its parts, written and oral, should be sung; there is no other way that serves. Music matches the mode of prayer: individuals, reciting their prayers on their own, yet in tandem. So too in song: all sing individually, in chorus. So when I say, God sings, I speak of Israel's response: the theological acts of the Judaic faithful, and I mean that as God speaks in organized, intelligible sound, so does Israel, and so do Israel. One by one and all together, Israel sings this song that God sings. In declaiming the Torah Israel responds to song with song, not in prose but in poetry, not in a monotone of speech but in the many colors of rhythm and nuanced voice and proper pitch and key, all forming harmony and bearing that ineluctable logic that only organized sound can convey. That is why I refer to the natural sounds of the Torah, its sung theology. God's singing, in the language of religious experience, corresponds, in the language of Israel's holy life, to the giving of the Torah, by which I mean, pressing our metaphor to its limit, the music of the spheres.

Since I have invoked the power of imagination, readers may suppose I treat music as a metaphor, telling us in one set of images how things are in some other realm. But that is not my meaning. To the contrary, when I say God sings and the Torah is God's song, I mean that statement literally: through the music of the Torah, God becomes known to us. And when we sing our learning in the Torah, God hears our song. The character of music serves because it helps us to define the character of the theology of Judaism, or, in the language I prefer to state matters, *God sings to Israel and the Torah is sung theology*. The norms of belief and behavior fully reveal themselves when we know how to hear the music and how to sing in tune: what makes notes into melodies, sound into music. To state my thesis in just a few words: speaking only descriptively, alluding to established and entirely familiar facts of the practiced piety of the faithful, I claim that, when Israel hears the Torah sung, Israel hears God's song. This constructive theology may be expressed, then, in a single sentence: since God's voice in the Torah is an active voice, in the Torah God sings to Israel.

What, then, of the theological propositions that, at a later point, take shape in a theological system? I have already stressed how God sings to Israel not only in music but also in very particular words. God sings a specific melody, saying particular words: "The Lord spoke to Moses saying, speak to the children of Israel and say to them . . . ," "You will love the Lord your God with all your heart . . . ," "Love your neighbor as yourself," "Remember the Sabbath day to keep it holy." That is why Moses did not need to see God's face; the back sufficed, for Moses had already heard God's voice in song. The particularities of God's song for Israel now come to the fore.

The first concerns the time and place of meeting: where and when do we meet God, and what happens in the meeting? Here we take up not only the record of the encounter but its consequences: when we meet God, God gives us the Torah, which tells us who we are and what we are, therefore, supposed to do. The liturgy of the synagogue itself insists that the synagogue right of proclaiming the Torah forms a moment of revelation: God giving the Torah. The language of the blessings recited before and after the reading of a Torah-lection says precisely that. The blessing speaks of the here-and-now, using as it does the present tense: "blessed . . . who gives the Torah." That refers to what happens here-and-now, in fact, and in effect, just as the blessing for bread, "who brings forth bread to the earth," speaks of what happens in the here-and-now. Other blessings using the perfect tense, "who has kept us in life, has sustained us, and has brought us to this season," show that the tense represents a matter of choice. Furthermore, even the blessing over the Torah fore and aft mixes tenses: "who has chosen us from all peoples and has given us the Torah . . . blessed . . . who gives," and at the end, "who has given us the Torah of truth and planted in our midst eternal life," and then again, ". . . who gives." The election took place in the beginning and endures; the Torah marked and marks the election. Through the authentic Torah eternal life has taken root among us. These statements reach far into the distant, governing past: time gone. But they speak to the present, especially to the present: ". . . who gives. . . ."

The choice of present tense is deliberate. It serves to say that Sinai is not a place nor a merely one-time, past-time historical event. It is a moment of eternity, when the eternal breaks into time and shatters one-time history with timeless truth: reliable mathematics replicates nature's uncertain processes. It is an hour beyond time marked specifically by what happens whenever in the holy community of the faithful the Torah is removed from the holy ark, danced with and paraded, displayed, read, opened full breadth to the community to inspect, paraded again, and reverently returned to its ark. That is what "giving the Torah" and "receiving of the Torah" by God and Israel, respectively, or, in theological language, what "revelation," means. And in the synagogue and academy that is not an act of commemoration or even replication but—once more I stress—of representation. When the Torah is given, then we are, we become, Israel, there we know God.

God is made manifest in the Torah and only there. People think otherwise, finding God in the stars or in ourselves, in the power of the seas or in the silence of the desert. But unless God tells us that there God is, we do not know it. Let me state matters in a simple and logical way: God is not made manifest in nature, outside of the Torah's account of natural creation. Nor is God made known through what happens in history, outside of the Torah's interpretation of events. That is to say, if the Torah did not tell us that the heavens tell the glory of God, how should we know? And if the Torah did not tell us that Assyria was the rod of God's wrath, how might we have come to such a conclusion? Contemporary confusion concerning the meaning to be drawn from our mortal wounds—the proclamation out of hell that God is dead, for example—shows the alternative: every one a theology for himself or herself; none left with personal doubt, but none with a faith susceptible to sharing either. But that is not how things are in the framework of the faith, the Torah ("Judaism"). So without the Torah, nature and history are speechless—or set forth messages too diverse to command universal assent. And, it goes without saying but has always to be repeated, Israel receives the Torah in community. There is no revelation to Israel that does not take place in the Torah or in entire unity with the Torah. The mountains danced—for Israel at Sinai. The kings heard the roar—of God at Sinai. Nature and politics or history find their sense—through God at Sinai, in this morning's giving of the Torah.

The theological encounter recorded in this morning's proclamation of the Torah takes form in propositions and becomes real in the specific words we hear and say. So while music may take the form of a song without words, the song that God sings has many words. Let me digress to provide an ample explanation of what is critical to the theology of Judaism, which is an enormous corpus of carefully criticized language. Up to now I have identified only the locus and the medium of God's self-manifestation, the Torah, but not explained either the character or the form that the Torah takes. I have, therefore, to pause and answer some questions about the Torah itself. First, its character: Why not a Torah that reveals

God's Presence not in words but in silence? Do we not meet God in the heights and in the depths, in joy or suffering when these take place? Why so much talk when God meets Moses, or when in the synagogue the Torah is set forth, why the flood of words, and, in the academy or yeshiva, why the waves and whole oceans of passionate words? Whence insistence upon the passion borne outward on wings of speeches, allegations, and points of insistence? Before the power of the song with many words can make itself manifest, we have to explain to ourselves why when God sings to Israel, God sings the words of a song, those specific words, no other words; and no song without words, and that particular song for those specific words.

To answer this question, we have to consult the Torah itself. There we find that the reason (from the perspective of the Torah itself) is that the other way—the way of wordless revelation in nature or in history—did not work, has not worked God's purpose from creation and the dawn of humanity in history. Uninstructed, with only a few perfectly natural responsibilities, the children of Noah missed the lessons of the flood. Nor did the history made, even by the elect family of Abraham and Sarah and their descendents, accomplish the goal. The children of Abraham and Sarah included Ishmael, of Isaac and Rebecca, Esau; Jacob and Leah cannot have boasted about all their sons and daughters, and Jacob's last word—brutal in its honesty about them, shocking in the absence of sentimentality—left no doubt of his views of matters. So genealogy was not enough; the presence, indeed even the blessing, could not suffice. Israel without the Torah knew only that God is, but not what God says.

Revelation required articulation: not only that God is, but what God wants. Humanity is like God in intellectual power, but not God: humanity has to be told what God knows. What makes humanity like God, to be sure, is that humanity at least can understand when told: can obey, or can sin. But even heirs of the patriarchs, in the elected genealogy, needed to be told what to do: to respond to the presence. That explains (at least from the perspective of the Torah) why, when God proposed to undertake self-revelation to humanity, in the end it was not through mere nature, with its mute testimony (no more floods), nor even through the lessons of consequential events called history (Ishmael and Esau had history but did not draw the right conclusions from it, as their disappointed parents learned). Not content with nature's, or history's, ambiguous message, God through the Torah, eloquent and unambiguous, conveyed what he wished and now wishes to say.

Nor would God rely only upon this man and that woman, even Abraham, even Sarah; family by itself could not suffice, for the reason just now given in the names Ishmael and Esau.[8] It would be to an "us" that was made up of not only the children of Abraham and Sarah and their children, but to "all Israel" that made a place for even the hangers-on who in the wake of freedom flooded out of Egypt in the flotsam. It was to that enlarged Israel that God would speak. Israel would not suffice only as one extended family; it would also have to be a kingdom—of priests; a people—that was holy. These other social metaphors besides family each bore its own paradigm. And so, too, once the Torah came forth at Sinai, it formed the paradigm of revelation with no further misunderstandings: creation could no longer be misread nor history misconstrued. Prophecy, then, would serve as a reminder, until sages uncovered in the Torah rules of rigorous analysis so reliable that even prophecy became redundant. The Torah sets forth what God chose through Moses to tell humanity, which is God's self-revelation in relationship to humanity: the story of nature's creation, Israel's revelation, humanity's end in redemption. So much for the reason that when God sings to Israel it is a song of many words.

8. The confusion of theology with sociology and politics, as has taken over the life of the Torah in America, need not detain us. It is the simple fact that genealogy without holy Israel yields merely secular facts, for example, a Jew in a family tree, or many of them, for that matter. Israel after the flesh, physical Israel, remains the Israel to whom God gives the Torah; it is the simple fact that no other Israel has shown much reason to endure. But in these pages I do not speak about social policy but what I take to be God's perspective as set forth in the Torah to, and about, holy Israel. The entire ethnicization of "Judaism" requires the purification of theological discourse, so that the Torah, that is "Judaism," may retain its integrity and exercise its remarkable power.

So much for a Torah made up of not only records of God's appearance but reports of God's points of insistence. Now to move to the next main point. It concerns the matter of attitude. In the context of music, the importance of attitude is easy enough to understand. What infuses music is our feeling in singing it: the joy of joyful music, the poignancy of the sad—these must come from our own hearts, or the music itself will not convey its message. If we sing, but not to God, it is not worship. If the Torah is sung, not to convey God's music but a merely secular song, it is not the true Torah. Our attitude takes the love songs collected in the Song of Songs (known to Christians as the Song of Solomon) and turns those songs into melodies of the love of God for Holy Israel, and of Israel for God. That transformation—an enchantment, really—underscores the power of attitude, the magic of intentionality. So when we think about meeting God in the song of the Torah, we introduce an element that only we can provide: the heart. That is why the Talmud says, above all, "God wants the heart," and, further, "the commandments"—actions that we carry out in submission to God's will expressed in the Torah—"were given only to purify us."

If we sing with all our heart and soul and might, the music resonates. In meeting God in the Torah, the encounter takes place not in random sound but in music made manifest in circumstance and occasion: intention and attitude above all. The attitude that draws Israel to synagogue worship or yeshiva learning makes all the difference, then, since the Torah may be read, not sung; cited as fact or studied as data, not at all received with reverence. God's self-manifestation in the Torah requires no footnotes and takes place elsewhere than in scholarly meetings. Not, just because a Jew opens Scripture, is God present. The giving of the Torah demands the receiving of the Torah and, therefore, requires holy Israel, assembled in sanctity. The attitude characteristic of authentic synagogue worship and yeshiva study enchants and transforms the act of learning. That at stake is not merely acquiring information, as in a classroom, but reverently receiving revelation, the setting itself reveals. In the synagogue the Torah is taken out of its holy ark with song and dance, psalms and hymns precede the act, blessings surround the proclamation, then the scroll is displayed and its claim conveyed: "This is the Torah"—this scroll from which we have just now read—"that Moses set before Israel at the command of God"—no ambiguities there.

We cannot imagine that we are sitting in the Library of Congress, or in a classroom of diverse students, all races and all faiths or none, of the vast and diverse University of South Florida—or even the Hebrew University of Jerusalem itself, for that matter. In the academy that is the yeshiva, when the Torah is studied through the teachings of the master to the disciples, rules of sanctity govern, and prayer concludes the action. That is why there is no confusing the yeshiva study hall with the university lecture room. We cannot suppose that a sage in a yeshiva is a professor in a university only with a long beard. In both cases, attitudes concerning what is done, where one is, transform what can be secular into what must be holy, the act of receiving the gift of the Torah.

So for the giving of the Torah—in secular language, revelation —to take place what is required is not place but identification of place, not just persons whom it may concern but the holy people. The right people, at the right time, with the right attitude receive the Torah, and what they do at such a time in such a place furthermore defines what it means for Israel to receive the Torah. In this context, "situation" speaks of circumstance, not location: God comes through the Torah to Israel, which is a utopian, not a locative, category. And God comes not promiscuously but in measured moments: at the time of finding, when in the Torah God wishes to be found. The circumstance of saying "Blessed . . . who gives the Torah," or reciting at the end, "Magnified and sanctified be the great name in the world that he created in accord with his will," defines the conditions of giving and receiving the Torah, that is, the act and moment of revelation.

This point forms the critical turning in my argument. I have explained how, in Judaism, we know God. But where, in Judaism, does the meeting take place? I raise the following proposition: where God is to be found, there, the words that are said, and the manner of their enunciation, will tell us whatever we are going to know about the actual encounter with God, or (once more the secular use) the theological voice of Judaism. Just as I invoke music as not metaphor but the theological medium, so I point to the encounter with God in synagogue and yeshiva not as a this-worldly description but as a statement of the norm of encounter and dialogue. How holy people act tells me what I need to know. My identification of the theological voice of Judaism accords with the implications of common conduct, past and present: the Judaism of real people.

In the nature of things it is especially in the synagogue and in the yeshiva or academy that the meeting with God is constant. "Seek God at the time of finding" speaks of where and when God is made manifest. There is where the Torah is taken out of its holy ark and declaimed; where people gather, in intense concentration, to examine its words and their logic and their structure. In the one place, through proper rite, all Israel embodied in a quorum of ten hears the words of the Torah. In the other, people who devote all their real time to learning in the Torah undertake to be changed by the Torah. So while when even one studies the Torah God is made manifest in its words, where Israel in community studies the Torah the Torah comes to full realization in the song that is sung only in chorus: God sings, Israel hears and responds in the Torah. The Torah is in two parts, however, and each introduces its own kind of meeting. In stressing throughout the singular encounter with God in synagogue and yeshiva, I should not represent the two meeting places as uniform or obscure that the two components of the Torah afford quite different kinds of meetings with God. God sings in one way here, in the other way there, as Moses and Elijah could have taught one another.

The two public occasions of God's self-manifestation in the Torah not only are alike but they also differ. They differ in the very obvious fact that in the synagogue the written part of the Torah is displayed and proclaimed, while in the academy the oral part of the same Torah is set forth. While, furthermore, the synagogue celebrates the Torah, in the academy the Torah gains its true voice and is heard in all solemnity. That is for two reasons. First, in the synagogue Israel sits and listens; affirms without a more than passive engagement. In most circumstances a rabbi explains what has been read, or no one does; the words speak for themselves. But in the academy Israel takes part in a colloquy of proposition and objection, analysis and argument, an on-going conversation and dialogue with allegations as to truth. In the academy's unique way of receiving the Torah, Israel pays the compliment of utter and total conviction: the tribute of sustained argument as to truth, along paths dictated by public reason and compelling rationality.

The second reason is that, in the academy, in theory and practice, disciples of sages through learning in the Torah are changed in mind and, therefore, also in character and soul. For the academy through Torah learning means to form right attitudes, in the language of the Torah itself, to purify the human heart. In the academy or yeshiva, that means to shape their minds in response to the rules of rigorous inquiry by which the inner order and sense of the Torah are uncovered, so that they too may think in the same way. The religious experience of encounter and dialogue with God that the Torah affords takes the form of prayer or study; but study is the more immediate, the more intense, the more intimate: there God gets inside our minds. The Talmud says that God wants the heart, and the Talmud also says that God gave the Torah only to purify our hearts. All that I said about the centrality of attitude and intentionality means only to bring to the surface the profound insistence upon the why of the encounter with God: What difference meeting God is supposed to make.

What makes the argument of the academy a medium of theological discovery, so that the modes of argument convey the melodies of the Torah? Right thinking in the academy affords access especially to those rules of intellection that governed when the Torah took shape and that express what was on God's mind. If God is made manifest in the Torah, then all can see how God forms thoughts, makes sentences, brings about connections (e.g., juxtapositions), and draws conclusions: how God thinks in a way we can understand, in a way we ourselves can think. Disciples of sages not only gain possession of teachings of the Torah but are possessed by the modes of thought that produced those teachings and, therefore, reformed. The reformation takes place in the heart and mind, where the Torah makes its mark. But even hearing the Torah in the synagogue may change minds and affect the intellect of hearers; properly proclaimed in careful song, the Torah in the synagogue touches the heart and soul.

Observing the difference between the giving of the Torah in the synagogue and the receiving of the Torah in the academy, we now note that synagogue and academy share the implacably public character of their activity. The religious encounter afforded by the Torah takes principal place not for the private person but in public, in a moment of community and of communion: Israel with Israel, Israel with God. In both cases, then, synagogue and yeshiva, the act consists in the shared act and moment of hearing and receiving the gift of the Torah. The gift has to be received, accepted, acknowledged, and, in the nature of the holy life of Israel, that means by Israel as a whole, as at Sinai. The unacknowledged gift is an insult.

How is this shared acknowledgment, this public engagement with the gift, to be accomplished? The Torah not only reveals that God is, but what God says and wants: propositions. And it follows, the way in which Israel receives the gift of the Torah is through its understanding, its capacity to persuade itself in all rationality to affirm and obey. That is why in the synagogue the Torah is not only displayed but read. That fact further explains why in the academy the Torah is not only read but analyzed. It is in the life of the mind that Israel receives the gift, that Judaism affirms revelation. The rigorous composition of theology then forms the counterpart, in secular language, to the act of rational affirmation, in the language of the Torah: we shall do, and we shall obey. And that fact brings us back once again to the center of matters, the public and communal quality of the meeting with God. It leads us to understand why we must understand the Torah as God's song. There is nothing so public, and that by definition, as intellect.

Now let us dwell on the requirements of the shared and public receiving of the gift of the Torah. When we have grasped what is required we will more vividly understand the necessity of singing, singing in particular, in the giving and receiving of the Torah.

The first rule of thought is the sharing of thought: to speak intelligibly to the other is to ascertain that what one thinks is intelligent. The contemporary philosophical words, "universalizability" and "generalizability," serve as the model. These refer to what can be shown to others to be true and can be demonstrated to apply to many cases. Where thought cannot be communicated by some protocol of rationality or convention of agreed signals that sustain communication, we deal with what is not asocial but insane. Rationality is always public, by definition. And, given the public character of the giving of the Torah, the propositional character of what is given, and the active and engaged character of the act of receiving the Torah, it is no surprise that the rule for studying the Torah and, therefore, also the requirement for meeting God, is as with Moses and Elijah. God gives the Torah through the prophet, to be sure, but always to the "us" of Israel. So "we" meeting the One may be embodied in the "I," the individual of whom Halafta speaks, but "we" always stands for the "we" of Israel. Rationality requires community.

If revelation is public and communal, how in the theology of Judaism does the individual relate to the community? I speak of theology that is shared, public, and communicable, not only solipsistic and personal. While the Torah may be studied in private, it is received and proclaimed only in the public square of shared worship or shared learning: synagogue, yeshiva. One's obligation to hear the Torah read can be fulfilled only in community, in a quorum. That is where we meet God. This is the point of R. Halafta of Kefar Hananiah, in a familiar saying of Torah learning that explains how we meet God in the Torah:

> Among ten who sit and work hard on Torah the Presence comes to rest, as it is said, "God stands in the congregation of God" [Ps. 82:1]. And how do we know that the same is so even of five? For it is said, "And he has founded his group upon the earth" [Am. 9:6]. And how do we know that this is so even of three? Since it is said, "And he judges among the judges" [Ps. 82:1]. And how do we know that this is so even of two? Because it is said, "Then

they that feared the Lord spoke with one another, and the
Lord hearkened and heard" [Mal. 3:16]. And how do we
know that this is so even of one? Since it is said, "In every
place where I record my name I will come to you and I
will bless you" [Ex. 20:24].

TRACTATE ABOT 3:6

So—Halafta maintains—Israel meets God in the Torah, and that
encounter may take place among many or even one on One. But
Halafta has spoken of even a single individual, and, it is manifest,
Israel is made up of individuals, each of whom is supposed to receive and reverence the Torah and its teachings. How hold the
whole together, making place for each along the way? I speak of a
theological voice, but in the adventitious accidents of personality
there may be only voices. The answer unfolds in yet another sequence of facts, to be specified and analyzed.

We recall how music serves to hold together individual voices
in a single moment of music. We now leave the medium of music
behind and identify the facts of the living faith and the propositions those facts convey. The first is that the character of the Torah
tells private persons what they are, all together, and it tells Israel,
all together, how the families of which Israel is comprised are to
conduct themselves.

1. Israel is made up of individuals in families, of families in
communities, of communities in all Israel.

2. And all Israel takes place when it is all together, all at once.

That assembly takes place on Sabbath after Sabbath when Israel is assembled, as at Sinai, to celebrate the Torah by paying attention to it and asserting who Israel too is, as the blessing before
the Torah states: "Blessed are you, Lord, our God, ruler of the
world, who has chosen us from among all the peoples by having
given us the Torah. Blessed are you, who gives the Torah." At the
end come similar words, referring to us, Israel: "who has given us
the Torah that is true and planted within us eternal life." So much
for individuals in families assembled in the synagogue: chosen
through the Torah. That is not the end of the matter of the public

character of the assembly with God, but it carries us far beyond the beginning.

What about God's presence, in secular language the theological voice itself? The second, and more important aspect already has impressed us: the immediacy of the presence of God in the Torah, despite Halafta's contrary assurance, really does require the presence of the many, for in fact the Torah insists upon Israel's presence, represented by some sort of quorum; Halafta does after all commence with a quorum. In the synagogue the quorum makes possible the public declamation: the reading of the Torah at the climax of the act of worship. Without a quorum Qaddish—the sanctification of God's Name in public—cannot be recited or the Torah read. This quorum by definition invariably marks the present tense; there is no quorum out of the past. Merely because, an hour earlier, ten people were present does not validate the public proclamation of the Torah. And merely because, an hour from now, someone will come to complete the quorum, does not permit us to remove the Torah from its ark and to read it now. God gives the Torah (so the blessing states) here-and-now, this minute, to these people, in this quorum. And that is where the academy (and its civilian counterparts, groups of Jews assembled for Torah study wherever they meet) comes into the picture. The Torah speaks in the hear-and-now when people learn how to listen.

So we come to the critical question concerning the giving and the receiving of the Torah, which is to say, how God is made manifest in Israel, in me, you, him, her: us: How to hold the whole together? The answer once more derives from the facts of the lived theology of Judaism, or, in the native categories of Judaism, from the moment when God gives the Torah: it is to listening Israel in the here-and-now, all of us, all together.

We form a quorum specifically to listen, which of course means to understand and to respond. Then the whole holds together in our shared act of understanding and responding: reasoning together, hearing at once and thinking along the same lines of rationality. In the ordinary world we understand through reasoning specifically, through a process of thought that we share with the other, that makes two minds work in one way so that both understand the same thing. In Torah study, properly conducted, we undertake the disciplines of reasoning that show us not only what the Torah says but how the Torah works: the way in which our minds work in correspondence with, therefore in response to, how the mind of the One who gives the Torah works.

So much for the exposition of the known. Now everything is in place, and I have evoked only entirely familiar, universally acknowledged facts concerning the practice of the faith. Our somewhat slow progress, with an occasional doubling back, through the facts of the giving and receiving of the Torah in the vivid existence of holy Israel, yields this conclusion: when Israel meets God, it is (1) in a public event, which (2) requires a meeting of minds, a shared rationality.

Then the mystery is: How, in what media, through what processes of ratiocination, joined through what shared rationality, do our minds join—and also meet—God's mind? How do we form a communion of intellects, and what are the media by which minds are brought into union? Several questions here are melded: (1) the question of the giving of the Torah to me through us, (2) the question of shared communication, (3) the question of the how of revelation. When we know the solution to that complex of mystery and paradox, we shall hear how the Torah is supposed to speak to us, which is to say, in the categories of the world at large, how to identify Judaism's theological voice. So now I have set the stage for the considerations of the critical issue: how the Torah makes intelligible statements, at once compelling and persuasive, to which we give uncoerced assent, that is, through our own rigorous reasoning coming to God's own conclusions.

I do not mean to deal in paradox or mystery. The evidence of faithful humanity tells that God speaks not only in silence but also in the mystery of what comes to us as contradiction. But in the Torah all things lie on the surface. The voice of Sinai was heard by the uneducated slave girl as much as by the sages of the day, and, when she heard, she heard more, and with more nuance and also more conviction, than sages later on with their acute logic, working with the mere memory of Sinai. Even the infants and babes in their mothers' wombs joined in the Song at the Sea:

Then [Moses and the people of Israel sang this song to
the Lord, saying "I will sing to the Lord, for he has tri-
umphed gloriously; the horse and his rider he has thrown
into the sea" [Exodus 15:1]:

R. Meir says, "Even embryos in their mothers' wombs
opened up their mouths and recited the song before the
Omnipresent: 'Bless God in full assemblies, even the
Lord, you who are from the fountain of Israel" [Ps. 68:27].

"And it was not Israel alone that recited the song before the Omnipresent.

"Even the ministering angels did so: 'O Lord, our
Lord, how glorious is your name in all the earth, whose
majesty is rehearsed above the heavens' [Ps. 8:2]."

MEKHILTA XXVI:I.17 = SHIRATA CHAPTER ONE

So there are no mysteries before God, though from the world that
God has made come many to us. How are we to accord uncoerced
assent to propositions that God has already reached and revealed?
The critical point lies in the character of God's self-manifestation,
which defines the conditions for communion of minds, ours with
one another, ours with God's. The fact, as we have already observed, is that God's self-manifestation proves in the Torah to
make a highly propositional statement, which forms facts into
truth and means to persuade us, to compel through a process of
thinking and feeling. So the medium by which minds are formed
into a communion affects intellect but also emotion, attitude and
also feeling, deed and also intentionality: how we are and what we
may become in the whole of our being.

Let me spell this claim out with some care, so that the final solution to the mystery of the giving and receiving of the Torah will
prove commensurate to the problem: What medium serves, or, to
adumbrate my goal at the end: why song in particular? And, to
signal what is coming, my answer will be, it had to be music, and
only music. That claim paraphrases what the Talmud itself states
in so many words.

Said R. Shephataiah said R. Yohanan, "Whoever recites
from the Torah without melody or repeats Mishnah-
traditions without song—concerning him Scripture states,

'Moreover I gave them statutes that were not good and ordinances by which they could not have life' [Ezekiel 20:25]."

BAVLI MEGILLAH 32A

Essential to learning Torah traditions and not forgetting them is song:

> R. Joshua b. Qorhah says, "Whoever studies the Torah and does not review it is like a man who sows seed but does not harvest it."
>
> R. Joshua says, "Whoever learns the Torah and forgets it is like a woman who bears and buries."
>
> R. Aqiba says, "A song is in me, a song always."

TOSEFTA AHILOT 6:8H–I = BAVLI SANHEDRIN 99A–B

So my insistence on the centrality of song in receiving the Torah once more is shown merely to paraphrase what our sages of blessed memory themselves maintained. But the point of relevance to the argument here is different. Why song in particular? The reason is that song uniquely bears the power to unite one person to the next, and also forms the union of feeling and intellect, proposition and sentiment. When we sing, we sing words, but we may also smile or laugh or cry; and pray, and, as I shall explain, also study.

Am I right to insist upon a medium for theological expression that unites feeling and thought? To respond, let me give a single compelling case of the union of the public and the private, the intellectual and the affective, the propositional and the emotional, conviction, attitude, and conscience. The Torah contains the words that say not only that God is one and unique ("Hear O Israel, the Lord is our God, the one God"), but also how we are supposed to feel and what we are supposed to think in that very context of the pronouncement of the doctrine concerning the one unique God: presence. The next words state, "And" (meaning, therefore) "you shall love the Lord your God with all your heart, with all your soul, and with all your might." Now love is a gift, not a given, and cannot be coerced by mere commandment. There is always, after all, the possibility of hypocrisy, or duplicity, or mere obedience; and coerced love is not love, nor are the formalities of love love.

Love, then, is the space in the heart left open for our own volition, the gift that, by definition, is never a given but must be presented, and unless an offense is intended must also be acknowledged and received. The commandment of loving God speaks of soul: Then what does the soul have to do in the transaction of the commandment to love? The soul, the being or person of each one, is formed of conscience and consciousness, which are the work of reason and persuasion, and it is in the soul that information is turned into truth, knowledge into conviction. Love flows from the union of mind and soul and fills the heart. So heart and soul form mind: where God meets humanity through, or in, the Torah. So let us think music.

Two

THINKING THE MUSIC

*I*ntegrity characterizes truth, when all things hold together and cohere. Thought, well crafted, flows like music, well conducted: compelling and inexorable from note to note. Then the connection between one thing and the next bears the aspect of self-evidence that governs throughout. In a well-ordered world, matters cohere so that all things say the same thing, and nothing disrupts to say the opposite. If, therefore, I can establish that many details make the same point, I can demonstrate the good order of the world or, in the life of intellect, the integrity of truth.

This I accomplish when I can explain how this detail fits with that, illustrating the rationality of connections. I do so by showing that when something is juxtaposed with something else, there is a connection to be made and, it must follow, a lesson to be drawn. All things depend upon juxtaposition and connection. Then the connection bears the message—asking, why this, not that, why here, not there—but also forms the medium for conveying rationality. These principles of the orderly and well-composed universe of thought guide us in our quest for the encounter with God in the Torah: the Torah's portrait of God's mind as God is made manifest in the words and sentences of the Torah.

Now to move forward in learning how to hear the Torah's

theological voice: if I can show what one thing has to do with something else, I produce the conclusion that the connection insists is there to be drawn. Everything depends upon making connections and drawing conclusions, and our path into the depths of the Torah leads us toward those profound layers at which one thing joins something else, while another thing does not. Accomplishing that work of exegesis of the given—the received juxtapositions, the points of self-evident intersections—I replicate the main exercise of thought: the demonstration of harmony, unity, coherence, which characterize truth of integrity. What I mean here will become concrete in due course, for, I hasten to emphasize, these altogether too abstract remarks will take on acutely detailed form in Chapters 3 and 4. At the outset, we do well to consider the prevailing proposition in whole form, only later on examining its concrete exemplification.

Now, right at the outset, the reader knows what to expect: a detailed examination of the problem of making connections and drawing conclusions. Three questions form the outline of our inquiry into how we think the music: What is this? Why this, not that? So what? To describe something, we ask how it is like something else, and we answer "what is this" by identifying what this is like. To analyze something, we compare and contrast something with something else, why this not that capturing the process of contrast. And to interpret our results we find the answer to the always-urgent question, So what? That means, If I know this, what else do I know?

To amplify: three stages mark the work of analysis. These are (1) describing, then (2) analyzing through comparison and contrast, and finally (3) interpreting the religious system at hand. "What is this?" refers to the first stage; "Why this, not that?" to the second; and "So what?" to the third. The first question is descriptive and inductive. The second is analytical, and, among the many ways in which we may analyze, I choose the comparative one: this thing in comparison with another that is in some ways like it, in others not like it. The third question invites interpretation. Among the many questions of interpretation one can raise, I want to know the answer to a single one, as I said: If this, then what else? So we move from one thing, to some things, to many things. Seeing something entirely in its own terms means we have to seek evidence about the character of that thing only within the thing itself. But when we have found that evidence, we shall find it difficult to make sense of it until we have established a context for it. And the context means we have to compare the thing we propose to describe with some other thing of its own sort. Otherwise, all we have are facts. But even when the work of comparison has been undertaken, so that we know that *A* exhibits the following three traits, and *B* three other traits, we have little more in hand than bits and pieces of information. Description without comparison yields a work of mere show and tell. Comparison without interpretation produces mere paraphrase. Both then serve to point toward a larger task, which is to answer the question, So what? All these steps in thinking bring us to the knowledge of how we are supposed to make connections and draw conclusions.

These, in concrete terms, are the modes of analysis of those processes of thought that in the Torah's words and wording show us the connections God has made, the conclusions God has drawn, for instructing us: how God thinks, how our minds correspond to God's mind. There, and there alone, in the making of (self-evidently valid) connections, we find the natural sounds of thought, counterpart to the natural sounds of music in synagogue worship and yeshiva learning. And, it goes without saying, in the conclusions drawn from those connections, we identify the propositions of the faith at their foundations: those points of self-evidence on which all else rests and everything is constructed. Now, why this shading over from the connection of sound to sentiment, the movement of music into meditation in words, as in a symphony that ends with a song that is sung in so many words—the music alone no longer sufficing? And how explain the connection between this, that, and the other thing: the making of connections and (consequent) drawing of conclusions? And why, moving from the insistence that God sings, do I speak of our "thinking" the music?

Unpacking the question yields its answer. We start with the simple explanation: why words with the music? The reason is that—as Chapter 1 has already shown us—the music of the spheres does not suffice, however inviting its harmonies. The holy God sings not music without words alone but music with words, a great many words: "I am the Lord your God who brought you out of the land of Egypt, out of the house of bondage, you shall have no other gods before me." That and many other words—all of the words of the Torah, both oral and written—join the music. For our God is not a Presence alone, nor yet a Person alone, but the one and only God that passionately propositions us: do this not that, this minute not later on, eat this not that—therefore, think this not that. Do and deliberate, draw conclusions from this for many other thats.

And it is at that point—the point of rationality and occasion of intellection—that we find the center of our inquiry into the sung theology of Judaism, the voice, the melody of the Talmud in particular. And a simple specification of the three steps of this part of my argument explains why: (1) Since the Torah sets forth the results of thought, our task is to move from those results—the words the Torah sings to us—(2) to the rules for forming words into sentences, that is, corresponding to the rules that (for the Torah) form sound into music. (3) For the counterpart to the theory of the music put forth by God's song, I refer specifically to the principles and rules of making connections and drawing conclusions.

Let me spell out the relationship between the sung theology of the Torah and our search for the principles of self-evidence and rationality that define the permissible harmonies, the match of sound to substantive statement to which I referred earlier. Our answer will be found—as we shall see in Chapter 3—when we make the movement from the surface to the depths, reversing the process that in ordinary thought leads us from premise to principle to coherent propositions. Our movement goes from proposition to principle to premise. Why does the Torah make possible that progress? Because—the premise of all constructive theology in the Torah—the Torah forms God's self-manifestation: it is what God wants us to know about all the questions we cannot on our own answer or even intelligently ask. Without the Torah we are like the simple child at the Passover seder, who can ask only, What is this? Or we are like the fourth child, who does not even know how to ask at all.

The Torah changes all that. In God's wording ("God spoke to Moses saying, Speak to the children of Israel and say to them . . .") the Torah shows us how sentences take shape, words form intelligible propositions, as God speaks, and from the sentences we can learn the grammar—moral, metaphysical, theological alike—of God's intellect. In context, then, we who can say only, What is this? or nothing at all, find ourselves able to master the language of God's mind, the processes of thought. That comes to us in the written Torah. In the conflict of the oral Torah, we show how we can try to speak that very same language, form our own part of the conversation. So in the written Torah we work our way back from the Torah to God's rationality, from the world to God's purpose and will. In the oral Torah we use the principles of thought that God has exposed. From the foreign language learned by rote in the classroom, we take our first steps in the country where that foreign language is not foreign at all, but where we are foreign and through the natural sounds of the country make ourselves intelligible. From the world to the Torah, from the Torah to God's mind—that is the path we can take, singing as we go, as the original Man in Australia sang his way across the continent and so created the world.

My claim in behalf of the Torah ("Judaism") proves less extravagant when I place on display the very words that express the claim that I have represented. This view that in the Torah God is made manifest and, in particular, that God's modes of thought become known is expressed in the claim that, when God made the world, God took the Torah, and, with the perspective of the architect, made use of the Torah as plan in hand at the outset of the building. Then the Torah, oral and written, affords us perspective on the building—but, in the nature of things, only from inspection of the finished edifice. Comparing the world to the Torah, and the Torah to God's plan and intent, and these to the shape and structure of God's mind, which correspond to ours—these are the breathtaking conceptions that the Torah itself opens up to us:

what is humanity, indeed, that through the Torah that manifests God we should think like God! The following expresses the point:

"In the beginning God created" [Gen. 1:1]:

R. Oshaia commenced [discourse by citing the following verse:] "'Then I was beside him like a little child, and I was daily his delight [rejoicing before him always, rejoicing in his inhabited world, and delighting in the sons of men]' [Prov. 8:30–31].

"The word for 'child' uses consonants that may also stand for 'teacher,' 'covered over,' and 'hidden away.'" . . .

Another matter:

The word means "workman."

[In the cited verse] the Torah speaks, "I was the work-plan of the Holy One, blessed be he."

In the accepted practice of the world, when a mortal king builds a palace, he does not build it out of his own head, but he follows a work-plan.

And [the one who supplies] the work-plan does not build out of his own head, but he has designs and diagrams, so as to know how to situate the rooms and the doorways.

Thus the Holy One, blessed be he, consulted the Torah when he created the world.

So the Torah stated, "By means of 'the beginning' [that is to say, the Torah] did God create . . ." [Gen. 1:1].

And the word for "beginning" refers only to the Torah, as Scripture says, "The Lord made me as the beginning of his way" [Prov. 8:22].

GENESIS RABBAH I:I.1–2

The Torah is the plan, fully in hand, so God created the way a philosopher or architect does, consulting the principles in laying out the lines of the building. God made the Torah so as to know how to make the world. And the burden of my argument is that that invites the reverse journey. From the world to the mind of the Creator of the world through the close encounter with the plan for creation. True, all that humanity now has for understanding the world as God wants it to be is the Torah. But, seen in light of the remarkably spacious claim at hand, that suffices for the labor at hand.

In creating the Torah, the sage thus maintains, God worked as a theologian, that is, God worked logically in exposing the logic of God the creator's intellect, thus the inner structure of the world. Then, through study of the Torah, the sage can uncover, out of the details, the plan of the whole—thus doing the work of the theologian. Working back from the correspondence of the world to the details of the Torah, guided by the Torah, not the data of the world, we, therefore, gain access to the plan that guides God: what is in God's own mind, how God's own intellect does its work. And in our context, our very capacity for understanding, for entering into the logic of the world, gives testimony to how our minds correspond to that of God's. It is in intellect, as much as emotion and attitude, that we can become *like God:* "in our image, after our likeness," as, the Creation narrative tells us, we have been created.

In the present context, then, the point is clear. If we want to know how to make connections and draw conclusions, we must learn how the Torah's connections are made and how its conclusions are drawn. The point then is a simple one: since the Torah is God's song, it must follow that the theology of Judaism reaches expression in some few, particular melodies, of which the Written Torah presents one, and the Oral Torah, in particular in the Talmud, another. The ultimate quest is for the harmony of the two melodies. So our task is to explain precisely how the voice is heard, the melody set forth. And at stake is not only music but mind, since God's is a song with many words.

My answer, Chapter 1 has already suggested, is that just as when we proclaim the written Torah in the synagogue we can sing God's song too, so also when we study the Talmud in the academy we can think as God does and wants us to. In the synagogue we talk to God through prayer and hear from God in the Torah, but in the yeshiva or in other locations for studying the Torah, we participate as active partners in the conversation. We talk but also listen; we listen but also respond. We are, then, at our most human: most like God.

The life of synagogue shows how we sing out the Torah, as God did to Moses, as Moses did to Israel. I have already spelled out in abstract terms the foundations of thought, specifically the intellectual premise of the yeshiva's study of the Torah. And that is, we think the way the Torah thinks, which is the way God thinks. That is why reasoned argument becomes plausible. We are joined to God by the common law of intellection, the shared sense of self-evidence, the given that is the gift of rationality. And that claim that I put forth in humanity's behalf—the correspondence of our mode of intellect to God's—is not merely the conceit of a professor, pleased with his own life and its promise. Nor is it attested to solely by the life of the contemporary Yeshiva, where sages and their disciples venture deep into the intellectual depths of the Torah. That very proposition emerges and is said in so many words by statements of the oral part of the Torah itself, first, that God thinks the way sages do and sages think the way God does, and, second, that God is coerced by the same logic and bound to the same rules of evidence.

This view that God thinks like us and, therefore, we like God, that God needs us and responds to our argument and insight as much as we need God and respond to God's logic as portrayed by the Torah, which forms the premise of all that follows, is expressed in the following tale:

> —*[Rabbah bar Nahmani] was in session on the trunk of a palm and studying.*
>
> *Now in the session in the firmament they were debating the following subject:*
>
> **If the bright spot preceded the white hair, he is unclean, and if the white hair preceded the bright spot, he is clean. [The Mishnah-paragraph continues: and if it is a matter of doubt, he is unclean.**
>
> **And R. Joshua was in doubt] [M. Neg. 4:11F–H]—** the Holy One, blessed be he, says, "It is clean."
>
> *And the entire session in the firmament say,* "Unclean." [We see, therefore, that in Heaven, Mishnah-study was going forward, with the Holy One participating and set-

ting forth his ruling, as against the consensus of the other sages of the Torah in heaven.]

They said, "Who is going to settle the question? It is Rabbah b. Nahmani."

For said Rabbah b. Nahmani, "I am absolutely unique in my knowledge of the marks of skin-disease that is unclean and in the rule of uncleanness having to do with the corpse in the tent."

They sent an angel for him, but the angel of death could not draw near to him, since his mouth did not desist from repeating his learning. But in the meanwhile a wind blew and caused a rustling in the bushes, so he thought it was a troop of soldiers. He said, "Let me die but not be handed over to the kingdom."

When he was dying, he said, "It is clean, it is clean." An echo came forth and said, "Happy are you, Rabbah bar Nahmani, that your body is clean, and your soul has come forth in cleanness." [The body would not putrefy.]

A note fell down from heaven in Pumbedita: "Rabbah bar Nahmani has been invited to the session that is on high."

BAVLI BABA MESIA 86A

The critical point in this story for my argument comes at three turnings. These points are so vital to all that follows that each requires articulation.

First, God and the sages in heaven study the Torah in the same way as the Torah is studied on earth.

Second, God is bound by the same rules of rationality as prevail down here.

Third, the sage on earth studies the way God does in heaven, and God calls up to heaven sages whose exceptional acuity and perspicacity are required on the occasion.

It follows that, when I claim our processes of analytical reasoning rightly carried out replicate God's, we can think like God and in that way be holy like God, I merely paraphrase in abstract language precisely the point on which this story and others bearing the same implication rest. My constructive theology undertakes only to state what is already in the Torah, in so many words, but set forth in other words than the received ones: theologians serve to paraphrase God's revealed truth, and the paraphrase recasts that truth in accord with God's revealed rules of thought. So much for the "what is this" of the claim that in the Torah we encounter God's mind.

Now to move onward, to the "why this, not that," and specifically: Why do the rules reveal to our minds the mind of God? It is because God is bound by the same rules of logical analysis and sound discourse that govern sages. That view is not left merely implicit but is stated explicitly as well. In the following story, also found for the first time in the second Talmud and assuredly speaking for its authorship, we find an explicit affirmation of the priority of reasoned argument over all other forms of discovery of truth:

> *There we have learned:* **If one cut [a clay oven] into parts and put sand between the parts,**
> **R. Eliezer declares the oven broken-down and therefore insusceptible to uncleanness.**
> **And sages declare it susceptible.**
> **And this is what is meant by the oven of Akhnai [M. Kel. 5:10].**
> *Why* [is it called] the oven of Akhnai?
> Said R. Judah said Samuel, "It is because they surrounded it with argument as with a snake and proved it was insusceptible to uncleanness."
> *It has been taught on Tannaite authority:*
> On that day R. Eliezer produced all of the arguments in the world, but they did not accept them from him. So he said to them, "If the law accords with my position, this carob tree will prove it."
> The carob was uprooted from its place by a hundred cubits—and some say, four hundred cubits.
> They said to him, "There is no proof from a carob tree."

So he went and said to them, "If the law accords with my position, let the stream of water prove it."

The stream of water reversed flow.

They said to him, "There is no proof from a stream of water."

So he went and said to them, "If the law accords with my position, let the walls of the schoolhouse prove it."

The walls of the schoolhouse tilted toward falling.

R. Joshua rebuked them, saying to them, "If disciples of sages are contending with one another in matters of law, what business do you have?"

They did not fall on account of the honor owing to R. Joshua, but they also did not straighten up on account of the honor owing to R. Eliezer, and to this day they are still tilted.

So he went and said to them, "If the law accords with my position, let the Heaven prove it!"

An echo came forth, saying, "What business have you with R. Eliezer, for the law accords with his position under all circumstances!"

R. Joshua stood up on his feet and said, "'It is not in heaven' [Deut. 30:12]."

What is the sense of, "'It is not in heaven' [Deut. 30:12]"?

Said R. Jeremiah, "[The sense of Joshua's statement is this:] For the Torah has already been given from Mount Sinai, so we do not pay attention to echoes, since you have already written in the Torah at Mount Sinai, 'After the majority you are to incline' [Ex. 23:2]."

R. Nathan came upon Elijah and said to him, "What did the Holy One, blessed be he, do at that moment?"

He said to him, "He laughed and said, 'My children have overcome me, my children have overcome me!'"

BAVLI BABA MESIA 59A–B

Through the ages, those concluding words have inspired the disciples of sages at their work: through intelligent argument the sage may overcome in argument the very Creator of heaven and earth, the One who gives the Torah—and is bound by its rules too. Here, in the Torah, humanity is not only like God but, in context, equal to God because subject to the same logic. In secular terms the conception of theoretical mathematics as the actual description of nature corresponds.

But with this difference: the testimony of nature on its own is null. The heavens declare the glory of God—but only because the psalmist says so. "You have seen what I have done . . . ," but only because God tells Moses that that is how events add up to meaning. And that is what I meant when, in Chapter 1, I argued that, uninterpreted by the Torah, neither nature nor history without the structure of meaning manifest in the Torah bears compelling messages. Only the Torah does, and the Torah imposes its messages upon nature and history alike.

But the Torah takes its stand against the arbitrary and capricious: God is bound by the same rules of logical argument, of relevant evidence, of principled exchange, as are we. So we can argue with the mere declaration of fact or opinion—even God's, beyond the Torah, must be measured against God's, within the Torah. The (mere) declaration of matters by Heaven is dismissed. Why? Because God is bound by the rules of rationality that govern in human discourse, and because humanity in the person of the sage thinks like God, as God does; so right is right, and nature has no call to intervene, nor does even God to reverse the course of rational argument. That is why the Torah forms the possession of sages, and sages master the Torah through logical argument, right reasoning, the give and take of proposition and refutation, argument and counterargument, evidence arrayed in accord with the rules of proper analysis.

That Torah of ours is a revelation of reason, and this in two ways: (1) reason itself is encompassed in what is revealed, and (2) through reason the divine imperative is made compelling. Then the majority will be persuaded, one way or the other, entirely by sound argument: and the majority prevails on that account. God is now bound to the rules of rationality that govern the minds of our sages, and if reason or logic compels a given decision, God is compelled too. Once more, the full meaning of "thinking the music" emerges, and it turns out that the Torah in its oral form makes that very point about (in my terms) the union of words and music, proposition and modes of thought.

Let us now turn back to the tales before us and ask, Precisely how do these stories say so? When Heaven sends for Rabbah, it is because Rabbah possesses the intellectual power that Heaven as much as sages require. And if God rejoices at the victory, in the give and take of argument, of the sages, it is because God is subject to the same rules of argument and evidence and analysis. Then, as I said, if we want to know God, we shall find God in the Torah: not in what the Torah says alone, but in how the Torah reaches conclusions, meaning, not the adventitious process of argument but the principles of thought. God's self-manifestation takes the form of not Presence alone ([1] there is a God in the world, and [2] God is one), nor of Person alone ([1] the one God hears prayer and answers, [2] loves us and accords us grace), but of intellectual incarnation: we are like God in the shared, self-evident rules of utter rationality. God has revealed these in the Torah, and in them we encounter God's own intellect. The theology of Judaism sets forth, out of that medium of self-revelation, the Torah itself, God's will and intellect. Now, rapidly, to recapitulate the main beam of this construction of theology: it is that Torah that is sung in fitting music that we can master, that Torah that is made up of words we know and sentences we can understand and forming connections we can follow and replicate, that we meet God. When I said, God sings to Israel, that is what I meant. Now, when I speak of thinking music, here is what is at stake.

Then how do we know right from wrong in the Torah? If we think the music, we know how. We know right notes from wrong, discordant ones. Rules of harmony tell us what works and what does not. That means, what notes work with what other notes, logically sound at the same moment, or logically connect in a sequence, fore and aft. When we know how to make the fitting connections, we can draw the right conclusions. Then identify—in sound—the sounds that count. Then we hear the melody within the music. In sentiment and substantive statement the music conveys the inner cogency and logic of what otherwise seems disorganized. The opposite for sound is not silence—God after all is in all silence, waiting to be heard—but cacophony, not music in any conventional sense at all; the opposite for substantive statement is nonsense, confusion, and chaos—the violation of the rules of self-evidence we know as rationality. So theology for Judaism is the quest for God's rationality, which we uncover in rigorous inspection of our own.

Up until now, I have used the word "theology" without an elaborate definition, assuming we all know what we mean, that is, well-criticized and coherent norms of belief and behavior. But that functional usage obscures the specific vocation of theology, contained in the preceding words. So a more locative definition is required. That is, to compose theology is to set forth in a cogent and coherent statement, in accord with rational principles of inquiry and argument, the norms of belief and behavior. In our case, theology comprises knowing the difference between what naturally sounds sweet and what does not, what self-evidently forms connections to something else and what does not: theology knows the difference, theology explains the reason why: not this but that. So, until this point, preferring to emphasize the native categories of "the Torah" rather than the academic categories of "Judaism," I have left open the question, When we speak of Judaism's theological voice, are we not discussing whatever pertains in general to Judaism, the religion? Why specify not religion in general but theology in particular? None of the implicit definitions that have served so well to this point responds to that question.

Since by "theology," however, we mean, at a minimum, cogent, well-examined truth about God, for Judaism, it is entirely appropriate to ask about Judaism's theological *voice,* and not only, or mainly, Judaism's theological *message.*[1] Absent the voice, while there are messages there is no single message: things that make

---

1. Indeed, it is only in systematic theology, not undertaken here, that a formidable agendum of theological propositions is to be set forth. Then a set of questions will define the systematic program, from start to finish. Distinguishing voice from message, to be sure, shades over into the disingenuous, since, self-evidently, this book is full of concrete theological propositions. But they serve a different argument from the systematic kind.

sense but no defining rationality. The voice not only conveys the message but invites the recognition that a message is to be conveyed. What is life like, before we recognize a voice, music governed by fixed rhythm, harmony, melody? It is as though we had two apples but no arithmetic, an atomic explosion without nuclear physics, a sturdy bridge without engineering: facts but no explanation, data without generalization, cases but no rule. That explains why, when I speak of "theology," I begin by seeking to identify the "voice" of the Torah: the voice not the notes, the voice not the devices by which truth is set forth. But that is not where we end. So, it must follow, when I wish to explain the priority of the Talmud in the theological formulation of Judaism (in the language of the Torah: the contribution of the oral Torah to the one whole Torah of Moses, our rabbi), I have in acute detail to expose the relationship of melody to proposition. Where, specifically, are we to find the notes to the music, and of what do the notes consist? That now defines the task to be carried out in the remaining pages of this book.

Theology then is not alone sound not only the union of sounds. Theology says things, theology thinks, theology speaks intelligibly and rationally about God: specifically, what we know about God out of God's self-manifestation. So we are drawn from the sung theology to identify precisely what that theology is that is sung. It is now time to learn where and how we are to think the music. How in our inner ear do we hear the melody of that theological voice of which we have spoken? The answer, of course, has already been set forth in Chapter 1, the requirements of the answer in what has been said in this chapter. And it is a simple answer: the theology of Judaism finds its voice in the melody of the two parts of the Torah, written and oral, the written sung in the synagogue, the oral sung in the academy, where the natural sounds find their voice in the Talmud. Matters have not even begun to show their complexity.

We can make no further progress until a more precise and nuanced account of our subject—the theological voice of the religion, Judaism, and the Talmud's distinctive melody for that voice—is in hand. Only with a clear answer shall we fully grasp

why synagogue and academy alike have chosen music as the medium for not religious experience in general but theological discourse in particular. Theological discourse then refers to the
statement of religious truth, in so many words. For music does not
limit the repertoire of religious experience and expression in the
lived faith of the Torah; deeds, transformed by attitudes expressed in liturgical formulas, serve equally well to give authentic
expression to the faith. But when it comes to the encounter with
God in the Torah, written and oral, music forms the medium of
communication, without which the words merely inform us; they
tell us about God but do not invoke God's presence. And words
without music do not serve for the same reason: they provide facts
but not truth, information not insight.

That is what I meant in the beginning when I asked for the
principles of cogency, which are the rules of juxtaposition. I insisted that we find out what one thing has to do with another and the
conclusions we are to draw from that fact. The religious form of
the intellectual question is best imparted once more by music;
when we sing the truths, our hearts feel what our minds profess,
and we are whole, intellect matching intention, sentiment united
with reason. That explains the place of liturgy, learning, and song
within the theological enterprise of the Torah: all three are necessary but not sufficient; and the words that are prayed or analyzed
or sung also are insufficient. But when they join together, we
come as close to God as, in this life, we ever shall.

Now, as a matter of fact, music need not have formed the medium for expressing the connections that are to be made, the conclusions that are to be drawn. Other religions find diverse, quite
suitable media for expressing in a rational and compelling way the
norms of the faith. Theater and dance, philosophy and debate, liturgy and prayer—all serve where they serve. And each medium
yields a message of an appropriate, specific character. Theology
for Christianities yields creeds, determined by councils of authorities, to be recited in church, rather than melodies to be sung in
chorus, polyphonic exchange; theology may take the form of laws,
decided by the consensus of the faithful, to be realized in the universal, uniform conduct of the Nation of Islam, rather than belief

and behavior embodied in the music of the synagogue and yeshiva that celebrate the Torah of our rabbi, Moses. Religions ordinarily concur that every medium must serve for an account of what it means to know and love God. But they differ. For no religion believes that all religions serve equally well. Judaism has its theater and its liturgy, but its voice is the sound of silence and speech. As we shall see, like Christianity, Judaism has been given its creeds and principles of faith; like Islam, Judaism has defined the norms in acts of faith, not only statements of conscience and conviction. But it is singularly, particularly[2] in the union of words through music when sung in synagogue or academy in the communion of faithful that Israel meets God. There, and only there, the Torah makes its statement (in the language of the faith). There Judaism identifies its creed (counterpart to the creed and dogma of Christianity). There and there alone the Torah defines its rules of divine service (counterpart to the law of the Nation of Islam).

So, deep into our argument, now let us consider a simple definition of what theology does and is. It is what I mean by "thinking the music." Theology is to religion as rational, rigorous thought is to impression and feeling. Theology employs the methods of philosophy for the reasoned inquiry into religion's revealed truth. Why so? Religion becomes theology—that is, makes a theological statement—when it adopts the rigorous discipline of philosophy. Philosophy takes the detritus of thought and composes a coherent and cogent statement, turns rubble into mortar and brick, and of them constructs a building that can stand. Only when religion formulates a statement that is coherent, proportioned, cogent, subject to sustained analysis for imperfections of disharmony with good result—only when religion says some one thing in many ways, and says so exceedingly persuasively—does religion become fully intelligible, wholly accessible to reasoned comprehension.

That analytical process, identifying disharmony and disproportion, pointing out contradictions in principle or in the premises of principle, reconstructing harmony and proportion and the

2. I avoid the word "uniquely."

unity of premises and consequently principles and cases, makes religion comprehensible. Comprehensibility in propositional terms corresponds to what I have called "the natural sounds," that is, the making of the ineluctable, obvious connection, the drawing of the necessary conclusion. So to define matters very succinctly: the process of reasoned knowledge of God made manifest finds its corpus of data in the Torah, its method in philosophy and its generative problem in religion. Then, allowed to run its course, that process defines theology.

Take for example the matter of God. The Torah presents a vast corpus of facts about God. Religion sets forth attitudes toward God, such as love and fear; traits attributed to God, such as justice and mercy; and definitions of God's place and presence, such as immanent and transcendent. Obviously, for ordinary rationality, which chokes on the union of opposites, one God cannot be both material and immaterial, omnipotent and weak, transcendent and immanent, able to govern history and also subject to rules beyond divine authority, and so on and so forth. The premise of monotheism certainly excludes the possibility of contradictions of such an order. Both merciful and just, perhaps, but never both strong and weak, or one and many, or unique and wholly other and also immanent and consubstantial with this world.

But for Judaism one source of knowledge of God, the written Torah, represents God through each trait and its opposite. And the other source of knowledge of God, the oral Torah in its various written versions, assigns to one and the same God a mass of traits of varying consequence and proportion, allowing no guidance as to the composition of the whole into a single cogent account. In just a moment, we shall see how the Oral part of the Torah embarrasses us with its riches of thought; no one can accuse our sages of blessed memory—those who give expression to the oral part of the Torah in their writing—of an economy of intellect or a poverty of imagination. That is why the problem of alleging about God everything and its opposite forms only one difficulty. The other is reckoning with truth in the right proportion, what is more important, what less; and the balance and order of truths, how they form, all together, a coherent and also elegant statement.

These too form tasks to be taken up by religious thinkers who call upon the methods of philosophy, which concern generalization and, therefore, take up contradiction, uniformity, balance, order, and harmony and rigorously form judgments upon issues of proportion and composition of thought.

Now, as a matter of fact, were philosophy to be asked to form an account of God or metaphysics, beginning with first principles and fundamental definitions, philosophy's God would surely exhibit none of the contradictions and disharmonies that the Torah's account of God reveals. That is in the nature of philosophy. But the nature of the revelation that contains the data of God and metaphysics confronting Judaic system framers, by contrast, does not permit the orderly progression from the observation of the facts of nature upward to the systematic construction of a well-composed world. It is not that, out of the raw data of the two parts of the Torah, sages did not make the effort to make theological statements. As we shall now see, they made every effort, with commendable results, to speak cogently and harmoniously.

But examining only four of those formulations of the fullness of the faith now shows the unsolved, and probably insoluble, problem. While trying to identify the messages of the parts as the statement of the whole—this, that, and the other thing as one thing[3]—our sages of blessed memory added disorder to the very chaos with which they began. When we have fully appreciated the obstacles to a proportioned and cogent theology that the Torah, oral and written, sets forth, we shall grasp the solution already offered: commencing in the lived theology of synagogue and academy, concluding in the sung theology of the Torah. The crux of the matter then is the multiplicity of voices bearing theological statements, the diversity of melodies that are sung.

Because of its prolixity, the Torah does not allow itself to be summarized, generalized, rendered in proportion. Everyone who has tried has succeeded—for himself or herself. No one has presented the final solution to the problem—or ever will. It is not a

---

3. The topical counterpart to the "why this not that" of my opening paragraphs.

question of mere quantity, the sheer volume of ideas and allegations; rather, it is the character of the Torah itself—its specific contents—that renders creed alone an unserviceable theological medium, and law alone (in the form of orthopraxy) an insufficient one. Neither part of the Torah, oral or written, sets forth generalizations that respond to philosophical thinking, though both address issues of a deeply philosophical character. The written part speaks of particulars, the oral part expresses its principles mainly through cases. Nor does orthopractic theology serve (anymore than it can serve in Islam), for orthopraxy there being too substantial a corpus of allegations to sustain a coherent statement of what God is, what Israel is to be, and how God's love for Israel, expressed through the Torah, shapes both the pattern of behavior and a passionately believed proposition as well.

The argument has moved beyond itself. So, before proceeding, let me once more recapitulate where we stand in its unfolding:

1. For Judaism, at stake in theology is what we know about God. That means, specifically, what we learn about God in the Torah.

2. The answer to that question lies in making the right connections between this fact and that one, or this rule and that one. There we find out what God wants of us: who we are, why we are together, what we are supposed to do.

3. In the community of holy Israel there is vast knowledge about God, a massive treasury of commandments and obligations, a richly detailed statement of God's love for us and how we are supposed to respond.

The task of theology finds its definition in the facts of religion; in the language of Judaism, the Torah sets forth commandments and teachings, and so tells us whatever we know about God's love for us and how we are to respond; study of Torah (the words in Judaism for "theology" in general) then shows us how the bits and pieces of knowledge hold together to form a coherent account.

And that is necessary because the knowledge is so rich, the facts so plural and diverse, that even within the setting of the Torah itself, forming a single, coherent statement presents a considerable challenge.

In turning to the third of the three stages of argument—the question, So what?—we move rapidly by reviewing four compelling efforts to meet that challenge. We want to find out how, in the Torah, our sages of blessed memory have determined what we learn about God. What we see is a sequence of formidable failures: success on the occasion, giving way to redundancy as others take up the challenge. Beyond the liturgy, which we can make mean whatever we wish, there has been no final statement of the central truths, the governing melody, no set of notes to replace all others, no formulations of words to form a single statement of the whole. Only when we recognize efforts that led nowhere shall we grasp the way taken, in the end, in the Talmud. In the compositions that follow, we identify serious and consequential theological initiatives to define the faith in a rational and propositional manner.

The theological enterprise in the four instances (and many others like them) consists of two steps. First, we try to identify principal facts. Then, we propose to make a cogent statement of those facts, with due proportion, with propositional clarity (if the proposition is not spelled out in so many words), with that accessibility of rational examination that depends upon a clear statement of facts and reasoning about the facts. These are not creeds in any limited sense, nor yet are they formulations of the norms of behavior and belief. But they do represent theological compositions. They make important statements, set forth fundamental propositions. Then, leaving nothing unclear, they show us why the very character of the Torah itself, oral and written, always prevents the formulation of theology in accord with philosophical conventions of a propositional character. At that point, having closed the old and other paths, the way that Judaism did take will open before us.

For my four examples of failed theological discourse within the Torah's framework, I have in mind not a mere saying but a systematic argument, flowing from facts to propositions, such as theology formulated in philosophical and propositional terms will have yielded. A saying by itself lays no claim on theological standing; it is an opinion or a datum, not a principle and a component of a system.

Summarizing the Whole Torah in a Few Words

Here, in the famous saying that follows, we deal with a theological generalization in the setting of a fable, no evidence, no argument, no reasoning being included. All we have is simply how a great sage said things should be seen. In a sequence of stories about defining the faith comes the following famous fable (the italics represent Aramaic, the plain type Hebrew):

> There was another case of a gentile who came before Shammai. He said to him, "Convert me on the stipulation that you teach me the entire Torah while I am standing on one foot." He drove him off with the building cubit that he had in his hand.
>
> He came before Hillel: "Convert me."
>
> He said to him, "*'What is hateful to you, to your fellow don't do.'* That's the entirety of the Torah; *everything else is elaboration. So go, study.*"
>
> B. SHABBAT 31A

The framer of this narrative setting for the Golden Rule has given us an allegation, not an argument; we do not know why the ethical principle of reciprocity ("love your neighbor as yourself," Lev. 19:18) takes priority over any of a dozen candidates; we cannot even say how the oral Torah, represented by Hillel's statement, relates to the written one, Lev. 19:18 not being cited at all. In stories such as this, we find instruction on proper attitude and action, but no sustained effort at a cogent, theological statement within the definition set forth just now.

The Theological Principle of Judaism: A Definition

Now, by contrast, we turn to systematic compositions that set forth theological propositions based on facts of the Torah. In the first, a syllogistic composition, three facts are made to make a single point contained in none of them but proved by all of them when juxtaposed. In it we are presented with a powerful argument on how the Torah forms evidence of divine grace: what we really know about God and ourselves we know because God's grace has permitted us to know—that alone. So the proposition is, the facts provided by the Torah themselves comprise an act of grace. This is demonstrated syllogistically, on the basis of three givens. These three fundamental truths govern throughout: humanity is made in the image of God; Israel are children of God; Israel possesses the most precious of gifts. These are givens. Wherein lies the gift? The act of grace is that we are told that they are God's gifts to us. We are not only in God's image—something we cannot have known on our own—but God has told us so. Israel are not only God's children—it would have been arrogance to have supposed so on their own—but God has so stated in so many words. Israel possesses the greatest gift of all. They know it: God has said so. So the syllogism draws on the three facts to make one point that is not stated but that lies at the goal of the argument.

> R. Aqiba says, "Precious is the human being, who was created in the image [of God].
>
> "It was an act of still greater love that it was made known to him that he was created in the image [of God], as it is said, 'For in the image of God he made man' [Gen. 9:6].
>
> "Precious are Israelites, who are called children to the Omnipresent.
>
> "It was an act of still greater love that they were called children to the Omnipresent, as it is said, 'You are the children of the Lord your God' [Deut. 14:1].
>
> "Precious are Israelites, to whom was given the precious thing.
>
> "It was an act of still greater love that it was made known to them that to them was given that precious thing with which the world was made, as it is said, 'For I give you a good doctrine. Do not forsake my Torah' [Prov. 4:2]."
>
> MISHNAH-TRACTATE ABOT 3:13–14.

These six statements form the paradigm of Judaic theology: not truth alone but truth enhanced because of the Torah's verification and validation.

Now what we have here, and the reason the passage defines the Torah's truth (in secular language: forms the paradigm of theological knowledge in Judaism), is the model of how theology does its work. By the definition just now given—theology forming the rigorous, rational investigation of what religion tells us about God—what we have is a theological composition. Specifically, theology takes out of the riches of religious truth facts, feelings, attitudes, emotions, sentiments, things known and things believed, and forms of the whole a cogent, coherent, and economical statement, as Aqiba's shows. He has selected fundamental considerations: Who are we, and who is God? Who and what is "Israel"? And how do we know? He has then not only answered in a cogent way the questions at hand, so that each answer leads us forward to the next, and the whole forms a complete statement of what we know about God and what, consequently, we are to do. He also has validated his statement by appeal to the Torah.

Now, what is wrong with this statement is not that it does not carry out the theological task: philosophical demonstration, based on facts properly established, principles of analysis correctly brought to bear. It is that this saying forms merely one among a rich succession of equivalent statements. Aqiba's task is not different from Hillel's, that is, to state "the whole Torah" standing on one foot, meaning, to state matters coherently and in an economical way. But whenever sages undertook the same work, and numerous cases of the endeavor lie ready to hand, they produced diverse results, no coherent theological system or structure at all.

How Everything Comes Down to One Thing

For the Torah, written and oral, is rich in statements such as this one. And while in general they cohere, in detail they scarcely intersect. Let me give a single example of the numerous counterparts to what Aqiba has said here. Here is a sustained effort to say the whole in a single authoritative way, drawing upon the facts provided by the written part of the Torah to permit the oral part of the Torah to make its point about the priority of trust in God above all else, surely a comprehensive theological principle:

Rabbi Simelai expounded, "Six hundred and thirteen commandments were given to Moses, three hundred and sixty-five negative ones, corresponding to the number of the days of the solar year, and two hundred forty-eight positive commandments, corresponding to the parts of man's body."

"David came and reduced them to eleven: 'A Psalm of David: Lord, who shall sojourn in thy tabernacle, and who shall dwell in thy holy mountain? (i) He who walks uprightly and (ii) works righteousness and (iii) speaks truth in his heart and (iv) has no slander on his tongue and (v) does no evil to his fellow and (vi) does not take up a reproach against his neighbor, (vii) in whose eyes a vile person is despised but (viii) honors those who fear the Lord. (ix) He swears to his own hurt and changes not. (x) He does not lend on interest. (xi) He does not take a bribe against the innocent' [Psalm 15].

"Isaiah came and reduced them to six: '(i) He who walks righteously and (ii) speaks uprightly, (iii) he who despises the gain of oppressions, (iv) shakes his hand from holding bribes, (v) stops his ear from hearing of blood (vi) and shuts his eyes from looking upon evil, he shall dwell on high' [Isaiah 33:25–26].

"Micah came and reduced them to three: 'It has been told you, man, what is good, and what the Lord demands from you, (i) only to do justly and (ii) to love mercy, and (iii) to walk humbly before God' [Micah 6:8].

"Isaiah again came and reduced them to two: 'Thus says the Lord, (i) Keep justice and (ii) do righteousness' [Isaiah 56:1].

"Amos came and reduced them to a single one, as it is said, 'For thus says the Lord to the house of Israel. Seek Me and live.'

"Habakkuk further came and based them on one, as it is said, 'But the righteous shall live by his faith' [Habakkuk 2:4]."

BABYLONIAN TALMUD MAKKOT 24A–B

Now the abundance of religious truths provokes the question that Simelai answers: How does the whole hold together? What makes this connect to that, so that different things adhere and also cohere? And how are we to know what really counts? Simelai's answer is to speak in abstract and general terms. He points not to cases but to principles; walking uprightly, after all, can be accommodated in more than a single posture; And what, after all, is oppression, or "hearing blood," or "looking upon evil"? Aiming at a vast generalization, "the righteous shall live by his faith," the formulation of the faith as a simple, single rule yields only abstraction, shading over into vacuity. But more to the point, Hillel's statement and Simelai's bypass one another, different sages talking about different things. Hillel identifies at the center the Golden Rule of Lev. 19:18, while Simelai finds living in faithfulness, clearly meaning, with God, to form the heart and soul of matters.

I cannot imagine a more successful theological discourse than this one. Certainly the character of the dual Torah permits no more compelling statement. And yet, it is the simple fact that one may readily construct another one, or two, or ten compositions just like it, yielding other conclusions, conclusions that do not coalesce with this one or even intersect with it. The character of the dual Torah, with its remarkably rich, but also discursive and diverse, corpus of sayings, stories, laws, and liturgies, accounts for the failure of Simelai's successful effort. What he wishes to accomplish —say it all in a single coherent statement—he achieves. But he cannot have hoped to make a statement to cover the whole of the Torah, anymore than Hillel did, anymore than Aqiba did. In the end, the theological statement turns cases into an example, but we do not know whether what we have as an example exemplifies much beyond itself; the nature of the Torah denies us that knowledge. It is not the way in which the Torah is going to make its governing statement, find its persistent and ubiquitous voice.

Then what about the written Torah's own theological discourse: its specific statement of the main thing, which holds many things together? How does the one whole Torah work with one of those generalizations?

The Commandment of Holiness

Yet a third formulation of the main point comes to us in the amplification of yet another encompassing principle, that of Lev. 19:1, the commandment of holiness. Here the oral Torah shows how the exposition focuses not on principles of the faith, the exposition of an accommodating structure, but only the sense of Scripture itself:

> "You shall be holy, for I the Lord your God am holy:"
>
> That is to say, "If you sanctify yourselves, I shall credit it to you as though you had sanctified me, and if you do not sanctify yourselves, I shall hold that it is as if you have not sanctified me."
>
> Or perhaps the sense is this: "If you sanctify me, then lo, I shall be sanctified, and if not, I shall not be sanctified"?
>
> Scripture says, "For I . . . am holy," meaning, I remain in my state of sanctification, whether or not you sanctify me.
>
> Abba Saul says, "The king has a retinue, and what is the task thereof? It is to imitate the king."
>
> SIFRA CXCV:I.2–3

The clarification of the comprehensive principle of Scripture contributes nothing to that store of abstraction and generalization of which theology is comprised.

The Union of the Two Parts of the Torah

Then let us move from the vast principles of divine grace, the human response in perfect faith and trust, and the sanctification of Israel. Perhaps a simple theological statement of how the two Torah's relate becomes possible out of the materials of the Torah itself. We turn to one final example of how broad and encompassing principles come under discussion. The problem at hand forms the counterpart to the issue with which we began, which is to say, the Torah as medium of divine grace. We revert now to the same absolutely fundamental issue of the theology of Judaism, namely, the character and definition of the Torah, which is the point of God's self-manifestation. The final theological formulation concerns the relationship of the two parts of the Torah, written and oral, and how the oral Torah sets forth a theological structure that is balanced and encompassing:

> Said R. Simeon b. Laqish, "What is the meaning of the verse of Scripture, 'And there shall be faith in your times, strength, salvation, wisdom, and knowledge' [Is. 33:6]?
>
> "'faith:' this refers to the Mishnah-division of Seeds.
>
> "'in your times:' this refers to the Mishnah-division of Holy Seasons.
>
> "'strength:' this refers to the Mishnah-division of Women.
>
> "'salvation:' this refers to the Mishnah-division of Damages.
>
> "'wisdom:' this refers to the Mishnah-division of Holy Things.
>
> "'and knowledge:' this refers to the Mishnah-division of Purities.
>
> "Nonetheless: 'the fear of the Lord is his treasure' [Is. 33:6]."
>
> B. Shabbat 32A

Here we find a rather successful exercise in large-scale definition, with the divisions of the Mishnah identified with theological virtues such as faith, salvation, wisdom, and the like, the whole culminating in fear of the Lord. If we wish to know how the two Torahs relate, we can ask for no better definition: the specificities of law in the Mishnah correspond to the abstract theological virtues of Scripture. Our four cases yield four absolutely fundamental, compelling statements of the whole Torah: principles and generalizations, golden rules and governing truths.

If everything is right, then what is wrong? What is wrong with our four theological formulations is not that they do not contain self-evidently valid statements, or that they do not match words to the music of the Torah, or that we cannot instinctively give our assent, or that we can intellectually withhold our concurrence.

None of those flaws characterizes any of our cases. Our problem is a different one. It concerns coherence, balance, proportion: perfection. Precisely how do we know what is important, what counts, what fits, and what holds together? None of our cases, in which we demonstrate out of the data of the Torah fundamental theological truths, guides us toward the central issue: Why this not that? How do things connect? What joins this to that? Whether we seek a generalization that conveys the main point of the Torah, or a careful demonstration of the unity of the two parts of the Torah, oral and written, whether we ask for a syllogism properly argued or an abstraction carefully instantiated, the result is the same: this, that, the other thing, many things, all of them plausible and true, but not some one thing that encompasses them all.

If, however, someone had put these four items together, side by side in an unfolding statement, our problem would have been, How do we account for the wild disproportions and disparities, and precisely what does *A* have to do with *B*, *B* with *C*, and so on down? And our answer can have set forth the theology yielded by juxtaposition and connection: the conclusion to be drawn from the connections that have been laid down. But these are discrete items. So in due course we shall have to examine not the connections that we make, for instance, by imposing our categories, but the connections that are dictated by the documents themselves. There, in Chapter 3, we shall see precisely where, in Judaism, God dwells.

Now to conclude: Why should it not have been possible to negotiate the differences and attain final solutions to problems of theological definition? Other scriptural religions, Christianity and Islam, found it possible to work with vast bodies of holy statements and out of them to formulate coherent and cogent statements, economical statements at that. Christianity found the means in its way, Islam in its manner. By contrast, in Judaism in the formative age the numerous candidates for inclusion in a theological summa continued to advance their claims, each name (Aqiba, Simelai, Simeon b. Laqish) allowed its full and complete statement, to the exclusion of no other. And, while the various sayings do not contradict, they also do not intersect with one another. It is difficult to find a more inviting occasion for cacophony than when many sages talk at the same time, each about his own interest, all in the name of a single Torah. In fact, the solution to the problem of theology derives from the character of the documents that form the Torah: Scripture on the one side, the Talmud on the other. There the connections are dictated that require explanation, there the conclusions are adumbrated that demand deliberation. All we know is that we are supposed to think the music, but, to this point, we do not know how to do that, let alone what sound is supposed to resonate.

Before turning to the specific case that will show the rule, let me now recapitulate the argument of this chapter. I have raised the question provoked by Chapter 1: How do we "think" the music so as to know what sounds are natural to the Torah, or, in the language just now used, so as to explain the principles of self-evidence? To state the governing question in all specificity, how are we to make the connections and draw the conclusions that echo in God's singing to us? We have to work our way back from the music to the theory of the music, from the Torah, oral and written, to the principles for making connections and drawing conclusions that the Torah embodies and realizes in its material melodies, its intelligible sound, in the exquisite match of word and sound to yield music. The answer to that question requires that we now define in a very specific way what we mean by "theology," and explain why, when in Judaism we speak of theology, in the language of the Torah we listen for the melody of the principal parts of the Torah, oral and written. We are ready to learn how to hear the melody of the Talmud.

The part of the Torah that sages and disciples sing in the academy, or yeshiva, is the oral part, which is written down in the Talmud of Babylonia. That document, properly understood, sets forth the way of making those connections in general that permit us to draw particular conclusions about what is right and wrong in belief and behavior, deliberation and deed. If, then, we want to know (to use secular language) how Judaism makes its theological statement, or, in the language of synagogue and academy, how the

Torah matches sound to significance and music to words, here is one of the two occasions of discovery. The match of the written Torah to its music, which takes place in the synagogue's representation of the giving of the Torah, is the other. Of the two, the yeshiva's way is the more important. The reason is that the written Torah sets forth the message, but, through right reasoning set on display, the oral Torah portrays the method of God's thought. If, therefore, we want to know how God manifests rationality and intellection, we do well to turn not to the synagogue but to the academy and its document. So, at last, after two chapters, we are nearly ready to open the Talmud and listen for its voice—but not quite.

Three

WHOLE HARMONY

The harmony between written and oral components of the Torah forms that one whole Torah of Sinai that God gives to holy Israel in synagogue and academy day by day. But finding the right notes to make the music, forming that whole harmony—that is not an easy task. While the words of the Written Torah are sung out just as they are written down, that is not the case with the written-down signs that make it possible for us to reproduce the oral part of the Torah. That oral document is aptly called "the Torah that is memorized," since the marks on paper—the Talmud itself—are elliptical, gnomic, unintelligible on their own, but accessible of thought only with the intervention of a teacher trained in the tradition. In the Talmud, in writing, all we have are brief signals, the gist of thought, which the sage and disciples have to recast into the form of a fully spelled-out proposition, argument, evidence, and analysis. We may say very simply that the oral Torah never was really written down at all, but preserved only in the chain of tradition formed of master and disciple, backward to God instructing Moses at Sinai, forward to the very moment, this morning, at which the sage gathers the disciples and teaches them their passage of the Torah for the hour.

So holy Israel uninstructed, the disciples without the sage, simply cannot gain access to the oral part of the Torah anymore than language can be learned only from a book, never spoken. Just as a writer writes for a "you," who forms the focus of thought in such a way as to make possible authentic communication, so the reader hears the voice of the book or grasps nothing at all. That is in the nature of writing and reading, respectively: both acts of deliberate dialogue. And the same is so when learning a language. To master a living language at some point one must enter into the oral discipline of the language. Without the voice of the language, the language remains alien with incomprehensible symbols, a merely formal structure.

To explain the problem, let us turn back to our governing medium of thought, the fact of music. Truth in sound, music, like the declaimed word, commands attention, compels assent. The oral part of the Torah, in the nature of things, forms the close counterpart to music. That is for two reasons. First, because, as we have noted, its fundamental orality means that it forms the record of a singing argument. But, second and more important, it also lives only in sound, not on the surface of the printed page. That is to say, the Talmud of Babylonia (ca. 600 c.e.) is made up of notes on the reconstitution of a conversation, signals of what we are to say and think, but not the complete record of the conversation, the spelling out of thought. The Talmud lives only when it is oral, and that means only when people take up its disciplines of thought and argument, even participating in them. Then, in the world of the Torah, an act of learning shades over into a moment of prayer: then God speaks, and we talk back. God sings, and we harmonize. God sets the melody, we make the improvisation. The glory of the Torah is the Talmud.[1]

1. Throughout, I refer only to the Talmud of Babylonia. A talmud is a gloss upon, ordinarily commentary to, the Mishnah, ca. 200 c.e. The first Talmud is the Tosefta, of no determinate date but possibly ca. 300 c.e., a compilation of three types of material: citation and amplification of the Mishnah; statements of rules that complement those of the Mishnah by providing further information on the same matters; and sets of rules that stand independent of the Mishnah's counterparts, sometimes on the subject subject, sometimes not. Hence the Tosefta forms a compilation of supplements to the Mishnah, offering clarifica-

The correspondence between music in written form and the oral Torah written down in the Talmud is concrete. The printed Talmud forms the exact counterpart to printed music. That is because to learn the Talmud we have to use its statements as signals of what is to be said, but not as exhaustive reports of precisely how we are to word our ideas, or even how we are to formulate them. Translated literally, the Talmud is comprehensible in detail, but not in its intent and program; we may understand words and even sentences but rarely the larger context of thought. So, to continue the comparison, just as the notes for the music are not the music, the words of the Talmud are not the statement of the Talmud.

When musicians read the notes however, in their inner ear they hear the music the notes represent. Then they know just how to make the music. And if sages look at the truncated and allusive words of the Talmud, they understand the thought that the words

---

tion and expanding on the information therein. The second Talmud is the Talmud of the Land of Israel, ca. 400 c.e., formulated in the Land of Israel by the clerks of the Jewish autonomous, ethnic government and their disciples. It moves beyond the Tosefta by taking up problems of an analytical character and forming propositions for study. The third Talmud is the Talmud of Babylonia, ca. 600 c.e., a massive and brilliant rereading of the Mishnah, in accord with a highly disciplined program of exegesis and hermeneutics, joined with large-scale composites of an other-than-exegetical character, which expound problems or principles of law distinct from the work of Mishnah commentary, or present large-scale and systematic analyses of passages of Scripture. The two Talmuds are made up of large-scale composites, many formed as Mishnah commentary, some for other purposes altogether. We have no need here to investigate the prehistory of the Talmuds, that is, the story of the formation of the compositions and then the composites that all together comprise the two documents. What is important here is that from ancient times to our own day, this Talmud has formed the authoritative statement of the Torah, oral and written, all together and all in one place. It defines the foundation curriculum of the yeshiva world, and in synagogue study sessions some of the simpler portions—Mishnah tractate Abot, the Fathers or the Founders, ca. 250 c.e., being a prime choice—are studied and explained. For further discussion of all of the principal components of the rabbinic canon beyond the written part of the Torah or Scripture, see my *The Doubleday Anchor Reference Library Introduction to Rabbinic Literature* (New York: Doubleday, 1994).

signal. The Talmud is rich in signals that form the counterpart to sharps and flats, rests and marks for crescendo and diminuendo.[2] Then they reconstruct the coherent discourse the verbal signals mean to convey, even recovering the contentious arguments the gnomic words intend for us to recapitulate. So while the musical notes to the ordinary eye scarcely hint at what its melody may be, in the inner ear of the musician the notes make music. And so it is with the Talmud, which, read without guidance, shades over into pure gibberish.

The reader can readily see the problem by examining a passage of the Talmud in the unadorned form in which it occurs in the original Aramaic (and Hebrew). Let me give one passage in English but otherwise as the passage appears in the Talmud, providing only punctuation (more than the original gives) but no explanation.[3] Faced with a naked rule, out of context, with pro-

2. For example, it is written in three languages, the Hebrew of the ancient Israelite Scriptures ("biblical Hebrew"), the quite different Hebrew of the Mishnah, and eastern Aramaic, the language spoken by the Jews in Babylonia until the advent of Islam. Each of these languages contains its own signal. The Hebrew of Scripture, of course, tells us that we are hearing the written part of the Torah. The Hebrew of the Mishnah, in addition to conveying the statements of the Mishnah and the Tosefta, serves to formulate fixed rules, propositions for argument. And Aramaic is the language of argument and sustained discourse. In my translation of the Talmud, I signal the difference between biblical and Mishnaic Hebrew by using quotation marks and supplying citations for Scripture for the former, and by printing Mishnaic Hebrew in simple roman type. When the Mishnah and the Tosefta are cited, I put the citations in boldface type. I then put in Aramaic the real language of the document, the language of thought. These signals leave no doubt on the way the document works. We shall return to this matter in due course. My translation of the document is *The Talmud of Babylonia: An American Translation,* 69 pts. (Chico, Calif., then Atlanta: Scholars Press for Brown Judaic Studies, 1984–93). Note also my *The Talmud of Babylonia: An Academic Commentary,* 37 vols. (Atlanta: Scholars Press for South Florida Studies in the History of Judaism, 1994–96).

3. This is how the Talmud is presented in the splendid British translation of the Talmud, *The Babylonian Talmud, Translated into English: With Notes, Glossary and Indices,* ed. I. Epstein (London: Soncino Press, 1948). The translation is pioneering, the scholars having had to invent a language suitable for rendering the document into intelligible English; I have found it masterful. But the translation

nouns lacking clear antecedents, with a statement of operative principles, what are we to make of this:

> He who leaves a jug in the public domain, and someone else came along and stumbled on it and broke it—he is exempt; and someone else came along and stumbled on it and broke it—[the one who broke it] is exempt: Why should he be exempt? He should have opened his eyes as he walked along! They said in the household of Rab in the name of Rab, "We deal with a case in which the whole of the public domain was filled with barrels." Samuel said, "We deal with a case in which the jugs were in a dark place." R. Yohanan said, "We deal with a case in which the jug was at a corner."

If, as I have alleged, the Talmud gives us hints on how to reconstruct an argument concerning a principle, the passage at hand shows how subtle are the hints.[4] Most of the main lines of thought are unarticulated; we have ourselves to identify the premise, define the problematic, even supply the data that form the raw material for analysis.

Uninterpreted, the passage yields a case ("He who leaves . . ."), a mystifying judgment ("he is exempt"—the one who left the jug? The one who stumbled on it?), and a voice otherwise unidentified ("Why should he be exempt?"). The three solutions to the problem have to be amplified, which, with a bit of imagination, we may accomplish; but then they also have to be differentiated,

---

in no way attempts to convey the character of the document, even failing to signal its units of thought through correct paragraphing. Since, as we shall see, the most difficult problem is to figure out the line of thought, the connection of one thing to the next, the Soncino translation leaves the document essentially opaque. Depending on the tractate, we have from four to ten translations of the Talmud produced after the Soncino volume, but none accomplished the work better, and many render the writing into an ugly and often unintelligible English. None conveys the character of the document better than the British pioneers did, nor its sense and meaning.

4. Later, in the next chapter, I shall re-present the same passage with the proper signals, and we shall see how the few words before us instruct us on the reconstitution of a conversation and an argument.

and that is not readily done. In due course, we shall return to this passage and use it the way it is to be used: as the occasion for the reconstruction of a case, the recapitulation of an argument, the representation of distinct and important principles in a wholly rational way.

As we see in the brief snippet at hand, in the Talmud we find not the script of the conversation but only the jottings out of which we reconstruct conversation. If we read only what is written on the page of the Talmud, we recite what is puzzling, and, at many points, mostly gibberish. We emerge with half-sentences and fourth thoughts. Vast quantities of facts, without which we cannot understand what is before us, are taken for granted. Premises of argument are inchoate, the upshot of exchange not articulated. Only when we bring to what is written the knowledge of a vast corpus of facts, on the one side, and mastery of modes of thought and inquiry, on the other, can we transform notes toward the re-constitution of conversation into a fully exposed dialectical exchange.

The Talmud cannot be read the way an ordinary book is read. Indeed, it cannot be "read" at all. To read the Talmud is to interpret its signals by rules the writing does not spell out but everywhere takes for granted. To learn, therefore, is to participate in the labor of re-creation. The Talmud imposes upon the reader or student the task of active engagement, beginning to end. And that is the key to its continuing character as an oral writing, for without a teacher the student ("reader") can never enter the document —ever. Everyone who has ever taken up the Talmud had to do so with a teacher and "read" by reciting a few words and then explaining them orally, or having them explained, until, after a long process of oral instruction, one-to-one really, the student has become a disciple of our sages of blessed memory and entered into their realm of speech and thought. Then, mastering the signals by which turns of an argument are conveyed, acquiring the concrete knowledge of detail required to make sense of a passage, and, above all, building upon accumulated experience of the kind of argument and analysis characteristic everywhere, the disciple may proceed to independent study—and also, therefore, to teach.

Every generation presents a danger to the oral part of the Torah for, if it fails in its task, the oral part of the Torah will be lost, beyond all access or reconstruction. Herein lies the orality of the Torah: if the pedagogical chain were to break, the document could never be understood again, and that is despite the fact that among its written commentaries are some of the truly great teaching intellects of all times, beginning with the incomparable R. Solomon Isaac of Troyes (1040–1105) or Rashi, and extending, through his restatement of the document in the systematic form of a commentary, to the greatest genius of the Torah, R. Moses b. Maimon (1135–1204) or Maimonides. Even guided by their sure hands, we could make only elementary progress in understanding the protean writing. But with the oral instruction of any experienced yeshiva master, in association with colleagues engaged in the same task and available for systematic public argument and inquiry, we can make our way quite well.

Then the Talmud becomes a vivid and exciting writing, notes that permit the reconstitution of sustained exchanges of thought. Living through the current generation and its capacity to take over the heritage, in writing and in oral tradition, of the long past, the document shapes the intellect of the coming generation too. It secures its own future, but only with the ephemeral collaboration of the transient, for the moment governing, age. Specifically, the master and disciple form the words into that contrapuntal conversation of dialectic that the Talmud offers as its part of the Torah. And therein we meet God: in the oral part of the Torah, by forming our minds to correspond to God's mind, so that we may understand and master and even realize the whole Torah, not only the truncated, written part. It follows that ours—we who are holy Israel in the academy—is the active role in receiving and handing on the oral part of the revelation—the giving, the receiving—of the Torah. The Torah forms the arena for the encounter with the living God, and what takes place there follows the script that is before us. Here is the kingdom, the power, the glory, of the Torah: realm of intellect, monarchy of imagination and sensibility, where we come to learn to imitate God, first in how we think, then in what we think, and, consequently, ultimately in what we do, are, and aspire to become.

The simple fact that the Talmud is not a book to be read or a book that can be read draws in its wake the further fact, the Talmud when it is learned surpasses all writing. That is why part of the Torah had to be formulated and handed on orally: in memory. The harmony of orality and memory form the melody of the Talmud. For these notes on how to reconstruct an eternal conversation comprise not the memorization of inert facts but the vivid reconstruction, the active replication of thought. I cannot overstate the consequence of the right reading of the notes: embodying here and now the Talmudic melody.

The Talmud's notes, properly interpreted, make possible an exchange of views and arguments—views concerning the Torah, arguments on principle with God, as we saw in Chapter 2: reasoned arguments concerning proposition, appealing to evidence, government by shared rules of analysis; balanced argument, each side matched by contrary proposition and the like. We are then supposed to reconstitute that conversation. That exceedingly odd mode of composing thought—not telling the reader everything but compelling the reader to participate in the writing of the book—is what sets the Talmud apart from all other documents of Judaism before its time or not connected to it. For other writings leave the reader passive, a recipient of what the author wishes to say. True, the imagination may be stimulated, the intellect engaged. But I cannot point to any other writing in Judaism, other than the commentaries and extensions of the Talmud itself, that pays the reader so warm a compliment as to make the reader partner of the writer. But that is what the Talmud does.

Let me revert once more to the facts of music to make sense of the facts of the Torah. The score of a piece of music tells only the notes we are to sing. Left for the musician are the challenges of musicianship: the craft, the art, the matters of taste and judgment. The notes, after all, merely signal in necessarily crude signs the way we are to sing them: fast or slow, but not just how fast or how slow. So much remains to the wit of musicians that singers and players are left alone to impart the nuance that makes music happen that minute. And the unpredictable is what makes performance heart stopping. For the conductor and performers take the major role in the momentary realization of the composer's thought, which, otherwise inert, perpetually lies lifeless in the merely written, therefore silent notes before us. So the notes are not the music, but only musicians make the music.

Their music, however, quickly fades into echo and then falls silent, merely remembered amid echoing applause. Why that fact matters has already been explained in Chapter 1: the Torah is given, here and now; is received, by the present Israel; the giving and receiving of the Torah is an activity in the acutely present tense, not even the continuing present: God gives, Israel receives—not God is giving, Israel is receiving, in their variations. So, too, the musicians make music for only here and now, for *that* audience. And the word is just: the audience—those who are to hear, even if it is only the musicians in their own inner ears. That third essential component in the miracle of music—the audience of hearers in addition to the composer and the performer—receives and responds to the moment and, holding its breath, makes the moment magic. So the communion formed in music—the whole harmony of composer, musician, and audience—is at once eternal and evanescent. In theory it never dies. In reality it lives for that brief moment as and where and by whom it is heard.

So music has always to be re-presented in a process that moves in a direction the opposite of nature's: not eternal, not perpetual, not natural, but always a matter of moment and amazement. The dead composer, living eternally, of course is never present. The musicians will follow, so will the audience. Preserved out of life, beyond death, then for the future—whether in memory or on tape—is only the record of that enchanted moment when eternity has once entered into time: sound into the silence of the merely printed music. That is the further meaning of whole harmony: a perfect union of composer, musician, audience—and, also, one-time occasion. True, all take their leave, one by one; like autumn leaves in their color, harmony lives but a moment, then falls away; whole harmony is like that, a communion that is ever so brief as it is perfect. And perhaps part of the perfection is brevity.

So it is with the Torah and its sung theology. The giving of the Torah is for that instant: the moment of hearing, the hour of en-gagement. The giving of the Torah (so the Hebrew for the English "revelation") is repeated wherever holy Israel assembles to witness God's self-revelation, which is to say, to receive the Torah. That defines the moment of whole harmony. But since—as I cannot overemphasize—revelation, the giving of the Torah to holy Israel in synagogue and academy—takes place in the acutely present tense of that minute, that perfect moment scarcely lasts. Attention flags, or distraction intervenes; the order of service moves forward; the disciples and masters take their leave. We have other things to do with our lives, nearly all of us. So revelation come to an end, until, once more, it takes place.

The moment the Torah is set forth and proclaimed in the synagogue, or is set forth and analyzed in the academy, the occasion of God's manifestation requires, as with the angels and Abraham at the oaks of Mamre, three presences: God, the Torah, and Israel—and they must for the moment become at one among themselves: God is made manifest in the Torah to Israel, which meets God in receiving the Torah. There consequently must be this communion of singularities: God to give the Torah, Israel to receive it, Moses and his surrogates—the reader of the Torah in the synagogue, the sage or master in the yeshiva—to proclaim it to the listening community, or to discover it for the contentious disciples. The composer, the audience, the musicians—now God, Israel, and sage—are assembled all three actively to participate in the realization of the giving of the Torah. Resting on the acknowledged facts of the lived faith and the sung theology of Judaism, that familiar allegation of mine concerning God's self-manifestation in the Torah where and when the Torah is sung suffices to establish the grounds for analogy and comparison.

But while, for the Torah, matters are comparable to the enchantment of music, in one definitive dimension they cannot be not exactly the same. The counterpart to the composer, God, is eternal, ever-present and everywhere-present. In the nature of things, as the Torah is proclaimed among us, not only Israel but God also forms the audience—so Halafta has told us in so many words. And it is God who, as the blessing for the Torah has already shown us, gives the Torah. So in one analogical version, the perfect harmony is realized in the one God of all creation. God is all in one—that after all is what we mean when we speak of monotheism. So—now capital letters convey the proper signal— Composer and Audience and Player in Heaven set a scene of incomparable intensity of presence, a wholeness of harmony that is scarcely to be sustained. The dimension of alterity disappears from the measure of the moment.

Even the power of music—and music alone—to capture that moment of the wholly engaged Presence falters and fails; nothing captures that moment, neither sound nor silence. That is for God alone: that is the music of the spheres of perfect harmony that God is supposed by the Qaddish to magnify among us. But the companion version of the same metaphor serves. It is the one that recognizes the transience of music, the evanescent enchantment. That is the version that alone can serve here in that finite space among us who die, on the earth that in its time perishes too. And here, too, through the notes of the Torah, God and Israel and sage make the music in perfect harmony.

So the synagogue and academy play for much higher stakes than the musicians in the concert hall. Performing for an audience of One, who also is composer of the music that they play and who, giving the Torah that moment in which it is received, shares in the performance. Israel is wise to replicate the notes with exquisite care. But as always in the Torah, there is an aspect of remission. Only God makes no mistakes; musicians do, sages do too.[5] For, if the stakes are more formidable in the giving of the Torah that is "Judaism," the Composer also parents the musicians. God come to hear Israel is more amiable than the ordinary composer; indeed, in no small measure he is avuncular, or, with Rachel in mind, like a loving Jewish mother, proud of her children's song: voice of bride, voice of bridegroom. To speak more plainly, God loves Israel and takes pleasure when Israel assembles to listen to the

5. And that is so even for those who regard themselves as the greatest sages of their generation. See for example my *Why There Never Was a "Talmud of Caesarea": Saul Lieberman's Mistake* (Atlanta: Scholars Press for South Florida Studies in the History of Judaism, 1994); and *Are There Really Tannaitic Parallels to the Gospels? A Refutation of Morton Smith* (Atlanta: Scholars Press for South Florida Studies in the History of Judaism, 1993).

Torah and to sing it, too. And God treasures the sound of the song, however sung, if sung with passion and conviction.

So much for the difference. Registering that difference we, of course, affirm the aptness of the analogy. For the written part of the Torah the comparison of composer, musician, and audience to God, Torah reader, and Israel at prayer serves quite neatly. Here, too, the written words, counterpart to the notes of music, become the proclaimed Torah only when the Torah reader sings them in a precise and musically proper manner, and then only when Israel has assembled for audience. But that is not the point of interest here. For at issue is understanding the Talmudic melody in the theological voice of Judaism. What of the oral part of the Torah set forth in the Talmud?

This explains why I argued in Chapter 1 that no act of imagination more immediately conveys humanity's encounter with God in the oral part of the Torah than imagining the giving and receiving of the Torah as an act of making and hearing music. The performance of music aptly captures the performance of the oral part of the Torah: in both circumstances uncertainty weighs in the balance against art and craft. The musician takes risks in realizing the music, the sage takes still greater risks—remember Who is the counterpart to the music critic!—in re-presentation of the oral part of the Torah. And that is for a simple reason. The written Torah demands only that we say properly what is before us. But the oral Torah does not exist in a fully spelled-out script; all we have are notes to guide us in reproducing the conversation—the dialectic, as I shall explain at the end of this chapter—of which the oral part of the Torah is comprised.

Now these observations bring me back to the here and now of this book: the "you" of the writer, the "I" of the reader. These form the counterpart to that "voice" of the Talmud, on the one side, and the sage who knows how to make sense of the sounds that the voice emits, on the other. Since our own encounter attests that what lies before the disciples in the Talmud is intelligible only to those who already know, access to the text requires the guidance of a living sage. (Later on, I shall carry out the responsibilities of the sage, talking you through the text we briefly encountered, and many others.) With this truly oral tradition, it is no wonder that the first significant point of progress is registered by the disciple's ability for the first time to prepare a page of the Talmud on his or her own, without the master's line-by-line tutelage. And that is not something that takes place so rapidly, or so painlessly, as the piano student's power to reproduce the notes on the page as a scale of *do re mi fa sol la ti.*

I met the Talmud for the first time at the age of twenty-two, scarcely knowing Hebrew, when I entered the Jewish Theological Seminary of America to get for myself a Jewish education (whatever that meant). A few days after the Festival of Tabernacles (Sukkot), classes began, and so did my life. I saw my first page of the Talmud and learned what it meant to study a document that can be opened only through a living relationship with a master. While I knew the meaning of every word on the page, I could make no sense whatever of what lay before me. So for the first five months of my daily encounter with the Talmud I simply memorized everything on the page, together with everything my tutor told me;[6] there was no other way. It took somewhat under a year for the signs on the page to make as much sense to me as *do re mi* make to the piano student in the first week of lessons.

A mark of the difficulty of the task derives from the use of the various aids to understanding, beginning with Rashi. For the first two years of study Rashi's commentary made matters more complicated rather than readily accessible, as he meant to do, and as, for the more experienced student, Rashi does do. Only later did Rashi become a source of intelligible signals, guides to not only what was said but to the order and continuity of discussion. Even then, after several years of pretty much full-time Talmud study with masters and fellow disciples, of course, instruction is required; but at that moment at which the disciple at least can prepare on his or her own, the disciple takes the first step toward becoming a sage: one who understands out of one's own resources of learning; people do reach that point. Presently, readers them-

---

6. He was Rabbi Dov Zlotnick. My first and certainly best Talmud teacher was the late Rabbi Seymour Siegel.

selves will see precisely what that means. As I have now under-scored: anyone can open the written Torah and make sense of most of what is there: the narrative, the prophecy, most of the law. But no one can encounter the oral Torah and make any sense of anything that is there, and if the beginning student imagines that he or she understands without help, that is a sure sign of ignorance.

The contrast then is clear. The musician reads the notes that draw the performer deep into the thought of the composer and help in the imagining of the music. While, with the written Torah, the scroll bereft of all annotation yields with a little learning of the accompanying vowels and trope, themselves simple and sensible, a complete account of the music, that is not the case with the oral Torah. There the sage and disciples play a role in the re-presentation of the Torah that demands of them a far more active role in the giving of the Torah. They are made partners of the One who gives the Torah in a way in which in the written Torah the one who declaims the Torah is not a partner at all. The realization of the oral Torah places the sage in the position of not only per-former but also partner with the composer. The sage knows not only the annotations that indicate how to replicate the conversa-tion, but also the rules of thought and argument that govern in the forming of a full and complete account of the conversation. And that means, the rules that we must observe in order to join in the conversation ourselves.

So the sage has to think (to shift back into our source of compre-hensible comparison) not only like a musician but like the com-poser of the music. The mastery of the master consists in the power to join in that conversation, share the work of composition, not only replication of thought. And the sage learns how thought takes place not in the pages of the Talmud but in the oral instruc-tion of the master when the sage was a disciple. The document contains little that is required; on our own we are to replicate its thought. The sage brings to the document and delivers to the dis-ciples all that is needed; the sage has mastered the rules of thought from the master who came before. Accordingly, the oral Torah is oral in the most profound sense, a vast corpus of thought that accompanies the document endures solely in memory and is handed on solely in oral form. Truly, therefore, the oral part of the Torah forms a tradition shaped of sounds unrecorded but never lost: the Torah that lives in memory, not in writing at all.

In the perfect union formed of the partnership of composer, audience, and performer—God, Israel, Torah—the sage takes the critical place as performer who also shades over into composer and, given the active role the sage takes in the re-presentation of the Torah, always forms part of the audience as well. The very character of the oral part of the Torah transforms the sage into a partner of the composer. But in the act of learning that is teaching, the sage with the disciples at hand undertakes also to cross and recross the line between audience and performer. For, we recall, if what the performer contributes to music is taste and judgment, which, in music, make the musician the key player, in the counterpart music of the spheres the sage enters the task of God: giving, not only receiving, the Torah, by reason of the active and formative role the sage undertakes in the academy's part of the Torah.

Let me underscore the reason for that remarkable fact, that the sung theology of Judaism demands the sage make up large stretches of the music, like the featured soloists in the time of early concerti and opera, who themselves made up the arpeggios as they went along. When it comes to the realization of the oral Torah, the notes scarcely serve by themselves but demand the active and creative participation of the musician; otherwise there is no music at all. A book is not the Torah, and printed notes are not the music. A book may become part of the Torah when received by Israel as part of God's giving of the Torah and when sung to Israel in synagogue or academy. Notes become music when performed by the musician for authentic audience. So the analogy illuminates the study hall even more than the synagogue. For there is one decisive point of difference: in the synagogue the reader of the Torah sings out the exact words in accord with the precise trope, and the audience follows in books that set forth both: no variations on a theme here, but in the academy the authentic work of giving of the Torah, that is, the re-presentation of revelation, takes place when sages and disciples sing the melody of the Talmud.

The musical form taken by the oral part of the Torah—contrapuntal song, that is, as I shall explain at the end of the next chapter, dialectical argument—therefore represents the sole form that the oral Torah can have taken. This point is vitally critical to the argument of this book: the written Torah need not have been sung, the oral Torah could only have been, and today can only be, sung. The oral Torah demands music, not for its metaphor but for its entire realization. There is no oral Torah without singing because only in the act of music does the full character of this mode of giving the Torah ("revelation") attain its goal: replicating in this moment the entire act of giving of the Torah. This is described in a single sentence: "Moses received Torah at Sinai and handed it on to Joshua," as at tractate Abot 1:1.

The process that actively engages the master and disciple in an exchange to which both are party is not one I have imagined; it is described in precisely the way I have said in the following:

A. *Our rabbis have taught on Tannaite authority.*

B. What is the order of Mishnah-teaching? Moses learned it from the mouth of the All-powerful. Aaron came in, and Moses repeated his chapter to him and Aaron went forth and sat at the left hand of Moses. His sons came in and Moses repeated their chapter to them, and his sons went forth. Eleazar sat at the right of Moses, and Itamar at the left of Aaron.

C. R. Judah says, "At all times Aaron was at the right hand of Moses."

D. Then the elders entered, and Moses repeated for them their Mishnah-chapter. The elders went out. Then the whole people came in, and Moses repeated for them their Mishnah-chapter. So it came about that Aaron repeated the lesson four times, his sons three times, the elders two times, and all the people once.

E. Then Moses went out, and Aaron repeated his

chapter for them. Aaron went out. His sons repeated their chapter. His sons went out. The elders repeated their chapter. So it turned out that everybody repeated the same chapter four times.

BAVLI ERUBIN 54B

What is important here is the active role of the disciples' repetition in the giving of the Torah—receiving, handing on, in the language of the opening of tractate Abot—that is assigned to sage and disciple. The master repeats, the disciple responds. But does mere repetition define an active role? Anyone familiar with the unfolding of a movement of a symphony or a quartet, with the polyphonic repetition of the melody, of course knows there is no such thing as mere repetition. Even in the repeating, in a different timber or voice, of precisely the same line, something changes.

Now the interchange of master and disciple in the labor of learning never finds sufficient the doltish repetition that the cited passage posits. To the contrary, students learn only when they teach themselves, turning the teacher's statement into their own words. And that kind of repetition always forms an exchange and defines a conversation.

That polyphonic, contrapuntal exchange is better represented in music, where polyphony and counterpoint bring life, than in any other of the media of creative expression I can imagine. When we consider in detail, as we shall, the dialectical argument that imparts life to the Talmud, the metaphorical character imputed to music will cease to govern; the Talmud will itself stand for music, and its melody will sound forth. The Talmud's dialectic, contrapuntal music (sometimes, to be sure, fugue in form) in which two or more voices participate is alone what makes a statement of sound, melody, and of notes. There we hear the Talmud's own melody in the theological voice of Judaism. The claim sounds extravagant; in yet a few pages it will appear an understatement.

It follows that this part of the Torah—the part that is called "the memorized Torah" (Torah she-be'al peh, the Torah that is memorized) and is not written down—always requires the act of communication of master to disciple. It is, therefore, clear now why I have insisted that by definition it is contrapuntal. In this act of speech the sage master states the melody, the disciple receives the melody—doing so by re-stating it, too. But then, the disciple restates the melody in the disciple's own voice. So it is by definition not precisely the same sound that the sage has expressed; it cannot be, it is no longer the sage's voice that sings the melody.

One melody, two voices—that is the beginning of the music. That is how it was with Moses and Aaron and Aaron's sons with the Mishnah, with Moses and Joshua with the oral part of the Torah. And the written Torah requires us to add: that is precisely how it was with God and Moses, the very point of the entire conception of tradition—receiving, handing on, as in the opening sentence of the tractate, The Fathers: "Moses received Torah at Sinai and handed it on to Joshua . . ." (Abot 1:1). The theological voice then is never one but always two (or more), and only contrapuntal music, two voices kept apart but held together, serves to capture the giving of the oral part of the Torah. That is why the oral part can only have been sung and can only be sung now, since, critical to the entire principle of orality is the role accorded to the sage in the process of receiving *and handing on* the Torah. The oral part of the Torah is so put down as to require oral formulation and oral transmission, generation by generation. Without the intervention of the sage, counterpart to the musician, and the disciples, counterpart to the audience, the writing, counterpart to the notes of the music, remains inert: Torah merely to be talked about, perhaps, in books such as this one, but never endowed with the passion and the power of enchantment and transformation.

It is only in the setting of disciples, hearing the document read aloud and extensively explained by the master, then joining in the song themselves, that we find the counterpart to the magical moment in which music lives: the moment of meeting among composer, performer, and audience. In the communion of Talmud, sage, and disciples, the oral part of the Torah finds its voice, and, being by definition oral, endures only in that living voice. This description will lead readers to imagine that the Talmudic melody is simply a Gregorian chant. But, as we shall see, the Talmud proposes a far more complex musical idiom than that.

The character of the Talmud's notes toward the re-constitution of contentious conversation makes all the difference. The melody belongs not to the twelfth century but to the twenty-first. The notes point to—remind the master and disciple of—facts, ideas, attitudes, modes of analysis and argument, that we are supposed to bring to the text. In this regard, the analogy of Talmudic phrases to musical notes is an exact one. Just as the musician in advance knows from the sign of an $A\#$ the sound he is to make and also by training has mastered how to make the music that that sign stands for, so is the case with the properly educated disciple. The notes remind, because the knowledge is implanted, whether by the teacher of music or of the Torah. And for both the young musician and the young disciple, learning is an active, transitive verb.

And this brings us once more to the question adumbrated in Chapter 1: Why orality as a medium of giving and receiving the Torah? For if I have given the impression that I maintain the dual Torah, oral and written, is the best possible Torah, I mean to say just that. So to understand why the oral part of the Torah, given its tasks, had to be oral and could never have been written down, wholly and completely, we have to dwell on that simple fact: the total engagement of the disciple's best energies by the classic issues. Engaged in the exchange of what are, in fact, very ancient and classic arguments and positions (a point I shall stress in Chapter 5), the disciples join in hoary arguments about enduring issues. In the acutely present tense of conflict about what counts today, in the confrontation with the received problems of thought, disciples find themselves compelled to rethink the ancient matter. They are charged not only with examining the facts, the law, the evidence, and the arguments. They are required to replicate the processes of thought that form the structure of argument. In that way they thus are forced by the character of the Talmud to play the principal role in the re-presentation of the Torah. And, in the nature of the task, that compelled engagement with the reason why requires an oral not a written Torah: a Torah that demands the sage's presence, the disciple's participation.

Our generative analogy once again clarifies the matter. The

composers' and performers' musicianship turns the score into actual music, on the spot. The intensely present tense in which music takes place once more sets the tone. The disciples' and the masters' power of lucid, abstract thought turns the Talmud into an exercise of compelling thought, that moment. But then the analogy also should not obscure this difference. The composer's score ordinarily contains sufficient markings to tell the musicians whether to play loud or soft music, slow or fast rhythms. But the Talmud's notes toward a conversation are all hint, no explication. A formidable process of thought is required before the sages and their disciples can reconstruct the ancient conversation, the exchange of reason and argument, the transaction of rigorous argument, that the Talmud preserves for them as a surpassing challenge of rationality. It follows that for the disciples of sages to replicate the harmony of Heaven's mind and theirs, they require models and instruction that the document itself does not provide. That explains why the part of the Torah presented by the Talmud had to be oral, realized in the lives of masters and disciples, fully exposed only in memory.

For therein lies what is oral about the oral part of the Torah. That same trait of the Talmud also is what makes that part, the oral part, of the Torah so critical to the theology of Judaism. Here is a document that presupposes a social setting for its reception: not an isolated reader, or even a reader at all, but a circle of sages and disciples, the sage always qualified by prior discipleship, the disciples always prepared for positions as sages for the coming generation. The Talmud cannot be studied other than with a living master, and that is why, when we speak of an oral tradition in Judaism, we refer to a simple fact: a document that serves as the truncated notes toward a script that aims at the re-constitution in the here and now of a long-ago conversation. Since, readers now realize, I take as the irrefutable, irreducible facts of the theology of Judaism the this-worldly embodiment of the Torah in synagogue and yeshiva, the basis of these statements is now fully exposed: this is not my fantasy of how Judaism might be in some imaginary world of intellect; it is how things really are lived out in the here-and-now of real people living real lives. It is time to read notes and make music.

Let us start with the Mishnah, the foundation document around which the Talmud organizes itself. To grasp its character in its own, Israelite context of the Torah, let us encounter the Mishnah at the very point at which its topic and problem intersect with Scriptures, thus seeing the different ways in which the written and the oral components of the Torah propose to deliver the same message. The Torah concerns itself with conflict, because God gives the Torah not to angels but to ordinary people more concerned with the here-and-now of jealousy and envy than the beyond of love for God and humanity in God's image and after God's likeness. The message of the Torah is to resolve conflict through a fair balancing of contradictory claims. Scripture gives that message in one way, the Mishnah in another—and it is the Mishnah's formulation of the Torah's principle that would govern from ancient times to our own day. We begin with the Mishnah's version of matters.

MISHNAH-TRACTATE BAVA MESIA 1:1–2

A. Two lay hold of a cloak—

B. this one says, "I found it!"—

C. and that one says, "I found it!"—

D. this one says, "It's all mine!"—

E. and that one says, "It's all mine!"—

F. this one takes an oath that he possesses no less a share of it than half,

G. and that one takes an oath that he possesses no less a share of it than half,

H. and they divide it up.

I. This one says, "It's all mine!"—

J. and that one says, "Half of it is mine!"

K. the one who says, "It's all mine!" takes an oath that he possesses no less of a share of it than three parts,

L. and the one who says, "Half of it is mine!," takes an oath that he possesses no less a share of it than a fourth part.

M. This one then takes three shares, and that one takes the fourth.

MISHNAH-TRACTATE BAVA MESIA 1:1

A. Two were riding on a beast,

B. or one was riding and one was leading it—

C. this one says, "It's all mine!"—

D. and that one says, "It's all mine!"—

E. this one takes an oath that he possesses no less a share of it than half,

F. and that one takes an oath that he possesses no less a share of it than half.

G. And they divide it.

H. But when they concede [that they found it together] or have witnesses to prove it, they divide [the beast's value] without taking an oath.

MISHNAH-TRACTATE BAVA MESIA 1:2[7]

Seeing the traits of the Mishnah as a piece of writing, we shall be able on the basis of merely formal evidence to distinguish the Mishnah from the *Gemara*. And, as a matter of fact, at every point in the Talmud we shall know which lines derive from the Mishnah and are commented upon, which derive from the *Gemara* or Talmud and form the commentary. The formal traits before us are unmistakable. The reason is that syntactically everything is matched with something else, and only one thing is left dangling —the final sentence, that alone. If we simply identify the pairs, we can see the compositions of which the composite as a whole is constructed.

The message of the Mishnah is this: *where there are equally valid claims, we split the object that is at issue equally between the claimants.* The Mishnah paragraph presents three exemplary cases, all of them following the same formal pattern and adhering to the same rules of syntax. We are supposed to form our own generalization out of the confluence of the three cases, formed in a single pattern to draw our attention to commonalities of form, yielding a shared proposition through discrete instances. We notice first of all a set of clauses, not complete sentences: 1:1A sets the issue, then

B, C form one set of conflicting claims; D, E the next; followed by F, G with a rule applying to each; and H, the resolution of the matter. This pattern is repeated at I–M, and at 1:2. It is clearly a pattern, then, to give us a group of three cases and their rules. We may point, then, to 1:2H as the line that breaks the pattern and, as it happens, marks the conclusion of the whole. Clearly, we are in the hands of a very careful author who formulates matters within tight patterns.

What are these patterns? For M. 1:1 they are three pairs, B-C, D-E, F-G, concluded at H; then I-J, K-L, concluded at M; and, for M. 1:2, C-D, E-F, ending with G; and H is tacked on. I cannot imagine a more disciplined piece of composition than this, and if you count the syllables you will find that each of the parts of the pairs, B, C, and so on, contains the same number of syllables as the other.

These formal traits serve a very simple purpose: to facilitate memorizing the passage. For it is hard to memorize random sentences but easier to memorize pairs or matched sentences. It is hard to memorize a series of one item, but it is easy to memorize groups of three items. So the Mishnah passage before us has been formalized, in part, to ease the task of memorizing the language (not just remembering the gist) of the passage. Then the author of the passage assumes that his writing is going to be memorized, and that strongly suggests he does not think his writing is going to be preserved and handed on only or even mainly in writing.[8]

What else does he assume?

To put matters very simply, our author thinks we are very careful readers (or listeners), who will put together the main point he wishes to make by seeing the patterns of not only language but

8. The circles of masters and disciples who produced the Mishnah and those who received it and over centuries studied it, formulating in the end the Bavli as we have it, included no women known to us. Only in the final quarter of the twentieth century have women found their rightful place as entirely normal participants within the circle of Torah study. It would misrepresent matters to say "he or she," "his or her," when in fact that was not the case before our own time. When we speak of the here-and-now, women as much as men, of course, are treated as entirely normal and in place.

thought. Just as he has so formulated his ideas in language as to make it easy for us to memorize what he says, so he has laid matters out in such a way that we, for our part, can see the main point that his three cases mean to make.

What are some of the generalizations that the passage yields?

1. In a case of conflict over right of ownership of an object, where the claims are of equal merit, we impose an oath on each party to assure that he or she is telling the truth, and then divide the object equally. That is, obviously, because each party claims the whole of the object. Then there is no choice but to give half to each.

2. The same principle—adjudicating the conflicting claims, once confirmed through an oath, by giving each party half of the part that he or she has claimed to own. If one alleges he owns the whole, and the other only half, then the second party has conceded the claim of the first to the other half. At issue then is only ownership of the second half, and that we divide, hence the first party gets three, the second one share of the whole.

3. The third case repeats the first. What it adds is only a procedural matter, H.

Then can we say that a single generalization covers the entire triplet? Of course we can: *where there are equally valid claims, we split the object that is at issue equally between the claimants.*

Does our author tell us that? No and yes. He gives us no generalization at all. But he assumes that we will see what the three cases have in common and recognize that that is the governing principle. Focusing upon his cases—the extent of the claim to the object, whole (1:1) or part (1:2), whether or not an oath is necessary to validate one's claim (1:3)—our author has made his main point by indirection. Yet he knows we will not miss it, and, of course, no one can. In fact, our author has given us an abstract representation of concrete events, which we might render as "if two lay hold of a cloak," "if this one says," "if that one says," then "this one takes, and that one takes, and they divide," and so on throughout. The omission of the "if," and the presentation of the whole in very brief clauses serve very well to give us what looks like a concrete case, a kind of event, but is in fact a general rule, yielding in the repeated statements of that rule an abstract generalization. Can a writer in the Israelite world say "Where there are equally valid claims, we split the object that is at issue equally between the claimants," in some other way than this? To answer the question we turn to Scripture's way of saying through narrative what the Mishnah says through an abstract case.

> Then two harlots came to the king and stood before him. The one woman said, "Oh, my lord, this woman and I dwell in the same house; and I gave birth to a child while she was in the house. Then on the third day after I was delivered, this woman also gave birth, and we were alone; there was no one else with us in the house. Only we two were in the house. And this woman's son died in the night, because she lay on it. And she arose at midnight and took my son from beside me, while your maidservant slept, and laid it in my bosom. When I rose in the morning to nurse my child, behold, it was dead; but when I looked at it closely in the morning, behold, it was not the child that I had borne."
>
> But the other woman said, "No, the living child is mine, and the dead child is yours."
>
> The first said, "No, the dead child is yours, and the living child is mine."
>
> Thus they spoke before the king.
>
> Then the king said, "The one says, 'This is my son that is alive, and your son is dead,' and the other says, 'No, but your son is dead, and my son is the living one.'"
>
> And the king said, "Bring me a sword."
>
> So a sword was brought before the king. And the king said, "Divide the living child in two and give half to the one and half to the other."
>
> Then the woman whose son was alive said to the king, because her heart yearned for her son, "Oh, my lord, give her the living child and by no means slay it."

But the other said, "It shall be neither mine nor yours; divide it."

Then the king answered and said, "Give the living child to the first woman and by no means slay it; she is its mother."

And all Israel heard of the judgment which the king had rendered, and they stood in awe of the king, because they perceived that the wisdom of God was in him, to render justice.

1 KINGS 3:16–28[9]

So the point is the same: where there are equally valid claims, we split the object that is at issue equally between the claimants. Will the author of our Mishnah paragraph have found the principle expressed in this story surprising? So far as the rule of law is concerned, the answer of course is negative. But the point of the story before us, and the purpose of the Mishnah paragraph at hand, are quite different. Each author has chosen to make his own point, and he has done so, as a matter of fact, by finding a medium of expression that matches his purpose.

Our Mishnah author wants to speak of principle and procedure: When is an oath required, when not? That is his main point. We know it, because it comes at the end; it is startling; there is no preparation for it; and it marks the climax and conclusion of the piece of writing at hand. My representation of matters earlier marked that matter; I treated H as a minor detail. But we see that, when the same thing is said three times, and then something else is tacked on, our attention is drawn to that new matter. When, then, we look back, and see how, in the prior writing, the oath has been introduced as integral, we realize what has happened. What will be the main point is introduced quite tangentially and repeated as a given; then we assume that given is not at issue. But at

9. Translation: *The Oxford Annotated Bible with the Apocrypha: Revised Standard Version,* ed. Herbert G. May and Bruce M. Metzger (New York: Oxford University Press, 1965), 4190–4200.

the end, we are told that what we took for granted is in fact not routine. An oath is required only if there is a conflict, but if each party concedes the other's claim, or if there are witnesses to establish the facts, then no oath is at issue at all. What was entirely tangential now turns up as the main point. The framer of the passage has made it certain we would be jarred and that our attention would be drawn to that surprising, and we now realize, critical issue.

That our narrator in the story of Solomon and the two widows has chosen a medium suitable for his message hardly requires specification. He sets the stage in the opening paragraph: the one party states her claim, the other the opposing claim. The rule of law is clear: split the difference. The issue of procedure is of no consequence to our narrator, so he does not say that each party must prove her claim, for example, taking an oath (or whatever procedure pertained at that point in Israel's history). The king then makes his elaborate preparation to carry out the rule of law. The woman who spoke first speaks again, then the other speaks as briefly as before. The king repeats the language of the first woman: "by no means slay it," now adding, "she is its mother." Is the point of the story the law that where there are equally valid claims, we split the object that is at issue equally between the claimants? Hardly! The point of the story is at the end: "And all Israel heard of the judgment which the king had rendered and stood in awe of the king because they perceived that the wisdom of God was in him, to render justice."

We see how cases of the same kind can be used for entirely different purposes, and, when an author proposes to set forth his purpose, he chooses language and syntax and forms of communication that serve that purpose. The author of the story about Solomon wants to say Solomon had divine wisdom; the case makes that point by showing how Solomon transcended the limits of the law through not (mere) mercy but profound understanding of obvious facts of human nature. The author of our Mishnah paragraph is talking about different things to different people, and his choices show the difference. He gives us not narrative, which serves no purpose of his, but brief and artful clauses, each free-floating, all of them joining together to create cases. He then finds for himself laconic and detached language, not the colorful and evocative phrases used by the other. Contrast the understatement with the overstatement, the one casual, the other rich in heightened and intense language:

> C. this one says, "It's all mine!"—
> D. and that one says, "It's all mine!"—

"Oh, my lord, this woman and I dwell in the same house; and I gave birth to a child while she was in the house. Then on the third day after I was delivered, this woman also gave birth, and we were alone; there was no one else with us in the house. Only we two were in the house. And this woman's son died in the night, because she lay on it. And she arose at midnight and took my son from beside me, while your maidservant slept, and laid it in my bosom. When I rose in the morning to nurse my child, behold, it was dead; but when I looked at it closely in the morning, behold, it was not the child that I had borne."

But the other woman said, "No, the living child is mine, and the dead child is yours."

The first said, "No, the dead child is yours, and the living child is mine."

Contrast, again, the undramatic resolution with the tension and the resolution of the tension that form the centerpiece of the narrative:

> F. this one takes an oath that he possesses no less a share of it than half,
> G. and that one takes an oath that he possesses no less a share of it than half,
> H. and they divide it up.

And the king said, "Bring me a sword." So a sword was brought before the king. And the king said, "Divide the living child in two and give half to the one and half to the other."

Then the woman whose son was alive said to the king, because her heart yearned for her son, "Oh, my lord, give her the living child and by no means slay it."

But the other said, "It shall be neither mine nor yours; divide it."

Then the king answered and said, "Give the living child to the first woman and by no means slay it; she is its mother."

It is difficult to imagine two more different ways of saying more or less the same thing. The two Torahs each take its own way to deliver its own message. Yet, we must concede, the message of each is truncated, and only with the two parts of the Torah side by side do we see the entire and comprehensive statement that Moses our rabbi wishes to make.

The Mishnah author speaks in brief clauses; he uses no adjectives; he requires mainly verbs. He has no actors, no "they did thus and so." He speaks only of actions people take in the established situation. No one says anything, as against, "the king said. . . ." There is only the rule, no decision to be made for the case in particular. There is no response to the rule, no appeal to feeling. Indeed, the Mishnah's author knows nothing of emotions, Scripture's narrator tells us "because her heart yearned," and the Mishnah's author knows nothing of the particularity of cases, while to the Scripture's narrator, that is the center of matters. The Mishnah presents rules, Scripture exceptions; the Mishnah speaks of the social order, Scripture, special cases; the Mishnah addresses all Israel, and its principal player—the community at large—is never identified. Scripture tells us about the individual, embodied in the divinely chosen monarch, and relates the story of Israel through the details of his reign.

When we remember that the author of our Mishnah passage revered Scripture and knew full well the passage before us, we realize how independent-minded a writer he is. On the surface he does not even allude to Scripture's (famous) case; he does not find it necessary to copy its mode of presenting principles. And yet what differentiates the main point, "they divide it up" and "divide the living child in two"? (And who requires "and gives half to the one and half to the other"?) Only these words make a material difference: *the living child.* Since our author knew Scripture, he had to have known precisely what he was doing: the affect, upon hearers or readers of his rule, of the utilization of the precise ruling of Solomon. All that changes is "living child" into "cloak." Everything is different, but everything also is the same: the law remains precisely what the narrator of the tale about Solomon knew, as a matter of fact, what it was. Then the law is not the main point, either of Scripture's tale, or of the Mishnah's rule. The Torah—God's revelation to Israel—lives in the details, and through our two authors, both of them immortal for what they wrote and perfectly capable of speaking to minds and hearts of ages they could not have imagined, God speaks through the details.

What we have seen thus far is how the Mishnah finds it possible to say in its way precisely the same thing that the scriptural narrator sets forth in his way, and to do so in such wise that the larger conceptions of the document—those concerning social order, regularity, routine, and concrete realization, always and everywhere, of abstract principles of justice and equity—register not only in what the writing says but in how it makes its points. So much for the harmony of the two Torahs, written and oral. Now it is time to meet the Talmud that receives the Mishnah and recasts it within a complete re-presentation of the whole Torah, oral and written.

$\mathcal{F}$our

READING NOTES, MAKING MUSIC

$\mathcal{T}$he time has come to read the music. But that is not so easy. For reasons amply set forth in the last chapter, the Talmud of Babylonia is easy to describe and difficult to re-present. The task is equivalent to describing music in words, or turning a painting into a story, or, for that matter, conveying an event in music or a painting in dance. What we need to know does not concern the history of the writing, nor its literary character, or even its religious qualities as a document of the faith but only its most basic formal traits. We need to learn how from the notes to sing the music, how from the verbal signals to realize the thought.

So let us turn to the writing and, in our own language, enter into its discipline. The labor of translation then is in two parts: putting Aramaic into American, putting ancient thought into contemporary language that accurately replicates the modes and message of the classic. Briefly described, the document consists of a law code, the Mishnah, ca. 200 C.E., joined to a sustained, systematic, and cogent commentary to the law code, the Talmud proper, written at ca. 600 C.E. The Mishnah is represented not whole and complete, in its original condition, but in brief sense units, sentences that obscure the character of paragraphs from which they are taken, paragraphs that in no way convey the larger formal and intellectual context of the cogent statements, or chapters, that they comprise. While a commentary, therefore, the Talmud obliterates the character of its base text and forms itself into a new statement altogether: sentences of the Mishnah together with sustained analytical discussions thereof.

The textual integrity—the autonomous textuality of the Talmud, its coherence, above all its self-portrayed claim of utter independence of all other writings—is underlined, also, by yet another fact.[1] While the Mishnah is in one language, (middle) Hebrew, the Talmud is in three, biblical Hebrew, Mishnaic Hebrew, and Aramaic.[2] The two languages occur side by side and in sequence, but each serves a distinct purpose and forms part of the document's convention of communication. If a saying is in one language, it enjoys one status and serves one purpose, and if in the other, it bears a different function altogether; so language accomplishes a taxonomic goal. Specifically, set-piece laws, authoritative statements, fixed rules, are given in Hebrew. Analytical discussions,

1. As between intertextual and intratextual writing, to use the passing jargon, the Talmud, like the Midrash compilations, is intratextual: freestanding, citing and quoting external writings with clear markings of its own alterity, and theirs. The contrary representative of all of the Rabbinic documents as examples of intertextuality does not take account of the autonomy of the various documents, their traits of particularity as to rhetoric, logic of coherent discourse, and, of course, topic and proposition. Any document that we compare whole with any other document underscores the fact that each is possessed of its own integrity. For my presentation of debates on this matter, see *The Integrity of Leviticus Rabbah: The Problem of the Autonomy of a Rabbinic Document* (Chico, Calif.: Scholars Press for Brown Judaic Studies, 1985); *Comparative Midrash: The Plan and Program of Genesis Rabbah and Leviticus Rabbah* (Atlanta: Scholars Press for Brown Judaic Studies, 1986); *From Tradition to Imitation: The Plan and Program of Pesiqta deRab Kahana and Pesiqta Rabbati* (Atlanta: Scholars Press for Brown Judaic Studies, 1987). [With a fresh translation of Pesiqta Rabbati *Pisqaot* 1–5, 15.]; *Canon and Connection: Intertextuality in Judaism* (Lanham: University Press of America, 1986). *Studies in Judaism Series;* and *Midrash as Literature: The Primacy of Documentary Discourse,* Studies in Judaism series. (Lanham: University Press of America, 1987). These books extensively cite, with sources and bibliography, the writings of the advocates of an intertextual reading of the same documents.

2. We have dealt with this matter at greater length in the preceding chapter, in the context of the signals the document gives on the reconstitution of its conversation. A brief reprise is now called for.

continuity of thought and inquiry, are presented in Aramaic. So Aramaic is the language of thought, Hebrew of conclusion and decision. The bilingual quality should not obscure the mono-lingual medium of thought: the Talmud does its work in Aramaic, only identifying its product—conclusions bearing authority and demanding harmonization among themselves—with Hebrew.

The textual and, therefore, intertextual integrity of the Talmud emerges in yet another quality of the document. While numerous authorities are cited, all appear by invitation of the commanding voice of the document itself. This is in two aspects. First of all, the continuity of discourse is established by the Talmud's own "voice," that anonymous, monotonous narrator of contention, al-ways speaking in Aramaic, always asking the logically consequent question, always pressing home the inconvenient fact, always con-trolling the ebb and flow of argument. So the formal quality of linguistic taxonomy finds its match. As we follow a few texts, we shall wonder who is speaking—this faceless disembodied voice that controls all thought and defines all discourse. And the sole answer is, that is the oral Torah itself, meaning, the voice of ap-plied reason and practical logic that guides us toward the making of connections and the drawing of conclusions. The integrity of the Talmud finds definition, then, in the sole and single voice that speaks throughout. It is that voice that carries the Talmudic mel-ody. What makes that voice a source of wonder is how that single, simple melody serves to carry the words that cover everything and its opposite; to yield infinite variations; to sound harmony that is whole and natural wherever the melody has been sung, by whom-ever it has been sung, whenever it has been sung, in times past and ages to come.

The next aspect is equally stark. The voice with its simple mel-ody is not only ubiquitous but utterly domineering.[3] Any given unit of thought bears its own problem, supplied by this anony-mous persona, which the author of a composition investigates in

3. This is fully spelled out in the conclusions set forth in my *The Bavli's Unique Voice*, Volume 7: *What Is Unique about the Bavli in Context? An Answer Based on Inductive Description, Analysis, and Comparison,* Studies in the History of Judaism (Atlanta: Scholars Press for South Florida, 1993).

its own terms; any statement that is admitted to the discussion gains entry because it serves the purpose of exposition and analysis that governs the formulation of the unit of thought; and no one gets to say very much that does not closely adhere to the unit's authors' plan. So personalities and marks of individuality, while occasionally present, play no role in the formulation of the document, which is governed by the authors and pronounced in their anonymous and prevailing voice. These two facts concerning the natural sounds of the oral Torah show us that the Talmud really does have a voice; it is the sole voice that prevails; and, I shall show, when we know how to hear that voice, we listen to whatever theological statement the oral part of the Torah is able to set forth: the norm, the authoritative, the coherent and cogent re-presentation of the whole, all at once, all together, in full rationality.

That voice of the Talmud utilizes many voices to make its statement. And that further trait of the document brings us back to this matter of whole harmony that occupied us in the preceding chapter. The analogy to music once more illuminates. The composer of a quartet uses four voices but makes one statement. The music is realized only through the union of the four distinct voices. In an opera five or six or ten voices, each with its own mood and message, may speak at once and convey a whole that vastly exceeds the sum of the parts. So too we find in the repertoire of our document capacities for simultaneous speech that ordinary writing scarcely imagines. The authors of the Talmud find it possible to speak through a variety of voices, soloists, duets, quartets, entire choruses. Their statement, however, in the end emerges in how they arrange one thing with some other, meaning once more, the connections that they impose by their editorial acts of juxtaposition. These, properly understood, convey the conclusion they wish us to draw, when we have recognized the problem they have set for us by some odd juxtaposition, or some apparently discontinuous presentation of free-standing but now contiguous, and (in the nature of the writing) continuous passages.

The voice of the Talmud corresponds to the recitative of classical opera, the sung talk that is chanted between the arias and choruses and holds them together. Therein lies the continuity, the narrative, the cogency—there and not in the flow of the music from aria to aria. But the recitative in opera joins free-standing set-pieces, while, in the Talmud, the recitative bears the burden of the whole. The set-pieces (the Hebrew-language propositions, e.g.) make their contribution to the entire sound, but they are isolated notes, not music, until joined by the Talmud's ubiquitous voice. So in the Talmud it is the voice of the document, anonymous and compelling and Aramaic, robust and feisty and unsentimental and unforgiving, that, like the recitative, guides and dictates discourse and turns this melody and that harmony into one entire, cogent piece of music. The counterpart to the aria is the free-standing saying: Rabbi X says . . . Ordinarily, Rabbi X is allowed to make his statement when it is relevant to the program of the anonymous Talmud and when it makes a point important in the realization of that program (whatever it is). Rabbi X may be juxtaposed with Rabbi Y and Rabbi Z, whom in life he never met; but, in the context established in the Talmud, Rabbi X engages in a dispute, on a common topic, with Rabbis Y and Z, and all three of them turn out to debate a single issue and differ on a single point, all three taking a position on that issue and directly confronting one another at that one point.

What that fact means is that the voice of the Talmud dominates. It overrides the voices of the Talmud's authorities. Not only so, but in general that same voice homogenizes the sounds of the voices of the diverse authorities. Now, as a matter of fact, the document comprises opinions of several hundred authorities, certainly a hundred who appear in the Mishnah itself, perhaps two hundred more who appear in comments on the Mishnah. These authorities talk pretty much in the same way; they may be differentiated as to opinion but not agenda; and they are permitted slight marks of individuality, except within the agenda dictated by the common topic or problem. They talk the same way about the same thing but have different views of that one thing.

But the same rules of thought, evidence, argument, form, and language govern throughout, so the decisions and program of the Talmud's authors homogenize the ideas and language of individuals and form of discrete and diverse minds and different times and places a single coherent statement. The categories that organize thought always are those of the document, never those of an individual; nothing accorded sustained attention makes space for idiosyncrasy. The effort always is to form one thing out of many, and that commanding principle shapes aesthetics and intellectual inquiry alike. That is, the statement that the Talmud's authors themselves wish to make defines the character of all the components that those same authors assemble to accomplish their goal. The implications of that fact for how we may use the Talmud to write the history of the period in which it took shape need not detain us; a document in which received writings are reshaped for the purpose of the final authors hardly claims to tell us precisely what was going on through the long period in which those writings were handed on, but only how the final authors wished to represent matters. We learn from the Talmud how its authors wished to see the world. From our perspective, the important result of these facts is that the document speaks for itself, through many voices making its own coherent statement.

What is more to the point, as we approach the document and begin to listen for its distinctive melody, What precisely does the document offer to its readers? And the answer is not what we expect of a piece of writing, whether the writing comes from ancient times or our own day. Only a few pieces of writing take for granted the givens that the Talmud's writers presuppose, for example, as I said, that there is a master to guide the reader, that the reader is in the status of a disciple, that there is a massive and thick layer of explanation intervening between the statements at hand and the full mastery by the reader/disciple of what the document wishes to say. Here is writing that presupposes explanation it does not provide, a purpose it does not define, cogency it does not effect, harmony and unity it never articulates but always and everywhere pursues.

Consider the contrast between the Talmud and other writings then or now. Ordinarily, we take up a book or article and assume we may make sense of it entirely on our own; that means, we suppose we know the rules of reading this writing. And the corollary is, we do not assume we require a teacher to make sense of what is in hand. But that is not how the Talmud communicates with us. It is a kind of writing that requires a different sort of relationship than the ordinary one between a book and its reader. Before us is a piece of writing that cannot be read the way we ordinarily read a book, because it presupposes knowledge that the text does not provide but that is required to make sense of the text. And that draws us back to the point at which we began: its framers, therefore, assume that a teacher intervenes between their writing and their reader.

How do we know that that is their presupposition? The reason is that the Talmud does not give us those signals that, in ancient times or today, afford direct access to the writing. To examine precisely how these writers propose to communicate with us, we turn to a specific passage, one that would correspond in any other book to the opening sentences. Let us examine the opening lines of the Mishnah and the Talmud, the first few statements of Mishnah tractate Berakhot, together with the Talmudic treatment of the same passage. I give the Mishnah sentences in boldface type, everything else in standard roman typeface; what is in Aramaic is in italics, Hebrew is in plain roman typeface.

A. **From what time do they recite the *Shema* in the evening?**

B. **From the hour that the priests [who had immersed after uncleanness and awaited sunset to complete the process of purification] enter [a state of cleanness, the sun having set, so as] to eat their heave offering—**

C. **"until the end of the first watch," the words of R. Eliezer.**

D. **And sages say, "Until midnight."**

E. **Rabban Gamaliel says, "Until the rise of dawn."**

F. **There was this precedent: His sons came from the banquet hall.**

G. **They said to him, "We do not recite the Shema."**

H. **He said to them, "If the morning star has not yet risen, you are obligated to recite [the Shema]."**

I. **And not only [in] this [case], rather, all [com-**

mandments] which sages said [may be performed] until midnight, their religious duty to do them applies until the rise of the morning star.

J. [For example], as to the offering of the fats and entrails—the religious duty to do them applies until the rise of the morning star.

K. All [sacrifices] which are eaten for one day, their religious duty to do them applies until the rise of the morning star.

L. If so why did sages say [that these actions may be performed only] until midnight?

M. In order to keep a man far from sin.

MISHNAH-TRACTATE BERAKHOT 1:1

The facts require only the briefest explanation. It is required to recite the prayer, the *Shema* ("Hear, Israel, the Lord, our God, the Lord is one"), morning and night. So the question at hand is, from what time is the action validly performed so as to carry out one's obligation? The answer specifies sunset, from the actual setting of the sun. Then, until what time may the obligation be carried out? The answer is for some hours. Then this is qualified, the act of reciting the prayer being valid until sunrise. That, sum and substance, is the Mishnah's rule. There commences the Mishnah, which is the first document that writes down (part of) the oral part of the Torah revealed by God to Moses at Sinai. Consider the contrast in the opening lines of the two parts of one Torah: "In the beginning God created the heaven and the earth," and "from what time do they recite the Shema in the evening?" We need no help at all to find our way into the written Torah, with its beginning, middle, and ending (at the death of Moses and the passage into the land). Without much assistance, by contrast, even the opening sentence of the oral Torah proves, if not gibberish, then very difficult of access.

When, earlier, I pointed out that the Talmud provides us with notes to a conversation but does not give us the script, emphasizing the necessity of the sage's intervention, I did not suggest that the Mishnah itself exhibited this same fragmentary quality. But when we reflect on what is before us, we realize that much is left without clear explanation. Now our first questions must be, Who is speaking? Where are we? What is the point of the Mishnah-sentence? None of these questions is answered here—or elsewhere in the Talmud. So the first thing we observe is, here is a document that takes for granted we know many things that the authors of the document do not tell us. But they are not the same things that are taken for granted, in the unarticulated compact between reader and writer, by the author of any of the sources of the Pentateuch on the one side, or by Plato on the next, or by the Evangelists on the third. Ordinarily, writers tell the readers where they are and what they propose to accomplish. Here we are nowhere in particular.

Nor does the Talmud, which follows, think it important to orient us, except in its own way:

> I. A. *On what basis does the Tannaite authority stand when he begins by teaching the rule,* **"From what time . . . ,"** [in the assumption that the religious duty to recite the Shema has somewhere been established? In point of fact, it has not been established that people have to recite the Shema at all.]

The voice of the Talmud now takes over and asks a question that proves routine in the Talmud and fundamental to its purpose. It wants to know the foundation for a rule that the Mishnah puts forth without specifying the authority or reason. From the answer, presently given, we further deduce the premise of the question. When the Talmud asks the basis for a Tannaite rule's statement, it means the basis in Scripture. So the Talmud wants to tell us what the Mishnah does not deem urgent: the scriptural basis for the rule of the Mishnah itself. But the basis that is requested is not only for the rule of the Mishnah—there is a specific time at which the obligation to recite the Shema may be fulfilled—but also the requirement for which the rule is made, which is the recitation of the Shema itself.

When I spoke of the Talmud as notes toward the reconstitution of a conversation, this is what I meant. What I insert in square brackets, what I have just now added—none of that necessary information is given. Then where does it come from? In the natural setting of the Talmud, it comes from the master. And how does the master know? The sage learned it from the teacher who taught the sage, and that teacher from the one before—backward to Sinai, forward to the end of time. Now the Talmud proceeds to extend its question:

> B. *Furthermore, on what account does he teach the rule concerning the evening at the beginning? Why not start with the morning?*

The second question involves not authority nor source but form: isn't it more sensible to discuss reciting the Shema in the morning, then in the evening, in the theory that that is the natural order of things? The answer now addresses both questions by seizing on the premise: that Scripture is at issue. The authority of Scripture is invoked to deal with both problems. Note once more the information that I have inserted, which is what, in the setting of the yeshiva, the master would have to tell the disciple.

> C. *The Tannaite authority stands upon the authority of Scripture, [both in requiring the recitation of the Shema and in beginning with the evening], for it is written,* "When you lie down and when you rise up" [Deut. 6:7].

That information carries us to the next question: having explained the source of the passage, we shall now paraphrase it and so amplify its meaning:

> D. *And this is the sense of the passage:* **When is the time for the recitation of the Shema when one lies down? It is from the hour that the priests enter [a state of cleanness so as] to eat their heave-offering [M. 1:1B].**
> E. *And if you prefer, I may propose that the usage derives from the order of the description of creation, for it is said,* "And there was evening, and there was morning, one day" [Gen. 1:5].

Up to this point, readers will have assumed that the Talmud's principal trait is its lucid, polyphonic presentation of information.

Through a process of question and answer, much as in a dialogue of Plato, we are led to see the facts of matters. But again like a dialogue of Plato, that is not where matters end, and in the few lines that follow is adumbrated the Talmud's deepest commitment: to rigorous argument, exposed in a moving or dialectical argument. That is, we set up that contentious conversation to which I made reference. The voice of the Talmud comes into play, arguing with itself, so to speak: "If that were so, then what about this . . . ?"

> F. *If there were the principal consideration, then let us take note of the formulation of the rules that occurs later on:* **In the morning one says two blessings before reciting the Shema and one afterward, and in the evening, one says two blessings before hand and two afterward [M. 1:4].** [The formulation therefore ignores the order of the description of creation.] *[By the reasoning just now proposed,] should not the Tannaite authority speak first of evening?*

The source of the objection is the evidence supplied by the Mishnah itself. We have maintained that we speak of the evening first because that is the way Scripture defines matters. But the Mishnah is not consistent with that pattern, and, therefore, any allegation that there is a compelling reason in Scripture must overcome the obstacle that the Mishnah here acknowledges, but elsewhere ignores, Scripture's alleged imperative. That, of course, is impossible. Scripture then cannot be at stake at all. And that carries us to the end of the passage:

> G. *The Tannaite authority at hand began by discussing matters pertaining to the Shema recited in the evening, and then he proceeded to take up matters having to do with reciting the Shema at dawn. While dealing with the matters having to do with the dawn, he proceeded to spell out other rules on the same matter, and then, only at the end, he went on to spell out other matters having to do with the evening.*
>
> BAVLI BERAKHOT 2A

The answer is, the objection is irrelevant. It does not prove what the person who raised the objection (in fact, the voice of the Talmud itself) wanted us to suppose. The author of the Mishnah paragraph began with the evening recitation of the Shema and dealt fully with that; then he turned to the morning recitation and examined that; and in that context, he moved on to secondary issues. So there really is no stylistic problem here at all; the normal rule of reasonable exposition—which keeps together matters of a common theme or category—governs.

That initial exposure to the Talmud—I here take the place of the sage in the yeshiva—brings us back to the character of the document and my representation of the Talmud, inclusive of the Mishnah, as of necessity oral, demanding the intervention of the living sage. The Mishnah begins abruptly, and any other tractate will have given the same jolt. Tractates ordinarily begin in the middle of things, rarely start with first principles. So it is a rare tractate that we can commence on our own, knowing nothing but what the tractate tells us in its opening lines. We are left to reconstruct the facts that are taken for granted, the verses of Scripture (if any) that are presupposed. These are not the only points of enigmatic silence. We do not know who speaks or why; we are not told the authority of the document; we are left ignorant of the context in which the rules matter.

As we saw, for the case at hand, much information is taken for granted: (1) what the Shema is; (2) why it has to be recited; (3) when the priests perform the specified action; (4) the identity of the named rabbis, Eliezer, sages, Gamaliel; (5) the purpose of the case or precedent; and these items only stand at the head of a long list of facts we are assumed to know. Not only so, but how and why the components of this paragraph hold together into a cogent statement is scarcely self-evident. What, after all, are "the priests . . . their heave-offering" doing here, and why are Gamaliel's sons exemplars? Much is taken for granted. And I think, the most profound premise of the document, both the Mishnah and the Talmud that re-presents it, is the obvious one: a teacher is there to help the student. For some of these facts or premises can have been assumed by reason of the ordinary practice of the people expected to receive the document, who will have known from Scripture and common practice what the *Shema* is. But the paragraph nonetheless cries out for amplification, and that amplification must not only spell out detail but specify the premise and goal of the rule: Why bother? What difference does it make?

And the characterization of the Talmud as a commentary to the Mishnah now turns out to reveal far less than meets the eye. To make sense of the Talmud that is before us, we have to accept without explanation the very givens that dictate the character of the statement at hand: this is what we need to know about this Mishnah paragraph—and not that. After all, if we present to the Talmud a list of our questions, its framers will dismiss most of them as inconsequential. They have their own issues. For it is a simple fact that a commentary may accomplish many purposes. That the Talmud forms a commentary to the Mishnah paragraph in no way prepares us to predict the character of that commentary. The kind of commentary we have has to be inductively defined.

First of all, the commentary assumes that the text requires clarification at its most basic level. Since we take for granted the Mishnah paragraph follows a logical program, we wonder why the framer has not established the obligation to recite the specified prayer. And, assuming that within the logic is the ordinary order of nature, we wonder why we do not commence with the morning, when people get up? The two questions draw a single answer, which itself represents a further datum: the Mishnah's laws rest upon Scripture's norms. The Mishnah has not cited the written Torah; the Talmud begins by moving us precisely in the direction of the other part of the Torah. The Mishnah imitates Scripture's formula, C, and then D accomplishes the work of exegesis based on the now-established hermeneutics. E offers a second explanation, challenged at F, with the resolution at G. I said earlier that the Talmud gives us the signals by which we reconstruct a conversation. The signals before us clearly mark the way: the question is not spelled out, but we readily identify the required amplification; the answers equally plausibly bear their own clear indications of the larger issues that we on our own must identify.

Note the difference between our first encounter, when I gave a sequence of unglossed sentences, clarified only with standard punctuation, and the present one. I gave this passage to the reader in the form that I myself have imposed, which converts the received text into its components and allows us immediately to reproduce the conversation about the Mishnah that the Talmud wishes us to replicate. Now let us take a step toward a more difficult confrontation with the character of the document: the way it is, not the way I have invented it so as to render it with a measure of clarity. I supply the signals routine for readers now, the periods and commas, more important, the paragraphing that separates thought from thought, the indication of the language that is used, and the like.

But what if I had given the text in the way in which we have it in the Talmud, which is to say, unpunctuated by sentences indicating where things start and stop, or paragraphs indicating where a complete thought has been set forth, or amplification in square brackets, which infuses the whole with continuity and clear sense. Now let us revert to the passage of the Talmud introduced earlier, in Chapter 3, and once more ask ourselves whether without the usual help of paragraphing and without the amplificatory material given by the contemporary translator (himself a commentator, of course), we still are able simply to read the passage as we would any other book, whether written by an ancient Israelite or by Plato or by one of the Evangelists or any other sort of writing.

First let us consider the Mishnah paragraph that is treated by the Talmud at hand, and then we examine the re-presentation of a piece of that paragraph in the Talmud.

A. He who leaves a jug in the public domain,

B. and someone else came along and stumbled on it and broke it—

C. [the one who broke it] is exempt,

D. And if [the one who broke it] was injured by it, the owner of the jug is liable [to pay damages for] his injury.

E. [If] his jug was broken in the public domain,

F. and someone slipped on the water,

G. or was hurt by the sherds,

H. he is liable.

I. R. Judah says, "In [a case in which he did so] deliberately, he is liable, and in [a case in which he did] not
[do so] deliberately, he is exempt."

MISHNAH-TRACTATE BABA QAMMA 3:1

Rather than speculate on the possible talmuds we might compose,
let us turn directly to the Talmud we do have. We begin with
a Mishnah rule, which again is distinguished from the Talmud
through the use of boldface type:

**He who leaves a jug in the public domain, and someone
else came along and stumbled on it and broke it—[the
one who broke it] is exempt,**

This is then cited verbatim and discussed as follows:

**and someone else came along and stumbled on it and
broke it—[the one who broke it] is exempt:** *Why should
he be exempt? He should have opened his eyes as he walked
along! They said in the household of Rab in the name of Rab,*
"We deal with a case in which the whole of the public
domain was filled with barrels." Samuel said, "We deal
with a case in which the jugs were in a dark place." R.
Yohanan said, "We deal with a case in which the jug was
at a corner."

Now I supply only punctuation, which is lacking in the original. I
also indicate the presence of the Talmud's voice, which speaks in
Aramaic ("why should he be . . . he should have . . .").

Let us take an inductive look at the passage. The Talmud's sentences clearly represent some sort of staccato phrases, question,
amplification of the question, then a set of three answers to the
question. But none of this is signaled in the unparagraphed presentation, so we clearly need guidance we are not given. But,
much more to the point, the three proposed solutions to the problem are set out without a trace of explanation, and that is curious.
The writer assumes that we know much more than we do. For
otherwise, why ask so simple a question as that which precipitates
the discussion, "He should have opened his eyes . . ."—if right

alongside we are going to be given three gnomic and unarticulated answers to the question.

Once more the point is clear: the authors assume a vast amount of knowledge. Then what do they think they are providing? This is once more a good example of what I mean by characterizing the Talmud as the notes that permit us to reconstruct a conversation —an argument, an analytical exercise. These are notes to the conversation but not the script of the conversation. Then how are we to move from the notes to the conversation? The answer is, of course, in the society of sage and disciple, where a living tradition explains how to read the text in such a way as to reconstitute the conversation that the text proposes to transmit to us: notes and not a script.

Now let us reconsider the same passage with the signs that we should routinely receive from a master in a yeshiva. That is, in his oral instruction, reading the text with us, he would teach us where the breaks are, who is talking to whom, and the sense of what is said. All this is conveyed in oral instruction, and the medium of that instruction, in the re-presentation of the text, will be song, as I explained in Chapter 1. The song will indicate in its phrasing, in its ups and downs, in its breathings and its rhythms, the beginnings and endings of sentences, the status of clauses, the force of questions. I, of course, cannot sing to the reader, but I do the equivalent by using the signals of my analytical annotation system. Taking the role of the master by my paragraphing, signals as to source (Mishnah, Talmud), language choice, identification of distinct sentences, I now spell out the passage by reconstructing the text through my own amplification of it:

II.1 A. and someone else came along and stumbled on it and broke it—[the one who broke it] is exempt:

B. *Why should he be exempt? He should have opened his eyes as he walked along!*

C. *They said in the household of Rab in the name of Rab,* "We deal with a case in which the whole of the public domain was filled with barrels."

D. Samuel said, "We deal with a case in which the jugs were in a dark place."

E. R. Yohanan said, "We deal with a case in which the jug was at a corner."

Now there can be no doubt about the structure of what is before us: a problem to be solved by three solutions. The problem is, why is one not responsible for his action? This is explained: a person should watch where he is going; this person has not taken due precautions. He has been irresponsible and so bears responsibility for the consequence.

The form of C–E is tight and disciplined, with three matched answers, differing only in the details. Then our problem becomes, since the authorities concur on the governing principle, what distinctions are they making through their respective solutions to the problem at hand. The question is answered in terms characteristic of the Mishnah: concrete and immediate; but the upshot is an abstract amplification of the law. The one who broke the jug would be exempt because the event of which the one who placed the jug in the street was the cause was by him rendered unavoidable (C), or preventable through the taking of proper precautions (D, E). It was not the result of overwhelming external force, and it also is not the consequence of anything the person who broke the jug has done or his failure to do something to prevent what was foreseeable to him. So the one who placed the jug is the necessarily efficient cause (absent the jug, no breakage!), and also the sufficient cause, there being no other participant to the incident, even though the one who actually broke the jug is the actual cause. That is the point at which responsibility parts company from the (mere) facts of the case. The hermeneutic of the Talmud requires dispute concerning the reading of the Mishnah; the result is clarification of the operation of the principles of the Mishnah.

A further characteristic of the second Talmud's hermeneutic, and the dynamic of its thought, is the spinning out of a dialectic argument, which we met briefly just now. Once more, we extend the analysis in a moving exchange of opinion, allegation, or proposition, objection, evidence, argument, counterallegation, and on and on. In the moving, or dialectic argument, we pursue the argument wherever it leads, and the close reading of the Mishnah's language vastly expands our understanding of the principles and how they apply:

> F. *Said R. Pappa, "A close reading of our Mishnah-rule can accord only with the view of Samuel or R. Yohanan. For if it were in accord with the position of Rab, then what difference does it make that exemption is accorded only if the man stumbled over the pitcher? Why not rule in the same way even if he deliberately broke the pitcher?*
>
> G. *Said R. Zebid in the name of Raba, "In point of fact, the same rule really does apply even if the defendant deliberately broke the jug. And the reason that the language,* **and stumbled on it,** *is used, is that the later clause goes on to say,* **And if [the one who broke it] was injured by it, the owner of the barrel is liable [to pay damages for] his injury.** *But that would be the case only* **if he stumbled on it,** *but not if he deliberately broke the jug. How come? The man has deliberately injured himself. So that is why, to begin with, the word-choice was* **and stumbled on it.**

Pappa's proposition is not required for the full interpretation of the three positions that precede. He adds a new point. He will prove that one position is discordant, that of Rab. This he does by pursuing the reasoning of Rab to its conclusion and asking why the distinction that he proposes makes a difference. To the Mishnah rule, it makes no difference. And this objection is met head on at G. When a person bears responsibility for his own injury, he cannot claim compensation. The conditions of the case are such as to validate all three positions.

It is, of course, the voice of the Talmud that carries the sounds of Pappa's and Zebid's statements. Absent the Talmud, we have no dispute, no analysis, no argument, no contention, but a set of freestanding statements. Did Samuel, Rab, and Yohanan assemble one day for a debate? (We ignore the fact that Yohanan lived in the Land of Israel, Samuel in Babylonia, Rab in both countries.) Then shall we imagine the following represents a transcript of what was said?

> *Why should he be exempt? He should have opened his eyes as he walked along! They said in the household of Rab in the name of Rab,* "We deal with a case in which the whole of the public domain was filled with barrels." Samuel said, "We deal with a case in which the jugs were in a dark place." R. Yohanan said, "We deal with a case in which the jug was at a corner."

When I characterize the writing as notes on the re-constitution of a dispute, the answer to that question indicates the sense of my remark. And, again, Pappa, coming some time later and not contemporary to the authorities, had access only to these same notes. He joined in the debate and made himself party to the conversation. And so, too, did Zebid. All we have before us, then, are the allusions to, the reports of, things thought—which we for our part must think through, too. Clearly, the Talmud's melody is stated in the dialectic: the variations prove each in its own way to express the theme. There will be more on that subject in the chapter that follows. If I may state what I think is at stake here, it is a very simple goal: the Talmud means to change the reader by reshaping the reader's mode of thinking, that is, the Talmud fully intends to undertake a process to convert the reader into a disciple: one who can hear the Talmud's voice and respond.

Having concluded the previous chapter with a Mishnah paragraph contrasted with Scripture's counterpart, let us complete our work here by considering the Talmud's reading of the same matter. We see the movement from the problem, resolving conflict, and the formulation of propositions in resolution thereof—Scripture's, the Mishnah's—to the Talmud's point of interest. It is, stated simply, not at all topical but methodical and methodological. The Mishnah and Scripture have talked about a problem and solved it. The Talmud will now place the entire matter in its own distinctive intellectual framework. The contrast between Scripture and the Mishnah on the one side, and the Talmud on the other, shows us why the two parts of the Torah, written and oral, require re-presentation in a single statement, and how the Talmud accomplished the task of holding together in one formulation the two components of the Torah of Sinai.

The Talmud wants to know why the Mishnah's author has formulated matters as he has. It pursues the question of whether the details in the Mishnah are necessary to communicate the message that is intended; whether they contain any ambiguity; whether they may prove even repetitious. While the premise, of course, is that the Mishnah cannot contain imperfections of formulation, the attitude toward the Mishnah is uncompromising and rigorous. The Talmud, we quickly see, by no means intends to compose a mere apologetic to the Mishnah. Nor does the Talmud paraphrase the Mishnah. Above all, the Talmud does not merely assemble information relevant to the subject of the Mishnah. Everything that the Talmud does say is purposive, directed toward the making of an important point, the construction of a significant argument. In other words, when we ask, What is this? Why this not that, and So what? we are taught to do so by the Talmud itself. Since a fair portion of contemporary academic discourse consists in a protracted labor of, first, paraphrase, then show-and-tell of episodic facts somehow deemed topically relevant, we do well to review the way in which first-rate minds carry on their inquiry. The people who now speak to us form a fine model of how to conduct intellectual life, especially in a time in which, in a fair part of the academy and, all the more so, the rest of the world of intellect, people find satisfaction merely in repeating what they find in their own words and then free associating so as to add to their paraphrase as much information as they can assemble, whether relevant or not. Here, when we ask, So what? we see the limits of mere topical information and follow an argument in which information is introduced when it is pointed and relevant to an argument, and in which discourse consists of something more to the point than mere paraphrase: rigorous argument about a sustaining proposition.

[Continuing Bavli Bava Mesia 2A]
I.1. A. *What need do I have to repeat in the Mishnah,*
   B. **this one says, "I found it!"**—

C. and that one says, "I found it!"—

D. this one says, "It's all mine!"—

E. and that one says, "It's all mine!"?

F. *Let the Tanna repeat only a single* [plea] [Salis Daiches, Soncino trans.: Surely one plea would have been sufficient.]

G. *It is only a single [formulation] that the Tanna has repeated* [Daiches:[4] It is only one plea], namely,

H. "this one says, 'I found it and it's all mine. . . .' and that one says, 'I found it and it's all mine. . . .'"

2. A. *Then let the Tanna repeat [the plea,]* "I found it," *and I shall [naturally] know the fact [that the litigant has claimed,]* "It's all mine"!

B. *Had the Tanna [repeated the formulation solely as,]* "I have found it," *I might have reached the conclusion,* "What is the sense of, 'I have found it'? 'I saw it, even though it did not actually come into my hands. Through merely seeing the object, I have effected acquisition of it.'"* [Daiches: The term I found it might have been explained as denoting, 'I saw it,' the mere seeing of the garment entitling him to claim it as his possession.']

C. *The Tanna* [has formulated the rule in the language of] **"It's all mine!"** *to indicate that merely by seeing the object, the man has not made acquisition of it.*

3. A. *But can you really maintain that the sense of* "I have found it" *must be* "I saw it"?

B. *Now lo,* Rabbanai has said, "'and you find' (Deut.

4. Where I cite "Daiches" (or, in later passages, other names in the same way), it is to the S. Daiches (and his colleagues') translation into English and commentary to the same tractate, published in London by Soncino Press in 1948. Daiches was one of the few British rabbis who first translated the Talmud of Babylonia (and other classics of Judaism) into English, and who solved nearly all of the translation problems by finding illuminating ways of rendering into intelligible English the elliptical language before them. None of the many other translations into English and American that have followed surpassed their work or much improved upon it. Daiches then serves as the guide to the sense of the passage, absorbing into his representation of it the important, received commentaries, beginning of course with Rashi's.

22:3: 'and so shall you do with any lost thing of your brother's, which he loses and you find').—[that is to say,] *that it has come into his possession."*

C. *Indeed so, when Scripture says, "and you find," the sense is, that it has come into his possession."*

D. *Nonetheless, [in the passage at hand,] the Tanna has employed the [commonplace and] prevailing usage.*

E. *[And, in accord with that usage, once] one has seen [an object], he takes the view, "I have found it," so that even though the object has not actually come into the man's possession, [he supposes that merely because] he has seen the object, he has effected possession of it.*

F. *The Tanna* [has formulated the rule in the language of] **"It's all mine!"** *to indicate that merely by seeing the object, the man has not made acquisition of it.*

4. A. *Then let the Tanna repeat [the plea], "It's all mine" and he then need not repeat in the passage the wording, "It's all mine"!*

B. *Had the Tanna [repeated the formulation solely as,] "It's all mine," I might have reached the conclusion that in general, when the Tanna uses the language, "I have found it," the sense is that merely by sighting an object in general, one has acquired possession of it.*

C. *He has formulated matters in the language of,* **"I have found it,"** *and then gone and formulated the passage further,* **"It's all mine,"** *so that, from this repetition we should draw the conclusion that merely by the act of sighting an object, one has not acquired possession of it.*

5. A. But can you really maintain that *it is only a single [formulation] that the Tanna has repeated,* namely, ["this one says, 'I found it and it's all mine. . . .' and that one says, 'I found it and it's all mine. . . .'"]? [Up to this point in its analysis of the Mishnah, the Gemara has sought to establish that the first two clauses, "I found it," and "All of it is mine," are two necessary features of a single, integral unit, dealing with one particular case. The Gemara now proceeds to attack this basic assumption and asks,

Can you say that the Mishnah in its two opening statements is teaching one particular case with one particular claim? Surely the wording indicates that the Mishnah is referring not to one but to two separate and distinct cases.]

B. Lo, The Tanna has repeated matters in the language, "This one says . . . and that one says. . . ."

C. [thus:] **this one says, "I found it!"—**

D. **and that one says, "I found it!"—**

E. **this one says, "It's all mine!"—**

F. **and that one says, "It's all mine!"?**

G. *Said R. Pappa, and some attribute the statement to R. Shimi b. R. Ashi, or assign it to Kadi, "The initial case involves an object that has been found, the succeeding one, a case of purchase and sale."* [Daiches: "But not to a case where each one maintains that he has made the garment, for then one of them is bound to be lying."]

H. *And both of these cases had to be addressed individually.*

I. [Bavli Bava Mesia 2B] *For if the Tanna had repeated the rule only concerning the case of a conflict over an object that has been found, I might have reached the conclusion that it is specifically in the case of an object that has been found that rabbis have imposed the requirement of taking an oath, since each party might allow himself to lay claim, saying, "My fellow loses nothing if I go and take possession of the object and split the object with him, [since the other never owned the garment to begin with and paid nothing for it]. But in the case of a dispute over who has purchased a given argument, where there can be no such calculation, I might say that [sages have] not imposed [the requirement of an oath.]*

J. *And if the Tanna had repeated the rule only concerning the case of conflict over an object that has been purchased [in which both parties claim to have purchased the same thing], the reason that rabbis have imposed the requirement of taking an oath in such a case in particular is this: the litigant may permit himself to lay claim, saying, "My fellow has paid for the object, and I can go and pay for the object. Now that I need it, I'll grab it, and let the fellow go and take the trouble to buy another object." But in the case of a dispute over an object that has been found, in which case such reasoning will not apply, I might say that that is not the rule. Accordingly, it was necessary [to impose the same rule in the case of a conflict over an object that has been purchased].*

6. A. *But in a case of an object that has been purchased, then [why should there be such a conflict between two equally valid claims, without evidence available to settle matters]?*

B. *Just see from whom [the seller] has accepted the money [and when he indicates who paid for the cloak, we know the resolution of the conflict].*

C. *Not at all, the [oath is] required in a case in which the seller has taken money from them both, one of them willingly, one of them under constraint, and we do now know from whom it was taken willingly, and from whom under constraint.*

The analysis of the Mishnah paragraph on the part of the Bavli begins with the analysis of the way in which it is formulated. The premise of the Bavli is that the Mishnah's framers do not repeat themselves, so that if there is what appears to be repetition, it is to make a point, for example, deal with a case that for some reason differs from the initial one. We begin with the question, 1.F, why has the matter been repeated, in that each party is assigned two pleas, first, I found the object, second, I wholly possess it. The first answer is as given at G–H. This is challenged at 2.B, and the reason for the specific wording is then adduced. It is to exclude misinterpretation of the law. Had the language been other than what it is, we should have misinformation on the rule. This position is again challenged and reenforced at no. 3 and no. 4, which goes over familiar materials.

The second fresh initiative commences at no. 5, which revises the grounds of analysis. Up to this point, we have assumed that we deal with a single case, one in which two people contest the possession of a single object, both of them claiming to have found it. But the language "It's all mine" can be read to speak of a quite distinct situation from one involving lost-and-found. Now we have two people who contest ownership of an object both claim to have purchased. This second initiative, fully worked out, is then challenged on the obvious ground that someone out there should have the facts, so why bother with an oath? Then, 6.C, we create a situation in which the seller cannot supply the required testimony, thus we still are in a case of equally valid claims and so invoke the oath. This concludes the analysis of the Mishnah's paragraph much in its own terms.

But the Mishnah's rule and case(s) bear a variety of implications, some of them right on the surface, and one of them demands analysis in its turn. It is that an oath is imposed in a case such as this—which, as we saw in Chapter 2, is the absolute given of our Mishnah paragraph and the purpose for which that paragraph of three cases has been composed. But are we not then engaged in a kind of entrapment, since we are imposing an oath on two parties in the certain knowledge that one of the two parties is going to swear falsely? That question now demands attention on its own terms. We now leave the Mishnah paragraph and turn to principles of law, embodied in the names of particular authorities. We move from cases to principles—the critical work of representation through generalization, which neither the Scripture's nor the Mishnah's statements of matters has contemplated.

The Talmud's second task, after its work on literary-critical reading of the language of the Mishnah, is to analyze the principles implicit in the passage before us. Since, as we ourselves noticed at the outset, the Mishnah's rule concerns the taking of an oath to resolve a dispute between two parties, we want to know whether there are other positions on the same matter. We immediately point out that at least some authorities do not think an oath should be imposed in a case such as ours. For one thing, how can we impose an oath on two parties when one of the parties is going to be a liar? We thereby entrap the liar and invoke upon him dire consequences, which follow from taking a false oath. That is hardly a good procedure. And, *mutatis mutandis,* if we permit both parties to split the disputed object merely by an oath, then one of them

—the liar—profits from his deceit. No bunko artist in the world will hesitate merely to take an oath and so grab half of someone else's property. These considerations emerge by indirection. We frame our critique of the Mishnah's premise in terms of whether or not a given authority, identified with a position contrary to that of our paragraph on the matter of the oath, will concur with our rule here. The first concerns the issue of entrapment: imposing an oath on two parties, when we know for certain one or the other will be swearing falsely.

> [Continuing on 2B:] **II.1.A.** *May one claim that the Mishnah-passage before us* [in requiring the taking of an oath to settle the matter] *does not accord with the principle of Ben Nannos.*
>
> B. For **Ben Nannos has said, "How is it possible that this party and that that party should be brought into the state of taking a false oath?"** [**M. Shabuot 7:5**] [Daiches: "For does not Ben Nannus express surprise at the decision of the Sages to impose oaths on disputants one of whom is bound to swear falsely?] [The reference is to M. Shabuot 7:1A, C: **These are the ones who take an oath and collect what is owing to him: . . . a shopkeeper concerning what is written in his account book.** M. Shabuot 7:5: **A shopkeeper concerning what is written in his account book—how so? It is not that he may say to him, "It is written in my account book that you owe me two hundred** *zuz.*" **But if the householder said to him, "Give my son two** *seahs* **of wheat," "Give my worker change for a** *sela,*" **and he says, "I already gave it to him," and they say, "We never got it"—the storekeeper takes an oath and collects what is owing to him, and the workers take an oath and collect what they claim from the householder. Said Ben Nannos, "How so? But these or those then are taking a vain oath! Rather, the storekeeper collects what is owing to him without taking an oath at all, and the workers collect what they claim not to have received without taking an oath."**]

C. [The case before us may accord] *even with the principle of Ben Nannos* [who will not impose an oath in a case in which it is clear one or another party will be taking the oath falsely].

D. *In the case to which Ben Nannos refers* [in stating his principle], *there is most assuredly going to be a false oath.*

E. *But in the present case, there is the possibility of claiming that there is no false oath.*

F. *One may say that the two of them at the same instant raised up the object* [and thereby effected possession of it, so both can be telling the truth].

2. A. *May one claim that the Mishnah-passage* [in requiring the taking of an oath to settle the matter] *before us does not accord with the principle of Sumkhos* (Symmachus)?

B. *For if it were to accord with Sumkhos, has he not said,* "As to money that is subject to doubt [and therefore contested ownership], that money is divided without the taking of an oath"?

C. *But then what* [alternative do you propose? Is it that the Mishnah-passage before us accords with the principle of] *sages* [vis-à-vis Sumkhos]?

D. *Lo, they have maintained,* He who proposes to take away [the property of another] bears the burden of bringing proof of the validity of his claim. [So they too will not concur that an oath will serve to settle the issue here.]

F. *Now if, as a matter of fact, you introduce the position of sages* [vis-à-vis Sumkhos], *in that case, in which both parties have not seized hold of the property that is disputed, rabbis indeed rule,* He who proposes to take away [the property of another] bears the burden of bringing proof of the validity of his claim.

H. *But in this case, in which both parties have seized hold of the property that is disputed, they indeed will divide the object upon the taking of an oath.*

I. *But if, on the other hand, you maintain that* [the *Mishnah-passage at hand] accords with the principle of Sumkhos,* [we may formulate matters in this way and so demonstrate the contradiction between his principle and the ruling before us]:

J. *If in such a situation, in which both parties have not in fact seized hold of the disputed object, they are to divide the object without the taking of an oath, here, in which both parties have seized hold of the disputed property, is it not an argument a fortiori* [that they should divide the object without taking an oath! Accordingly, the present ruling cannot accord with the position of Sumkhos.]

K. *You may even take the view that the Mishnah-passage before us accords with the principle of Sumkhos.*

L. *When Sumkhos took the view that he did, it is in the situation in which each party is uncertain* [as to the facts of the matter, so neither of them can be made to take an oath], *but in a case, such as this one, in which both parties express certainty about their rights of ownership, he would take a different view.*

M. *And in the view of Rabbah bar R. Huna, who stated, "Sumkhos said, 'Even in a case in which both parties express certainty about their rights of ownership, [an oath is taken to settle the conflicting claims],'" what is there to be said?*

N. *You may even maintain that in such a case, it is still in accord with the view of Sumkhos.*

O. *When Sumkhos took the view he did, it was in a case in which there would be a loss of money* [Daiches: For Symmachus expressed the view as quoted only in a case where a verdict in favor of one would involve a loss to the other, but where no actual monetary loss is involved, as in our Mishnah, he would take a different view.]

P. *But does that view not yield an argument a fortiori* [which will prove that Sumkhos does not accord with our Mishnah-paragraph]?

Q. *If in the case to which reference is made, a loss of money to one party is involved, and a loss of money to the other party is equally involved,* [3A] *and, further, one may maintain that the whole of the disputed item may belong to one party, and one may maintain that the whole of the dispute*

*item may belong to the other party, and, in such a case, Sum-
khos has adopted the principle,* "As to money that is subject
to doubt [and therefore contested ownership], that money
is divided without the taking of an oath," *here* [in the case
of the Mishnah's rule], *in which case there is no question of
a loss of money to either party, for one may rule that the disputed property belongs to both parties* [and so may be divided without an oath taken by either one], *is it not an
argument a fortiori* [and hence the Mishnah cannot accord
with Sumkhos, who will have the property equally divided without the taking of an oath]!

R. *You may, indeed, still hold* [that the Mishnah-
passage accords with the principle of] *Sumkhos.*

S. *This oath* [of which the Mishnah speaks] *is imposed
only by the authority of the rabbis* [and not on the authority
of the Torah. There are then two kinds of oath, and when
Sumkhos avoids imposing an oath, as in the cases just
now discussed, it is an oath on the authority of the Torah.
The distinction between the two kinds of oaths permits
us to allow that, in the present case, Sumkhos would concur that an oath is invoked, while in the cases of which he
speaks elsewhere, it is not invoked. The difference then
vitiates the argument *a fortiori.*]

T. *And that accords with the view of R. Yohanan, for* said
R. Yohanan, "This oath [to which our Mishnah-passage
refers] happens to be an ordinance imposed only by
rabbis,

U. "so that people should not go around grabbing the
cloaks of other people and saying, 'It's mine!'" [But, as a
matter of fact, the oath that is imposed in our Mishnah-
passage is not legitimate by the law of the Torah. It is an
act taken by sages to maintain the social order.]

3. A. *May one claim that the Mishnah-passage* [in requiring the taking of an oath to settle the matter] *before us does
not accord with the principle of R. Yosé?*

B. *For if it were to accord with R. Yosé has he not said,*
[Two who deposited something with one person, this

one leaving a maneh [one hundred zuz], and that one
leaving two hundred zuz—this one says, "Mine is the deposit of two hundred zuz," and that one says, "Mine is the
deposit of two hundred zuz"—he pays off a maneh to
this one and a maneh to that one, and the rest is left until
Elijah comes. Said R. Yosé,] "If that is the case [that one
may take an oath and (merely in that way) acquire possession of property subject to dispute], then what does a
liar lose? But let everything be left until Elijah comes
[and settles matters]"?

[M. B.M. 3:4F–G].

C. *But with whom then may we say the passage accords?
Is it with the possession of rabbis vis-à-vis R. Yosé?*

D. *But since rabbis [vis-à-vis R. Yosé] have said,* "Let the
remainder [of the property under dispute in the cited
passage] remain until Elijah comes [and settles mat-
ters]," *lo, [the cloak in the Mishnah-paragraph before us is in
the status of] the remainder [in the case under discussion, for
it is subject to doubt.*

E. *How now!* [Daiches: What a comparison!] *If you
have invoked the position of rabbis in that other case, in
which the money at issue assuredly belongs to one of the two
parties, so that, in that case, sages have ruled,* "Let the remainder [of the property under dispute in the cited pas-
sage] remain until Elijah comes [and settles matters]," *in
the present case, in which there is the possibility of claiming
that it belongs to both of the claimants, rabbis would [reason-
ably] take the position that it should indeed be divided upon
the taking of an oath.*

F. *But if you take the position that the passage before us
accords with R. Yosé,* [that is quite a difficult view, for] *if in
the case* [of M. B.M. 3:4], *where it is certain that each claimant beyond doubt is entitled to a maneh, R. Yosé has said,*
"Let the remainder [of the property under dispute in the
cited passage] remain until Elijah comes [and settles
matters]," *in the present case, in which one may claim that*

the cloak belongs to only one of the two parties, is it not an argument a fortiori [that the property should be left in the custody of the court and not divided by means of an oath].

G. *[To the contrary,] you may even maintain that the Mishnah-paragraph represents the view of R. Yosé. In that other case, there most assuredly is a liar. But here, who will say with certainty that there is a liar? I should claim that the two of them at one and the same moment raised up the cloak.*

H. *Or in that other case, R. Yosé imposed an extrajudicial fine upon the liar so that he would be impelled to confess his deceit, while here, what loss is incurred that would impel the deceiver to confess?* [He will incur no loss if he forfeits the garment.]

I. *That argument suffices for the case of an object that has been found [to which the two lay claim], but what is there to be said about the case of an object that has been purchased [and subject to dispute as to who has paid for it]?*

J. *But the initial answer* [Daiches: that in the other case one claimant is certainly fraudulent, while in our case both may be honest] *is the better one.*

4. A. [With reference to M. Shabuot 7:5, cited above, **A shopkeeper concerning what is written in his account book—how so? It is not that he may say to him, "It is written in my account book that you owe me two hundred zuz." But if the householder said to him, "Give my son two seahs of wheat," "Give my worker change for a sela," and he says, "I already gave it to him," and they say, "We never got it"—the storekeeper takes an oath and collects what is owing to him, and the workers take an oath and collect what they claim from the householder. Said Ben Nannos, "How so? But these or those then are taking a vain oath! Rather, the store collects what is owing to him without taking an oath at all, and the workers collect what they claim not to have received without taking an oath,"]** *whether with regard to the position of rabbis or to that of R. Yosé,* [who concur that the liar should not profit from his lying], in the case involving the storekeeper, at

which it is repeated, **the storekeeper takes an oath and collects what is owing to him, and the workers take an oath and collect what they claim from the householder,** *how is that case to be differentiated from this one, in that there we do not rule, let the money be taken from the householder [who certainly owes it to either the storekeeper or the workers, who were to be paid in kind through their purchases at the company store], and* **Let the remainder [of the property under dispute in the cited passage] remain until Elijah comes [and settles matters]?**

B. *For lo, in that case,* [one or another of the parties to the dispute] *most certainly is a liar!*

C. *In that case, here is the reason [for the ruling as it is given]: the storekeeper may say to the householder, "I was your agent in this matter and have carried out your mission. What business have I to do with the worker* [who claims not to have been paid]? *Even though he may take an oath to me, even when he takes an oath, he is not credible to me. You were the one who laid your trust in him, for you did not say to me, 'Only in the presence of witnesses are you to pay him off.'"* ["You were the one who trusted the worker, now you are the one who has to be penalized if he takes the oath."]

D. *And along these same lines the worker may say to the householder, "I did my work for you. What business do I have with the storekeeper? Even though he takes an oath to me, he is not credible to me."*

E. *Therefore both claimants are to take oaths and collect what is owing from the householder.* [Daiches: It would thus be wrong to make either party forfeit the amount claimed. As the shopkeeper and the employees have had no direct dealings with each other and have entered into no mutual obligations, they may regard each other as entirely untrustworthy and refuse to believe each other even on oath.] [In that way we differentiate the case cited in connection with Ben Nannos from the case at hand involving Yosé. The two cases have nothing to do with each other, by reason of differing circumstances.]

The sustained exposition of II.1–4 shows how a single hand—
one editor or a hundred, it hardly matters—has put together a
systematic study of the problem of settling a dispute by taking an
oath. Framing matters in terms of named authorities, the author
before us has raised principles that must be brought into relationship, and if possible harmonized, with the rule before us. The Talmud, therefore, engages in a vast labor of detailed comparison and
contrast of cases and rules, aiming at a single cogent statement of
the whole. No. 1 raises the question of allowing an oath to settle
a dispute, since liars take oaths as much as do God-fearing folk.
At no. 1 we point out how our passage accords with—does not
contradict—the view of Ben Nannos. Where there is the certainty
that one party to a dispute must be lying, we do not invoke the
oath; but here there is no such certainty. But, quite to the contrary,
no. 2 asks, why require an oath at all? If both parties can be telling
the truth, then let them divide the disputed property without the
fearsome procedure. The solution to this problem is to differentiate the cases. No. 3 proceeds to a third authority, Yosé, who raises
the same question as Ben Nannos: Why permit a liar to benefit?
The solution once again is to differentiate the cases. And, no. 4
shows, we may also harmonize the views of Ben Nannos and Yosé
and our passage. I cannot think of a more perfect execution of the
task, which is to introduce all pertinent cases and principles and
show how they either accord with one another or do not contradict one another. Nothing is omitted; everything is satisfactorily
ordered.

To conclude, let us dwell for a moment on the consequence
of the transformation of the reader. First, the very sense of the
conception of "harmony," which has engaged us for some time,
deepens. Now we require a harmony not only of ideas, but of engaged participants in the formation of ideas. That peace that prevails in Heaven and on earth, the union of rationalities, human
and divine,—these are turned into an active and engaged process
involving all who encounter the document that stands for the entire oral part of the Torah. So, second, now we must make ourselves party to the process of thought, sharing in the question,
making our own the objection, passionately concerning ourselves

with the outcome. What this means is that, in exchange for the high compliment of writers who think we may share in the process of their thought, we must agree ourselves to be changed by the outcome: to take the argument seriously and at face value. Once we enter into the work of recapitulating, reconstituting the ancient conversation, we run the risk of reconsidering our own rules of rationality—for the condition of discourse with the Talmud because submitting to the process of shared rationality and so accepting the consequence of persuasion.

Having spoken the language of the document, let us now take a step back and from the outside speak about it. The power of the Talmud to exercise intellectual hegemony in Judaism flows from its pathos. As a writer, I have envied the power of the Mishnah's writers for lapidary expression but have never admired the writing of the Talmud. If, from my very first encounter, I found myself wholly drawn in, completely engaged by what I met, it was not by reason of the aesthetic elegance of the sentences and paragraphs. The document is so poorly framed that the reader—now a student —requires a teacher; the writing cannot be read on its own without at least some years of sustained instruction from a teacher near at hand. It is so elliptical, so gnomic, so self-referential, that its rules of thought require explanation that the writing does not convey.

Not only so, but the ubiquitous substrate of facts, taken for granted in the argument, is nowhere excavated and examined but everywhere formed into the foundation of inquiry. These writers assume at each point that we know the entire document, all of the facts required to make sense of any one point therein. That fact accounts for the postpublication history of the document: it never again stood on its own, but almost from the beginning attracted to itself commentaries of explanation, clarification, and expansion. Now, since its original authors' own work necessitated the extension of their writing, but since they themselves (so far as we know) added nothing to what they originally said in their composition, that must mean they imagined a history for their writing other than the history that ensued. The Talmud's one voice truly accomplished the Talmud's writers' goals.

What I think they expected was that theirs would be the document of an institution, the document around which an institution would take shape and from which that institution would draw nourishment and purpose. Specifically, they anticipated that their notes on the reconstruction of conversation would be sung in a living chorus of disciples led by masters; that is the meaning, the deepest meaning, of "oral tradition," that is what is received in vivid and corporate explanation—not merely read in the privacy of a study—and what is then handed on through exchange, the give and take of the circle of master and disciples—not merely accepted in the dumb silence of the reader's mind. And why should that anticipation not have governed the kind of writing they set forth when, as a matter of fact, they themselves, for some four hundred years, had received the oral part of the Torah—the Mishnah in particular—within that same institutional setting: the circle of master and disciples.

So we deal not with an ordinary book—a piece of writing with a beginning, to tell us its purpose and program; a middle, to instruct us on its specific propositions; and an end, to persuade us to accept what we have been given. We confront an extraordinary kind of writing, not a book at all, in the sense in which any of the compositions of Scripture, Deuteronomy, or Jeremiah or Job, for instance, are books: situated somewhere, coming somehow to closure. The Talmud is situated nowhere in particular and, as we shall see, neither begins nor ends but records a kind of discourse that moves as rapidly but as open-endedly as the middle movements of a set of variations on a theme.

The analogy is apt, for, just as there are endless variations on a theme, the repertoire limited only by the imagination of the composer and the skill of the musicians, so for the Talmud, when we understand how it works, we are given the opportunity ourselves to invent endless variations on a few, simple themes. And, when we can identify those themes, we shall know that Talmudic melody that forms a paramount part of the Judaic theological voice. And that brings us to what is unique in the Talmud, which is the formation of practical reason and applied logic into an unfolding argument, which is to say, the document's dialectics.

Five

THE MELODY OF MIND

$\mathcal{T}$he melody of mind in the Talmud is the dialectical argument, and that argument serves uniquely to establish the Talmud's part of the Torah's song. "Dialectical" means, moving or developing an idea through questions and answers, sometimes implicit, but commonly explicit. What "moves" is the argument, the flow of thought, from problem to problem. The movement is generated by raising contrary questions and theses. What differentiates the dialectical argument of the Talmud from the dialectical argument of a dialogue of Plato, however, is the Talmud's quality of meandering, moving hither and yon, contrasted with the rigorous cogency of the Platonic dialogue, which never loses its way or forgets its initial purpose. Many beginners in Talmudic studies realize, halfway through an argument, that they have forgotten where they started and the goal they wished to reach. The Talmud, therefore, exhibits a meandering quality—this, that, the other thing—that may frustrate easy access to its purpose. Philosophical dialectics and Talmudic dialectics part company.

The dialectical argument—the protracted, sometimes meandering, always moving flow of contentious thought—raises a question and answers it, then raises a question about the answer, then does the same; it moves hither and yon; it is always one, but it is never the same, and it flows across the surface of the Talmud. Those second and third and fourth turnings differentiated a dialectical from a static argument, much as the bubbles tell the difference between still and sparkling wine. The always-sparkling dialectical argument is one principal means by which the Talmud accomplishes its goal of showing the connections between this and that, ultimately demonstrating the unity of many thises and thats.

These efforts at describing the argument serve precisely as well as program notes to a piece of music: they tell us what we are going to hear; they cannot play the music. So let us turn to a specific passage, and as we walk through it line by line, I shall show precisely how the dialectical argument moves along. From this example of the formation of a melody line in the Talmud, we may hope to form a picture of the line itself: the Talmudic melody. When we follow the dialectical argument—the movement of thought through contentious challenge and passionate response, initiative and counterploy—we hear those ineluctable combinations of individual notes that make up a sustained melody, even a long melodic line. The Talmud takes over the natural aggressions, even the violence, that define us and transforms the energy into intellectual electricity. Here is no mere exchange of information, nor even a fideist trade of opinion: I think this, you think that. Nor is there space for negotiation about what is true: you are right for you, I am right for me. The Talmud's is an uncompromising, implacable standard: relativism finds no place at all.

Why the passion and the vigor of contention? The reason is that, in the sustained conflict provoked by the testing of proposition in unpitying contention, argument turns fact into truth. Making a point forms of data important propositions. And time and again, at the end of the dialectic argument we find ourselves with the same, few notes, so abstract as to yield an infinity of variations, yet always variations on a single theme. The notes are the melody, the dialectics the mind that hears, rejecting all other possible combinations of notes, that one combination, that single melody—one entirely capable, as a matter of fact, of yielding all possible variations.

The exchange of propositions and arguments, objects and ripostes, hold together, however protracted. Now, in the nature of the document, these moving or dialectical arguments cover a vast number of issues. Readers may rightly ask, therefore, how we may speak of the Talmudic melody, when, in fact, what we have (by the metaphor in hand) are only melodies made up by many minds. And not only so, but if my description captures some of the sound of the academy when the oral part of the Torah is taken up, then we have not so much melodies as shouts, screams, banging of books, and slapping of tables: What sort of music is that? Even Charles Ives, even John Cage, may have found the sound of learning a challenge to musicianship.

What then is at stake in the dialectical argument? I see two complementary results. Both of them, in my view, prove commensurate to the effort required to follow these protracted, sometimes tedious disquisitions. First, we survey the entire range of possibilities, which leaves no doubts about the cogency of our conclusion. Second, by the give-and-take of argument, we ourselves go through the thought processes set forth in the subtle markings that yield our reconstruction of the argument. We not only review what people say but how they think: the processes of reasoning that have yielded a given conclusion. When I claimed that, in the Talmud, sages and disciples become party to the modes of thought, thus joining in the creative labor of writing the music, this is precisely what I meant. Here, turning the signs into statements, we find ourselves required to replicate the thought-processes themselves, and only when we do so are we able ourselves to read what is before us. We, of course, require the work of the composer, but the analogy of early concerti and opera holds true: we make up the arpeggios and much else.

When we grasp the dynamics of the dialectical argument, the power of a pertinent, purposeful response to an important argument, we realize that before the melodies there is a model for music in general: what is fitting, what sounds right. (And, in due course, I shall explain why what sounds right in the Talmud's context is right.) And the melody within all melodies, the one that forms the paradigm of music as much as the eight-note scale has served for Western music until nearly our own time, is the how of argument. In the method of sustained, rigorous exchange we discern the Talmud's tune: the "how" of thought, repeated enough times, turns into the "what" of the document's statement. A melody emerges from notes, more often than note, when the same notes are repeated enough times to form a pattern; the pattern then to our ears sounds out the melody.

Let us leap directly into the text. The passage that we consider occurs at the Babylonian Talmud Baba Mesia 5B–6A, which is to say, Talmud to Mishnah Baba Mesia 1:1–2. In Chapter 4, we have already examined the earlier part of this same composite, which serves the opening Mishnah paragraph of Baba Mesia 1:1. Now our interest is in the twists and turns of the argument and what is at stake in the formation of a continuous and unfolding composition:

> **[5B] IV.1.A. this one takes an oath that he possesses no less a share of it than half, [and that one takes an oath that he possesses no less a share of it than half, and they divide it up]:**

The rule of the Mishnah, which is cited at the head of the sustained discussion, concerns the case of two persons who find a garment. We settle their conflicting claim by requiring each to take an oath that he or she owns title to no less than half of the garment, and then we split the garment between them. Note, as before, the difference between my representation of the passage, inclusive of explanatory material, and the stark and, on their own, inaccessible words of which the passage is made up.

Our first question is one of text criticism: analysis of the Mishnah paragraph's word choice. We say that the oath concerns the portion that the claimant alleges he possesses. But the oath really affects the portion that he does not have in hand at all:

> B. *Is it concerning the portion that he claims he possesses that he takes the oath, or concerning the portion that he does not claim to possess?* [Daiches: "The implication is that the terms of the oath are ambiguous. By swearing that his share in it is not "less than half," the claimant might mean that it is not even a third or a fourth (which is 'less than half'), and the negative way of putting it would justify

such an interpretation. He could therefore take this oath even if he knew that he had no share in the garment at all, while he would be swearing falsely if he really had a share in the garment that is less than half, however small that share might be.]

B. *Said R. Huna, "It is that he says, 'By an oath! I pos-sess in it a portion, and I possess in it a portion that is no less than half a share of it.'"* [The claimant swears that his share is at least half (Daiches).]

Having asked and answered the question, we now find ourselves in an extension of the argument; the principal trait of the dialecti-cal argument is now before us: (1) but (2) maybe the contrary is the case, so (3) what about—that is, the setting aside of a proposition in favor of its opposite. These three explosive events—but, to the contrary, and what about—express the essence of dialectics.

For the definitive trait of the dialectic argument emerges in its insistence on challenging every proposal with the claim, "Maybe it's the opposite?" This pestering question expresses an attitude of unremitting contention, a love of argument. That is critical, since contrary argument forces us back upon our sense of self-evidence; it makes us consider the contrary of each position we propose to set forth. It makes thought happen. Dialectics provides the provo-cation, the energy and vigor, the source of rigorous thought, that marks the Talmud as remarkable. In our setting, dialectics invite us to join the conversation with God—as the stories in Chapters 2 and 3 have already shown. God needs Rabbah's reasoning. God responds to Joshua's rebuke. Dialectics form the shield of the questing mind in the encounter with the divine authority. When we meet God, it is to conduct a rigorous argument, respectfully to be sure. But the issue is not Job's: we do not ask God to explain God. The issue is our own: we share with God the curiosity to ask, Why? What if? and Why not?

True, the Talmud's voice's "but"—the whole of the dialectic in one word!—presents a formidable nuisance. But so does all criti-cism, and only the mature mind will welcome criticism. Dialectics is not for the puerile, the politicians, the propagandists. To argue with God, our "I" must stand up to God's "I." We cannot encounter God before we know ourselves. Here we see of what that knowledge consists: applied reason, practical logic.

Genuine curiosity about the truth shown by rigorous logic forms the counterpart to musical virtuosity. So the objection proceeds:

> C. *Then let him say,* "By an oath! The whole of it is mine!"

Why claim half when the alleged finder may as well demand the whole cloak?

> D. *But are we going to give him the whole of it?* [Obviously not, there is another claimant, also taking an oath.]

The question contradicts the facts of the case: two parties claim the cloak, so the outcome can never be, one will get the whole thing.

> E. *Then let him say,* "By an oath! Half of it is mine!"

Then—by the same reasoning—why claim "no less than half," rather than simply half.

> F. *That would damage his own claim* [which was that he owned the whole of the cloak, not only half of it].

The claimant does claim the whole cloak, so the proposed language does not serve to replicate his actual claim. That accounts for the language we specify.

> G. *But here too is it not the fact that, in the oath that he is taking, he impairs his own claim?* [After all, he here makes explicit the fact that he owns at least half of it. What happened to the other half?]

The solution merely compounds the problem.

> H. *[Not at all.]* For he has said, "The whole of it is mine!" [And, he further proceeds,] "And as to your contrary view, By an oath, I do have a share in it, and that share is no less than half!"

We solve the problem by positing a different solution from the one we suggested at the outset. Why not start where we have concluded? Because if we had done so, we should have ignored a variety of intervening considerations and so should have expounded less than the entire range of possibilities. The power of the dialectical argument now is clear: it forces us to address not the problem and the solution alone but the problem and the various ways by which a solution may be reached; then, when we do come to a final solution to the question at hand, we have reviewed all of the possibilities. We have seen how everything flows together, nothing is left unattended.

The dialectical argument in the Talmud, therefore, undertakes a different task from the philosophical counterpart. What we have here is not a set piece of two positions, with an analysis of each, such as the staid philosophical dialogue exposes with such elegance; it is, rather, an analytical argument, explaining why this, not that, then why not that but rather this; and onward. When we speak of a moving argument, this is what we mean: what is not static and merely expository, but what is dynamic and always contentious. It is not an endless argument, an argument for the sake of arguing, or evidence that important to the Talmud is process but not position. To the contrary, the passage is resolved with a decisive conclusion, not permitted to run on.

But the dialectical composition proceeds—continuous and coherent from point to point, even as it zigs and zags. We proceed to the second cogent proposition in the analysis of the cited Mishnah passage, which asks a fresh question: Why an oath at all?

> 2. A. Now, since this one is possessed of the cloak and standing right there, and that one is possessed of the cloak and is standing right there, why in the world do I require this oath?

Until now we have assumed as fact the premise of the Mishnah's rule, which is that an oath is there to be taken. But why assume so? Surely each party now has what he is going to get. So what defines the point and effect of the oath?

B. Said R. Yohanan, "This oath [to which our Mishnah-passage refers] happens to be an ordinance imposed only by rabbis,

C. "so that people should not go around grabbing the cloaks of other people and saying, 'It's mine!'" [But, as a matter of fact, the oath that is imposed in our Mishnah-passage is not legitimate by the law of the Torah. It is an act taken by sages to maintain the social order.]

We do not administer oaths to liars; we do not impose an oath in a case in which we may end up turning an honest man into a liar either. The proposition solves the problem—but it is hardly going to settle the question. On the contrary, Yohanan raises more problems than he solves. So we ask, How we can agree to an oath in this case at all?

D. *But why then not advance the following argument: since such a one is suspect as to fraud in a property claim, he also should be suspect as to fraud in oath-taking?*

Yohanan places himself into the position of believing in respect to the oath what we will not believe in respect to the claim on the cloak, for, after all, one of the parties before us must be lying! Why sustain such a contradiction: gullible and suspicious at one and the same time?

E. *In point of fact, we do not advance the argument: since such a one is suspect as to fraud in a property claim, he also should be suspect as to fraud in oath-taking, for if you do not concede that fact, then how is it possible that the All-Merciful has ruled,* "One who has conceded part of a claim against himself must take an oath as to the remainder of what is subject to claim"?

If someone claims that another party holds property belonging to him or her, and the bailee concedes part of the claim, the bailee must then take an oath in respect to the rest of the claimed property, that is, the part that the bailee maintains does not belong to the claimant at all. So the law itself—the Torah, in fact—has sustained the same contradiction. That fine solution, of course, is going to be challenged:

> F. *Why not simply maintain, since such a one is suspect as to fraud in a property claim, he also should be suspect as to fraud in oath-taking?*
> G. *In that other case, [the reason for the denial of part of the claim and the admission of part is not the intent to commit fraud, but rather,] the defendant is just trying to put off the claim for a spell.*

We could stop at this point without losing a single important point of interest; everything is before us. One of the striking traits of the large-scale dialectical composition is its composite-character. Starting at the beginning, without any loss of meaning or sense, we may well stop at the end of any given paragraph of thought. But the dialectics insist on moving forward, exploring, pursuing, insisting; and were we to remove a paragraph in the middle of a dialectical composite, then all that follows would become incomprehensible. That is a mark of the dialectical argument: sustained, continuous, and coherent—yet perpetually in control and capable of resolving matters at any single point.

Now, having fully exposed the topic, its problem, and its principles, we take a tangent indicated by the character of the principle before us: when a person will or will not lie or take a false oath. We have a theory on the matter; what we now do is expound the theory, with special reference to the formulation of that theory in explicit terms by a named authority:

> H. This concurs with the position of Rabbah. [For Rabbah has said, "On what account has the Torah imposed the requirement of an oath on one who confesses to only part of a claim against him? It is by reason of the presumption that a person will not insolently deny the truth about the whole of a loan in the very presence of the creditor and so entirely deny the debt. He will admit

to part of the debt and deny part of it. Hence we invoke an oath in a case in which one does so, to coax out the truth of the matter."]

I. For you may know, [in support of the foregoing], that R. Idi bar Abin said R. Hisda [said]: "He who [falsely] denies owing money on a loan nonetheless is suitable to give testimony, but he who denies that he holds a bailment for another party cannot give testimony."

The proposition is now fully exposed. A named authority is introduced, who will concur in the proposed theoretical distinction. He sets forth an extralogical consideration, which, of course, the law always will welcome: the rational goal of finding the truth overrides the technicalities of the law governing the oath.

Predictably, we cannot allow matters to stand without challenge, and the challenge comes at a fundamental level, with the predictable give-and-take to follow:

J. But what about that which R. Ammi bar Hama repeated on Tannaite authority: "[If they are to be subjected to an oath,] four sorts of bailees have to have denied part of the bailment and conceded part of the bailment, namely, the unpaid bailee, the borrower, the paid bailee, and the one who rents."

K. *Why not simply maintain, since such a one is suspect as to fraud in a property claim, he also should be suspect as to fraud in oath-taking?*

L. *In that case as well, [the reason for the denial of part of the claim and the admission of part is not the intent to commit fraud, but rather,] the defendant is just trying to put off the claim for a spell.*

M. *He reasons as follows: "I'm going to find the thief and arrest him." Or: "I'll find [the beast] in the field and return it to the owner."*

Once more, "if that is the case" provokes yet another analysis; we introduce a different reading of the basic case before us, another reason that we should not impose an oath:

N. *If that is the case, then why should one who denies holding a bailment ever be unsuitable to give testimony? How come we don't just maintain that the defendant is just trying to put off the claim for a spell. He reasons as follows: "I'm going to look for the thing and find it."*

O. *When in point of fact we do rule,* He who denies holding a bailment is unfit to give testimony, *it is in a case in which witnesses come and give testimony against him that at that very moment, the bailment is located in the bailee's domain, and he fully is informed of that fact, or, alternatively, he has the object in his possession at that very moment.*

The solution to the problem at hand also provides the starting point for yet another step in the unfolding exposition. Huna has given us a different resolution of matters. That accounts for no. 3, and no. 4 is also predictable:

3. A. *But as to that which R. Huna has said* [when we have a bailee who offers to pay compensation for a lost bailment rather than swear it has been lost, since he wishes to appropriate the article by paying for it, (Daiches)], "They impose upon him the oath that the bailment is not in his possession at all,"

B. *why not in that case invoke the principle, since such a one is suspect as to fraud in a property claim, he also should be suspect as to fraud in oath-taking?*

C. *In that case also, he may rule in his own behalf, I'll give him the money."*

4. A. *Said R. Aha of Difti to Rabina, "But then the man clearly transgresses the negative commandment: 'You shall not covet.'"*

B. *"You shall not covet" is generally understood by people to pertain to something for which one is not ready to pay.*

Yet another authority's position now is invoked, and it draws us back to our starting point: the issue of why we think an oath is suitable in a case in which we ought to assume lying is going on; so we are returned to our starting point, but via a circuitous route:

5. A. **[6A]** *But as to that which R. Nahman said, "They* impose upon him [who denies the whole of a claim] an oath of inducement," *why not in that case invoke the principle, since such a one is suspect as to fraud in a property claim, he also should be suspect as to fraud in oath-taking?*

B. *And furthermore, there is that which R. Hiyya taught on Tannaite authority:* "Both parties [employee, supposed to have been paid out of an account set up by the employer at a local store, and store-keeper] take an oath and collect what each claims from the employer," *why not in that case invoke the principle, since such a one is suspect as to fraud in a property claim, he also should be suspect as to fraud in oath-taking?*

C. *And furthermore, there is that which R. Sheshet said,* "We impose upon an unpaid bailee [who claims that the animal has been lost] three distinct oaths: first, an oath that I have not deliberately caused the loss, that I did not put a hand on it, and that it is not in my domain at all," *why not in that case invoke the principle, since such a one is suspect as to fraud in a property claim, he also should be suspect as to fraud in oath-taking?*

We now settle the matter:

D. *It must follow that we do not invoke the principle at all, since such a one is suspect as to fraud in a property claim, he also should be suspect as to fraud in oath-taking?*

What is interesting is why walk so far to end up where we started: do we invoke said principle? No, we do not. What we have accomplished on our wanderings is a survey of opinion on a theme, to be sure, but opinion that intersects at our particular problem as well. The moving argument serves to carry us hither and yon; its power is to demonstrate that all considerations are raised, all challenges met, all possibilities explored. This is not, as I said, merely a set-piece argument, where we have proposition, evidence, analysis, conclusion; it is a different sort of thinking altogether, purposive and coherent, but also comprehensive and compelling for its admission of possibilities and attention to alternatives.

Let me give a single example of the power of the dialectical argument to expose the steps in thinking that lead from one end to another: principle to ruling, or ruling to principle. (One of the glories of Talmudic dialectics is that we can frequently move in either direction and reach the same result. Climb up or climb down, the ladder is always the same.) In the present instance, the only one we require to see a perfectly routine and obvious procedure, we mean to prove the point that if people are permitted to obstruct the public way, if damage was done by them, they are liable to pay compensation. First, we are going to prove that general point on the basis of a single case. Then we shall proceed to how a variety of authorities, dealing with diverse cases, sustain the same principle. That result is what makes the passage interesting to us in our effort to identify the Talmudic melody.

TALMUD BABA MESIA 10:5/O–X

O. He who brings out his manure to the public domain—

P. while one party pitches it out, the other party must be bringing it in to manure his field.

Q. They do not soak clay in the public domain,

R. and they do not make bricks.

S. And they knead clay in the public way,

T. but not bricks.

U. He who builds in the public way—

V. while one party brings stones, the builder must make use of them in.

W. And if one has inflicted injury, he must pay for the damages he has caused.

X. Rabban Simeon b. Gamaliel says, "Also: He may prepare for doing his work [on site in the public way] for thirty days [before the actual work of building]."

We begin with comparing the rule before us with another Tannaite position on the same issue, asking whether an unattributed, therefore authoritative, rule stands for or opposes the position of a given authority; we should hope to prove that the named authority concurs. So one fundamental initiative in showing how many cases express a single principle—the concrete demonstration of the unity of the law—is to find out whether diverse, important authorities concur on the principle, each ruling in a distinctive case; or whether a single authority is consistent in ruling in accord with the principle at hand, as in what follows:

> I.1 A. *May we say that our Mishnah-paragraph does not accord with the view of R. Judah? For it has been taught on Tannaite authority:*
>
> B. **R. Judah says, "At the time of fertilizing the fields, a man may take out his manure and pile it up at the door of his house in the public way so that it will be pulverized by the feet of man and beast, for a period of thirty days. For it was on that very stipulation that Joshua caused the Israelites to inherit the land" [T. B.M. 11:8E–H].**
>
> C. You may even maintain that he concurs **with the Mishnah's rule [that while one party pitches it out, the other party must be bringing it in to manure his field].** R. Judah concedes that if one has caused damage, he is liable to pay compensation.

If we take the position just now proposed, then Judah will turn out to rule every which way on the same matter. And that is not an acceptable upshot.

> D. *But has it not been taught in the Mishnah:* **If the storekeeper had left his lamp outside the storekeeper is liable [if the flame caused a fire]. R. Judah said, "In the case of a lamp for Hanukkah, he is exempt" [M. B. Q. 6:6E–F],** because he has acted under authority. *Now surely that must mean,* under the authority of the court [and that shows that one is not responsible for damage caused by his property in the public domain if it was there under the authority of the court]!

The dialectic now intervenes. We have made a proposal. Isn't it a good one? Of course not, were we to give up so quickly, we should gain nothing:

E. *No, what it means is, on the authority of carrying out one's religious obligations.*

By now, the reader is able to predict the next step: "But isn't the contrary more reasonable?" Here is how we raise the objection.

F. *But has it not been taught on Tannaite authority:*

G. in the case of all those concerning whom they have said, "They are permitted to obstruct the public way," if there was damage done, one is liable to pay compensation. But R. Judah declares one exempt from having to pay compensation.

H. *So it is better to take the view that our Mishnah-paragraph does not concur with the position of R. Judah.*

The point of interest has been introduced: whether those permitted to obstruct the public way must pay compensation for damages they may cause in so doing. Here is where we find a variety of cases that yield a single principle:

2. A. *Said Abayye, "R. Judah, Rabban Simeon b. Gamaliel, and R. Simeon all take the position that* in the case of all those concerning whom they have said, 'They are permitted to obstruct the public way,' if there was damage done, one is liable to pay compensation.

B. *"As to R. Judah, the matter is just as we have now stated it.* Simeon b. Gamaliel and Simeon now draw us to unrelated cases:

C. *"As to Rabban Simeon b. Gamaliel, we have learned in the Mishnah:* **Rabban Simeon b. Gamaliel says, 'Also: He may prepare for doing his work [on site in the public way] for thirty days [before the actual work of building].'**

D. *"As to R. Simeon, we have learned in the Mishnah:* **A person should not set up an oven in a room unless there is a space of four cubits above it. If he was setting it up in the upper story, there has to be a layer of plaster under it three handbreadths thick, and in the case of a stove, a hand-**

> breadth thick. And if it did damage, the owner of the oven has to pay for the damage. R. Simeon says, 'All of these measures have been stated only so that if the object did damage, the owner is exempt from paying compensation if the stated measures have been observed' [M. B.B. 2:2A–F]."

We see then that the demonstration of the unity of the law and the issue of who stands, or does not stand, behind a given rule, go together. When we ask about who does or does not stand behind a rule, we ask about the principle of a case, which leads us downward to a premise. We forthwith point to how that same premise underlies a different principle yielding a case—and also question how X can hold the view he does, if that is his premise, since at a different case he makes a point with a principle that rests on a contradictory premise. The Mishnah and the Talmud are comparable to the moraine left by the last Ice Age, fields studded with boulders. For the Talmud, these are those many disputes that litter the pages and impede progress. That explains why much of the Talmud is taken up with not only sorting out disputes but also showing their rationality, their meaning. Reasonable people have perfectly valid reasons for disagreeing about a given point, since both parties share the same premises but apply them differently; or they really do not differ at all, since one party deals with one set of circumstances, the other with a different set of circumstances.

To what end? We now know the answer. The dialectical argument proves the ideal medium for the assertion, through sustained demonstration alone, of the union of laws in law. The words to the Talmud's theological melody are always the same and only a few: the integrity of truth. That truth—how all things point to the union of everything—is what is given in the Torah, set forth in God's wording, but, still more, in accord with the principles of reasoned thinking that govern in the intellect of the one God who is truth. When I said that theology utilizes the method of theology to convey the message of religion, that is what I meant. The perfection of the Torah consists in its capacity to allow us to see into the heart of matters, the point of it all.

Specifically, if all we know is laws, then we want to find out what is at stake in them? Accordingly, the true issues of the law emerge from the detailed rulings of the laws when, guided by the correct formulation of the Torah and its issues, we attain discernment. That discernment consists in knowing how to generalize from the specific case, or, more to the point, knowing that we must do so. Generalization takes a variety of forms, some yielding a broader framework into which to locate a case, others a proposition of consequence. Let me give an obvious and familiar instance of what is to be done. Here is an example of a case that yields a principle:

TALMUD BABA MESIA TO 9:11

A. (1) A day worker collects his wage any time of the night.

B. (2) And a night worker collects his wage any time of the day.

C. (3) A worker by the hour collects his wage any time of the night or day.

I.1 A. *Our rabbis have taught on Tannaite authority:*

B. How on the basis of Scripture do we know, **A day worker collects his wage any time of the night?**

C. "[You shall not oppress your neighbor or rob him.] The wages of a hired servant shall not remain with you all night until the morning" [Lev. 19:13].

D. And how on the basis of Scripture do we know, **and a night worker collects his wage any time of the day?**

E. "[You shall not oppress a hired servant who is poor and needy] . . . you shall give him his hire on the day on which he earns it, before the sun goes down" [Deut. 23:14–15].

F. *Might I say that the reverse is the case [the night worker must be paid during the night that he does the work, in line with Lev. 19:13, and the day worker by day, in line with Deut. 23:15]?*

G. Wages are to be paid only at the end of the work [so the fee is not payable until the work has been done].

What do we learn from this passage? Specifically, two points, that Scripture yields the rule at hand; that Scripture also imposes limits on the formation of the law; but one generalization, that the law of the Mishnah derives from the source of Scripture. And, if we take a small step beyond, of course, we learn that the two parts of the Torah are one. The hermeneutics instructs us to ask, How on the basis of Scripture do we know . . . ? Its premise then is that Scripture forms the basis for rules not expressed with verses of the written Torah. The theological principle conveyed in the hermeneutic expressed in the case is that the Torah is one and encompasses both the oral and the written parts; the oral part derives its truths from the written part. A step further would carry us to the consideration of the formula, *Our rabbis have taught on Tannaite authority:* which would lead to the consideration of the place and position of "our rabbis" in the formulation and formation of the Torah. But enough has been said to make the point quite clear.

Now if I had to identify the single most important theological point that the Talmud sets forth, it is that the laws yield law, the truth exhibits integrity, all of the parts—the details, principles, and premises—holding together in a coherent manner. To understand how generalizations are attained, however, we cannot deal only with generalizations. So we turn to a specific problem of category formation, namely, in the transfer of property, whether or not we distinguish between a sale and a gift. That is, in both instances property is transferred. But the conditions of transfer clearly differ; in the one case there is a quid pro quo, in the other there is not. Now does that distinction make a difference? The answer to that question will have implications for a variety of concrete cases, for example, transfers of property in a dowry, divisions inheritances and estates, the required documents and procedures for effecting transfer of title, and the like. If, then, we know the correct category formation—the same or not the same category—we form a generalization that will draw together numerous otherwise unrelated cases and (more to the point) rules.

One way to accomplish the goal is to identify the issue behind a dispute, which leads us from the dispute to the principle that is established and confirmed by a dispute on details, for example, whether or not the principle applies, and, if it does, how it does. In this way we affirm the unity of the law by establishing that all parties to a dispute really agree on the same point; then the dispute itself underlines the law's coherence:

TALMUD BABA BATRA 1:3

A. He whose [land] surrounds that of his fellow on three sides,

B. and who made a fence on the first, second, and third sides—

C. they do not require [the other party to share in the expense of building the walls].

D. R. Yosé says, "If he built a fence on the fourth side, they assign to him [his share in the case of] all [three other fences]."

In the following dispute, we ask what is subject to dispute between the two named authorities, B–C.

2. A. *It has been stated:*

B. R. Huna said, "All is proportion to the actual cost of building the fence [Simon: which will vary according to the materials used by the one who builds the fence]."

C. Hiyya bar Rab said, "All is proportionate to the cost of a cheap fence made of sticks [since that is all that is absolutely necessary]."

To find the issue, we revert to our Mishnah rule. The opinions therein guide the disputing parties. Each then has to account for what is subject to dispute in the Mishnah paragraph. Then the point is: the Mishnah's dispute is not only rational, but it also rests upon a shared premise, affirmed by all parties. That is the power of D.

D. *We have learned in the Mishnah:* **He whose [land] surrounds that of his fellow on three sides, and who made a fence on the first, second, and third sides—they do not require [the other party to share in the expense of building the walls].** Lo, if he fences the fourth side too, he must contribute to the cost of the entire fence. *But then note what follows:* **R. Yosé says, "If he built a fence on the fourth side, they assign to him [his share in the case of] all [three other fences]."** *Now there is no problem from the perspective of R. Huna, who has said,* "All is proportion to the actual cost of building the fence [Simon: which will vary according to the materials used by the one who builds the fence]." *Then we can identify what is at issue between the first authority and R. Yosé. Specifically, the initial authority takes the view that we proportion the costs to what they would be if a cheap fence of sticks was built, but not to what the fence-builder actually spent, and R. Yosé maintains that under all circumstances, the division is proportional to actual costs. But from the perspective of Hiyya bar Rab, who has said,* "All is proportionate to the cost of a cheap fence made of sticks [since that is all that is absolutely necessary]," *what can be the difference between the ruling of the initial Tannaite authority and that of R. Yosé? If, after all, he does not pay him even the cost of building a cheap fence, what in the world is he supposed to pay off as his share?*

We now revert to the dialectics, but a different kind. Here we raise a variety of possibilities, not as challenges and responses in a sequence but as freestanding choices; the same goal is at hand, the opportunity to examine every possibility. But the result is different: not a final solution but four suitable ones, yielding the notion that a single principle governs a variety of cases. That explains why we now have a set of four answers, all of them converging on the same principle:

> E. *If you want, I shall say that what is at issue between them is the fee to be paid for a watchman. The initial authority holds that he pays the cost of a watchman, not the charge of building a cheap fence, and R. Yosé says that he has to pay the cost of building a cheap fence.*
>
> F. *But if you prefer, I may say that at issue between them is the first, second, and third sides, in which instance the ini-*

tial Tannaite authority has the other pay only the cost of fencing the fourth side, not the first three, and R. Yosé maintains he has to pay his share of the cost of fencing the first three sides too.

G. *And if you prefer, I shall maintain that at issue between them is whether the fence has to be built by the owner of the surrounding fields or of the enclosed field if the latter pays the cost of the whole. The initial Tannaite authority says that the consideration that leads the owner of the enclosed field to have to contribute at all is that he went ahead and built the fourth fence, so he has to pay his share of the cost of the whole; but if the owner of the surrounding fields is the one who went ahead and did it, the other has to pay only the share of the fourth fence. For his part, R. Yosé takes the position that there is no distinction between who took the initiative in building the fourth fence, whether the owner of the enclosed field or of the surrounding field. In either case the former has to pay the latter his share of the whole.*

H. *There are those who say, in respect to this last statement, that at issue between them is whether the fourth fence has to be built by the owner of the enclosed field or the surrounding fields so that the former has to contribute his share. The initial Tannaite authority holds that, even if the owner of the surrounding fields makes the fourth fence, the other has to contribute to the cost, and R. Yosé maintains that if the owner of the enclosed field takes it on himself to build the fourth fence, he has to pay his share of the cost of the whole, because through his action he has shown that he wants the fence, but if the owner of the surrounding fields builds the fourth side, the other pays not a penny [since he can say he never wanted a fence to begin with].*

The premise of E is that the owner of the land on the inside has a choice as to the means of guarding his field; but he, of course, bears responsibility for the matter. F agrees that he bears responsibility for his side, but adds that he also is responsible for the sides from which he enjoys benefit. And, of course, G concurs that the

owner of the inner field is responsible to protect his own property.
H takes the same view. What we have accomplished is, first, to lay
a foundation in rationality for the dispute of the Mishnah paragraph and, further, demonstrate that all parties to the dispute affirm the responsibility to pay one's share of that from which one
benefits. Justice means no free lunch.

The Talmudic melody insists on near monotony, a melody
wishing to repeat only a few notes, but in many variations. I suppose an obvious comparison is to Beethoven's Fifth Symphony,
with its tedious use of the C-major scale, up and down, whole or
in part, first movement and last; then the fourth movement's restatement is the same. But the secondary developments and the
variations—ah, the variations! Compare the first movement to
the fourth, and we hear the whole story. The counterpart, the
unity of the law, forms a simple melody. But the authors of the
Talmud's compositions knew how to vary them without limit.

In what follows, the unity of the law extends from agreements
behind disputes to a more fundamental matter: identifying the
single principle behind many, diverse cases. What do diverse cases
have in common? Along these same lines, that same hermeneutics
wants us to show how diverse authorities concur on the same principle, dealing with diverse cases; how where there is a dispute, the
dispute represents schism versus consensus, with the weight of argument and evidence favoring consensus; where we have a choice
between interpreting an opinion as schismatic and as coherent
with established rule, we try to show it is not schismatic; and so
forth. All of these commonplace activities pursue a single goal:
limit the range of schism and expand the range of consensus, both
in political, personal terms of authority and, more to the point, in
the framework of case and principle. If I had to identify a single
hermeneutical principle—that is, defining melody—that governs throughout, it is the quest for harmony, consensus, unity,
and, above all, the rationality of dispute: reasonable disagreement
about the pertinence or relevance of established, universally affirmed principles.

Here is a fine instance of the working of the hermeneutic that
tells us to read the texts as a single coherent statement, episodic

and unrelated cases as statements of a single principle. The principle is: it is forbidden for someone to derive uncompensated benefit from somebody else's property. That self-evidently valid principle of equity—"Thou shalt not steal" writ small—then emerges from a variety of cases; the cases are read as illustrative. The upshot of demonstrating that fact is to prove a much-desired goal. The law of the Torah—here, the written Torah, one of the ten commandments no less!—contains within itself the laws of everyday life. So one thing yields many things; the law is coherent in God's mind and retains that coherence as it expands to encompass the here-and-now of the social order.

The details as always are picayune, the logic practical, the reasoning concrete and applied; but the stakes prove cosmic in a very exact sense of the work. Once more we take up the reasoned resolution of irrational conflict. Like the opening lines of the same tractate, which we examined in Chapters 3 and 4 and earlier in this chapter as well, here we ask applied reason and practical logic to bring about a fair result. I cannot imagine a more suitable example of the excellence of the Torah than what follows:

MISHNAH-TRACTATE BABA MESIA 10:3 AND TALMUD BABA MESIA 117A–B

A. A house and an upper story belonging to two people which fell down—

B. [if] the resident of the upper story told the householder [of the lower story] to rebuild,

C. but he does not want to rebuild,

D. lo, the resident of the upper story rebuilds the lower story and lives there,

E. until the other party compensates him for what he has spent.

F. R. Judah says, "Also: [if so,] this one is [then] living in his fellow's [housing]. [So in the end] he will have to pay him rent.

G. "But the resident of the upper story builds both the house and the upper room,

H. "and he puts a roof on the upper story,

I. "and he lives in the lower story,

J. "until the other party compensates him for what he
has spent."

At issue is a principle, which settles the case at hand. It is whether
or not one may gratuitously derive benefit from someone else's
property. We shall now show that Judah repeatedly takes that position in a variety of diverse cases:

I.1 A. [117B] Said R. Yohanan, "In three passages R. Judah has repeated for us the rule that it is forbidden for
someone to derive benefit from somebody's else's property. *The first is in the Mishnah passage at hand. The next is
in that which we have learned in the Mishnah:* He who gave
wool to a dyer to dye it red, and he dyed it black, or to dye
it black, and he dyed it red—R. Meir says, "The dyer pays
him back the value of his wool." And R. Judah says, "If
the increase in value is greater than the outlay for the process of dyeing, the owner pays him back for the outlay for
the process of dyeing. And if the outlay for the process of
dyeing is greater than the increase in the value of the
wool, the dyer pays him only the increase in the value of
the wool" [M. B.Q. 9:4G–K]. *And what is the third? It is as
we have learned in the Mishnah:* He who paid part of a debt
that he owed and deposited the bond on the remaining
sum with a third party, and said to him, "If I have not
given you what I still owe the lender between now and
such-and-such a date, give the creditor his bond of indebt-
edness," if the time came and he has not paid, R. Yosé
says, "He should hand it over." And R. Judah says, "He
should not hand it over" [M. B.B. 10:5A–E].

B. *Why [does it follow that Judah holds that it is forbidden for someone to derive benefit from somebody else's prop-
erty]? Perhaps when R. Judah takes the position that he does
here, it is only because there is blackening of the walls* [Freed-
man: the new house loses its newness because the tenant is
living there, so the house owner is sustaining a loss, and
that is why the tenant has to pay rent]; as to the case of the
dyer who was supposed to dye the wool red but dyed it

black, *the reason is that he has violated his instructions, and we have learned in the Mishnah:* **Whoever changes [the original terms of the agreement]—his hand is on the bottom [M. B.M. 6:2E–F].** *And as to the third case,* **the one who has paid part of his debt,** here *we deal with a come-on, and we infer from this case that R. Judah takes the position that in the case of a come-on, there is no transfer of title.*

Yohanan's observation serves the purpose of showing how several unrelated cases of the Mishnah really make the same point: you shall not steal. The voice of the Talmud then contributes an objection and its resolution, making Yohanan's statement plausible and compelling, not merely an observation that may or may not be so.

An ideal way of demonstrating the unity of the law is to expose the abstract premise of a concrete rule, that without regard to the number of discrete cases that establish the same rule. Here is a case in which the theological principle—a stipulation may not be made contrary to what is written in the Torah—is shown to form the premise of a concrete case; then the case once more merely illustrates the principle of the Torah, which delivers its messages in just this way, through exemplary cases:

2. A. And said R. Judah said Samuel, "He who says to his fellow, ' . . . on the stipulation that the advent of the Seventh Year will not abrogate the debts'—the Seventh Year nonetheless abrogates those debts."

B. *May one then propose that Samuel takes the view that that stipulation represents an agreement made contrary to what is written in the Torah, and, as we know, any stipulation contrary to what is written in the Torah is a null stipulation? But lo, it has been stated:*

C. He who says to his fellow, "[I make this sale to you] on the stipulation that you may not lay claim of fraud [by reason of variation from true value] against me"—

D. Rab said, "He nonetheless may lay claim of fraud [by reason of variation from true value] against him."

E. Samuel said, "He may not lay claim of fraud [by reason of variation from true value] against him."

F. *Lo, it has been stated in that connection: said R. Anan,*

*"The matter has been explained to me such that Samuel said,
'He who says to his fellow, "[I make this sale to you] on the
stipulation that you may not lay claim of fraud [by reason of
variation* from true value] against me"—he has no claim
of fraud against him. [If he said,] " . . . on the stipulation
that in the transaction itself, there is no aspect of fraud,"
lo, he has a claim of fraud against him.'"

G. Here too, the same distinction pertains. If the stipulation was "on condition that you do not abrogate the
debt to me in the Sabbatical Year," then the Sabbatical
Year does not abrogate the debt. But if the language was
"on condition that the Sabbatical Year itself does not abrogate the debt, the Sabbatical Year does abrogate the
debt."

TALMUD TO MAKKOT 1:1L–N, 1:2, 1:3/I.2

What is at stake in this issue is, of course, not only jurisprudential
principles but theological truth concerning the power of language. In the Torah, language is enchanted; it serves, after all, for
the principal medium of the divine self-manifestation: in words,
sentences, paragraphs, a book: the Torah. So what one says forms
the foundation of affective reality: it makes things happen, not
only records what has happened.

But what happens if one makes a statement that ordinarily
would prove affective, but the contents of the statement contradict
the law of the Torah? Then such a stipulation is null. Why? Because the Torah is what makes language work, and if the Torah is
contradicted, then the language is no more affective—changing
the world to which it refers, the rules or conditions or order of
existence—than it would be if the rules of grammar were violated. Just as, in such a case, the sentence would be gibberish and
not convey meaning, so in the case at hand the sentence is senseless
and null. Now the principle that the power of speech depends
upon the law of the Torah forms a theological conception of profound weight and nearly infinite consequence; and it is expressed
in the concrete case at hand; the hermeneutics' task is to identify
the principle behind the case—a perfectly routine operation—

and then theology takes over, making that abstract principle concrete through the intervention of the Torah.

Thus far our cases have focused upon practical matters. When I called the Talmud excellent, it was because I find in its modes of thought the media for the formation of a just and orderly society. But intellect transcends the here-and-now, though in the end it always ends there. The issues of the law concern not only concrete principles—for example, you shall not steal; as well as specific theological truths, for example, human language works only when it accords with God's usages—but also abstract philosophical generalizations. And these too bear theological weight, but in a different way. Let us take up an example of the Talmud's way of dealing with not the social order nor the theological moment but the perennial philosophy.

A central problem for philosophy is the relationship between the potential and the actual. The issue addresses "the shape of what is to come, all set and ready to go in the constitution of the present. The present is not cut off from ensuing outcomes."[1] There is a contrary position, which is that "a thing has the potentiality of acting only when it is engaging in action, and that potentiality is absent when the actuality is absent." For Aristotle, the principle that potentiality is treated as actualized is a fundamental point of physics, as Edel states:

> . . . Aristotle has built into his conception of motion the very idea of potentiality's being actualized. . . . The character of this process is indicated in Aristotle's formal definition of motion: the fulfillment of what is potential as potential. . . . Change can now be seen as a dynamic, teleological unfolding of the potentialities . . . in a situation. . . . [As to actuality:] primarily it means the acting or being acted on of the subject whose potentiality is being realized; the subject is . . . at work. . . . His concept

1. Abraham Edel, *Aristotle and His Philosophy* (Chapel Hill: University of North Carolina Press, 1982), 83. All further quotations in this setting are from Edel's work. The literature I consulted is somewhat larger, but Edel struck me as reliable and ample for my limited purpose in this chapter.

of actuality thus involves a situational or transactional character as the determinate form of activity; several subjects may participate in that activity and be expressing their potentialities.

Now this issue of metaphysics hardly demands restatement in theological terms—unless one is attempting to demonstrate the character of creation and the mind and intentionality of the Creator. And then, metaphysics in general, and the issue of potentiality and actuality in particular, will gain acute relevance. For what more profound issue in the disposition of materials, transactions, and persons can there be then to know whether what will be is to be treated as what is?

What the Talmud contributes here is to identify the presence of the issue of the potential or the actual in a statement of the Mishnah. To recapitulate: Do we treat the potential as though it were actual because it is surely going to become actual, or do we insist that what is potential is null until it comes into being? That somewhat abstruse question underlies the problem in the following, where we want to know whether or not one may consecrate what is not now in being, as the Talmud will now formulate the issue:

M. NEDARIM 11:4

A. [If she said,] "Qonam if I work for father," or "For your father," or "For your brother," he cannot annul that vow.

B. [If she said,] "Qonam if I work for you," he need not annul [that vow, which is null to begin with].

C. R. Aqiba says, "Let him annul it.

D. "lest she place a burden upon him more than is appropriate for him."

E. R. Yohanan b. Nuri says, "Let him annul it, lest he divorce her, and she be prohibited from returning to him."

I.1 A. Said Samuel, "The decided law is in accord with the position of R. Yohanan b. Nuri."

Now the issue is formulated in so many words: Can one sanctify what does not now exist? If what is potential is treated as part of actuality, then the act of consecration is valid, if not, it is null:

> B. *Is that to imply that Samuel takes the view:* a person may sanctify something that is not yet in existence? *And by way of objection:* **He who sanctifies to the Temple the fruits of his wife's labor [her wages], [85B] lo, this woman [continues to] work and eat [maintain herself]. And as to the excess—R. Meir says, "It is consecrated." R. Yohanan Hassandlar says, "It is unconsecrated"** [M. Ket. 5:4]. And said Samuel, "The decided law accords with the position of R. Yohanan Hassandlar," *which proves that [in his view here,]* a person may not sanctify something that is not yet in existence. *And, moreover, should you say that, when he said,* "The decided law accords with the position of R. Yohanan Hassandlar," *it was only with reference to the excess [but not other wages that she would receive in the future], then he should have said,* "The decided law in respect to the excess accords with the position of R. Yohanan Hassandlar," *or, otherwise,* "The decided law accords with the position of the initial, anonymous authority," *or, otherwise,* "The decided law accords with R. Aqiba."

The issue that interests us enters through a side door, the implication of Samuel's statement being that he takes the position that is specified, even though, in another setting, it is clear that he takes the opposite view. So we harmonize the two positions assigned to Samuel rather than analyze the issue before us. What this tells us about how the Judaic sages thought it important to set forth the great tradition is clear: part of the power of the tradition lies in its formal perfection; not only does the Mishnah not repeat itself or tell us obvious things, but the authorities of the Mishnah and those in charge of its exegesis are perfectly consistent in all their positions.

Does the issue truly inhere? In the world of dialectical argument, no statement can be left unchallenged; the result would be a lifeless, unpersuasive allegation of mere fact. So the issue may not inhere at all; or ours may be a special case. The process of harmonization, however, permits us to state why a vow may indeed affect what has not yet come into existence, even though, in general, we do not treat as substantive what does not yet exist. It is because in general one has the power to affect by a vow a variety of future actions and events. Just as someone can take a vow not to derive benefit from what belongs to his neighbor—which is one of the key points that makes vowing attractive—so one can take a vow concerning other matters that may or may not come about in the future. But that distinction does not help; it depends upon a flawed analogy.

> C. *Rather, said R. Joseph, "The case of Qonam-vows is exceptional,* since someone thereby prohibits himself from enjoying his neighbor's produce, so he can also prohibit himself from deriving benefit from what is not then in existence."
>
> D. *Said to him Abbayye, "Well, there is no problem understanding that* a person may prohibit his own deriving benefit from the produce of another party, for lo, a person may prohibit another party from deriving benefit from his own produce. But can he also forbid another party's deriving benefit from what does not then exist, since in any event he cannot prohibit another party from deriving benefit from that other party's own produce?" [Freedman, *Nedarim.:* the analogy is thus defective, since in both cases cited by Joseph, the one who takes the vow controls one element of the vow, namely, the person himself; but as to a woman who prohibits her earnings to her husband, neither her husband nor her future earnings are subject to her control at the moment at which she takes the vow.]

We have now completed our analysis of the problem that has led to the introduction of the issue of interest to us; we shall now solve the problem of consistency in another way altogether. But the same point recurs: if one retains power over what is to be in the future, his vow is valid; if not, it is invalid. So we sidestep the issue of potentiality and actuality altogether by resolving matters in favor of what is actual. The working out of matters that follows is important, since it shows us how practical reason and applied logic recast abstract metaphysics through concrete cases and rules; in the interplay the Talmud is created; in the energy, the Talmud works; in the outcome, the Talmud persuades. Aristotle's metaphysics demands the attention of a handful of philosophical sages; the Talmud's translation of issues of metaphysics into the everyday world defined as rational and singular the social order of holy Israel. Onward to the details, where God lives, because of peoples' action and intentionality:

> E. Rather, said R. Huna b. R. Joshua, "It is a case in which she says, 'Let the work of my hands be sanctified in respect to what they will produce.' In this case, the vow is valid even after she is divorced, *since her hands are already in being.*"
>
> F. *But if she made such a statement, are the hands consecrated? Surely the hands are subject to the husband's lien!*
>
> G. *It is a case in which she said, "When he divorces me. . . ."*
>
> H. *But now, in any event, she has not been divorced, so how do you know that such a statement, if she made it, would prove effective anyhow?*
>
> I. **[86A]** Said R. Ilaa, "*[So why not?]* If someone said to his fellow, 'Lo, this field that I am selling to you, when I buy it back from you, will be consecrated,' *is it not consecrated [from that later point]?*"

In the foregoing we see yet another modulation of the metaphysics. Now we have once more to try to exclude the principle of the potential as actual:

> J. *Objected R. Jeremiah, "But are the cases really comparable? In that case, the man has the power to consecrate the field, but in this case, the woman has not got the power to secure her own divorce! So the cases are hardly parallel.*

Rather, the point of comparability is to a case in which one says to his fellow, 'This field that I have sold to you, when I shall buy it back from you, will be consecrated,' *in which case the field is certainly not consecrated."*

K. *Objected R. Pappa, "But are the cases comparable? There [in the case of the field that has been sold], both the field and the produce belong to the buyer, but here, the wife's person remains in her own domain. Rather, the point of comparability is to a case in which* one says to his fellow, 'This field that I have mortgaged to you, when I shall redeem it from you, will be sanctified,' *in which case the field is certainly consecrated."*

L. *Objected R. Shisha b. R. Idi, "But are the cases properly compared? In that case, the man has the power to redeem the field, but in this case, does the woman have the power to arrange her own divorce? Rather, the point of comparability is to a case in which* one who says to his fellow, 'This field that I have mortgaged to you for ten years, when I shall redeem it from you, will be consecrated,' *in which case it is consecrated."*

M. *Objected R. Ashi, "But are the cases properly compared? In that case, the man has the power to redeem the field after ten years, but in this case, the woman will never have the power to arrange her own divorce."*

The Talmud—as distinct from the materials its framers assemble—clearly wishes to make one point, which is, we are not going to affirm, here at any rate, that the potential is classified as actual. So the framer of the composite, itself a composition, makes the theological point, never in so many words, but always by clear act: in the match between free will, therefore authentic, consequential change, and the inertia of natural law on the one side, or habit or continuity on the other, free will must win, if only on points:

N. **[86B]** *Rather, said R. Ashi, "Oaths that use the language, qonam are exceptional, for they effect the sanctification of the body itself. And it is in accord with Raba, for* said Raba, 'Sanctification of cattle [mortgaged for a liability] or of leaven and the freeing of a slave remove these things from subjection to the mortgage that may have previously pertained to them.'" [Slotki, Ketubot 59A: similarly here, the consecration cancels the husband's claim on the body or work of his wife; hence the validity of her consecration.]

O. *But then why say,* **lest he divorce her, and she be prohibited from returning to him?**

P. *Repeat the passage as,* moreover, **"lest he divorce her, and she be prohibited from returning to him."**

The problem that interests us remains tangential to the Talmudic analysis. Still, it is clear, both the priest and the sage have introduced the same problem, taking account of roughly parallel considerations in producing the same answer: all depends on the attitude of the one who vows, when that person has power over that concerning which he takes the vow.

We have now ranged far and wide, yet traveled along a single path. I set out to identify the Talmud's melody. We now see in detail how the melody is formed. Notes hold together in the dialectical argument. The melody finds its beginning, middle, and end in the demonstration of cogency: the unity of the law.

Perhaps the power of the Talmud flows from its ideas, not only, or mainly, from its modes of thought, specifically, the dialectical argument. I have argued so one-sidedly that the dialectical argument bears unique intellectual promise that readers must wonder. But can we not find the same power in the factual representation of the same propositions? We have considered a deeply engaging one: the issue of the potential versus the actual. Can we not gain the same intellectual result if we investigate that issue in some form other than the dialectical one? To answer that question, I turn aside briefly to show how a document of the same era, the dusk of late antiquity, deals with the same question. It is *The Pahlavi Rivayat of Aturfarnbag and Farnbag Srosh.*[2] Collecting the Zoroastrian tradition in the aftermath of the rise of Islam,

2. Translated by Behramgore Bahmuras Anklesaria (Bombay: Kaikhusroo M. Jamasp Asa, 1969).

Aturfarnbag answers 147 questions, and his questions and answers were collected in book form; but the unit of thought is the question and the answer. The relevance to our inquiry is simple. Aturfarnbag is asked a question that at the metaphysical level precisely corresponds to the one at hand. The question is, Can one transfer ownership of what has not yet come into existence?

Since both Zoroastrian and Judaic traditions recognize the validity of vows, and accord to believers the power through vows to transform the status of things, both the priests and the sages had to speculate on theoretical questions concerning vows with intensely concrete consequences for those who took them. And here, as a matter of fact, the intersection is nearly verbatim. In the present instance, we deal with two distinct questions that meet in a problem of high abstraction: Can one take a vow (Zoroastrianism) or by a statement transfer title of ownership (Judaism) to something not now in existence? The first question concerns the affect of a vow upon what is intangible at this time but will become tangible, for example, an object one will make, a meal one will cook. The second, a deeper, perennial philosophical issue, concerns the reality of the potential. Framed in neutral terms, Can I dispose of an oak when only the acorn is in hand? Is what is potential classified, because of what will come about inevitably and inexorably, as what is actual? Or do we distinguish the here and the now from what might come about? Left as an abstract question, the issue of the potential and the actual cannot have come up in either the Talmud or the Rivayat, neither of which knows how to frame philosophical questions in a philosophical way. But stated in concrete terms, both writings prove highly qualified to analyze philosophical problems.

The Rivayat states matters in language that with only slight revision can have appeared in the Mishnah. If one takes a vow to dedicate for someone else whatever actions of merit he may carry out in the future, is this a valid act of dedication? Aturfarnbag's answer is virtually identical to language that we can find in the Talmud, translating the question into the status of "property that has not come to his possession," which is difficult to distinguish from "something that has not yet come into the world." Not only so, but the Talmud knows the problem of whether one can transfer title to what does not exist ("something that has yet come into the world," such as an unborn baby), or of something that has not yet come into the world (a crop in the sowing stage).

LXXIV

QUESTION

1. Whoever makes a solemn vow with this sort of colloquy: "I have dedicated to such and such person all acts and good deeds which I may perform from this day onward," what is your opinion of this case: this as to whether they will have been dedicated by him or not?

REPLY

2. If he declares as "dedicated" that property which has not come to his possession, it will not have been dedicated; and if he speaks of that good deed which has not become his, he shall not have dedicated in the same manner; if he speaks of that property which has not come to his possession, or of that good deed and property which have not together come to his possession, if a fear, or a difficulty, or a trouble, or depressing thought, or a defect has not come, such as that which is said in detail in the ordeal section of the Husparam, if he speaks of one who is worthy; then when that property came to his possession, or that good deed came to achievement, then he shall have been dedicated, in the same manner, to him to whom they are dedicated, if even now that worthiness has not elapsed; it can be dedicated for that one fear of fears when one dedicates anything to worthy persons for fear of the wicked existence; if he says, "I will dedicate a good deed, not for any earthly gain, but for the friendship of the soul of a person who is worthy," it will be his to whom he said, "I will dedicate," when he has performed it; and it will not be the less of him who performed it; it will come to him in the same manner as if he had performed it for the sake of his own soul; since he declared that colloquy, "I will dedicate," for the love of righteousness, he ad-

vances this in the path of a soul, even this munificence
which he advances with a good deed will be such as his
who performs a worship, without earthly reward and
gain, for the souls of persons.

Aturfarnbag's answer leaves nothing in ambiguity: one has not
got control of what is not now in the world or subject to one's
possession. When he rapidly qualifies matters, it is to make an obvious point, one that is irrelevant to the question. Once the deed
has been done, it does indeed go to the credit of the person for
whom he has dedicated it. What makes the difference is the mo-
tive. If one does the act for the sake of his own soul, it serves for the
other. The main point throughout is that we take account not only
of the dedication of what does not exist but also the intentionality
of the person who makes that statement. Then, if the intentionality is valid, the statement before the fact takes effect; if the
intentionality is invalid—coercion having led to the pledge, for
instance—then the act later on is not classified by the initial language. To state matters simply, the Zoroastrian priest's statement
takes account of three considerations, not two: (1) the power of a
person to make such an affective statement, (2) the distinction between what is potential and what is actual, (3) the character of the
intentionality that has brought about making the statement. The
person with the right attitude and intention indeed can make
such a statement stick.

The Talmud frames matters in a comparable way: Can a person sanctify something that is not yet in existence? The act of
sanctification is a statement that a person makes concerning an
object that he owns that is donated to the Temple, for example, for
sale with the proceeds to go to the upkeep of the altar and the
building. Can he make such a statement concerning what is not
now in existence? A glance at Mishnah tractate Nedarim 11:4 and
its Talmud shows us that that is an exact parallel, controlling for
the differences in systemic detail, to the problem that interests
Aturfarnbag.

How then does the Talmud differ even when going over the
same concrete episode in the life of home and family? It is at the

dialectical argument, which is to say, through the exposure of a layer of analytical thought, the exegesis of rules, the imposition of a hermeneutical program that reshapes the Mishnah and makes something more dense of it, that differentiates the Talmud from the Rivayat of Aturfarnbag. But, after all, that is the point: the Talmud, not the Mishnah, forms the statement of the great tradition. So at the very point at which the Talmud differs from the Mishnah, it also, as a matter of fact, differs from the Rivayat. Where the rules run parallel, the presentation does not, and the difference in the presentation proves not merely stylistic—stylistic differences have struck me as trivial and readily ironed over—but in the deepest, most penetrating and substantive sense, hermeneutical. Saying the same thing through their dialectics, the Judaic sages set forth a message quite different from that of the Pahlavi tradition. That message bears a sense and a meaning not to be found on the surface of things.

What is at stake in the dialectics of the Talmud? This comparison brings us back to the simple point that the dialectics distinguishes our document from all others, both within the Torah and beyond. If, therefore, I had to choose only one consequence of the formation of the Talmud through dialectical arguments more than through any other mode of thought and writing, it would be the power of that mode of the representation of thought to show us—as no other mode of writing can show us—not only the result but the workings of the logical mind. When we follow a proposal and its refutation, the consequence thereof, and the result of that, we ourselves form partners to the logical tensions and their resolutions; we are given an opening into the discourse that lies before us.

Here we see precisely how and why the Torah is not the repository of tradition, or, in secular language, Judaism is not a traditional religion. The character of thought and expression have shown us why not. Specifically, as soon as matters turn not upon tradition, to which we may or may not have access, but upon reason, specifically challenge and response, proposal and counterproposal, "maybe matters are just the opposite?" we find an open door before us. For these are not matters of fact but of reasoned judgment, and the answer, "Well, that's my opinion," in its "traditional form," namely, that is what Rabbi X has said so that must be so, finds no hearing. Moving from facts to reasoning, propositions to the process of counterargument, the challenge resting on the mind's own movement, its power of manipulating facts one way rather than some other, and of identifying the governing logic of a fact—that process invites the reader's or the listener's participation. In general, the Yerushalmi presents facts and explains them; the Talmud presents a problem with its internal tensions in logic and offers a solution to the problem and a resolution of the logical conflicts.

What is at stake in the Talmud's capacity to move this way and that, always in a continuous path, but often in a crooked one? The dialectical argument opens the possibility of reaching out from one thing to something else, and the path's wandering is part of the reason. It is not because people have lost sight of their starting point or their goal in the end, but because they want to encompass, in the analytical argument as it gets underway, as broad and comprehensive a range of cases and rules as they possibly can. The movement from point to point in reference to a single point that accurately describes the dialectical argument reaches a goal of abstraction, leaving behind the specificities of not only cases but laws, carrying us upward to the law that governs many cases, the premises that undergird many rules, and still higher to the principles that infuse diverse premises; then the principles that generate other, unrelated premises, which, in turn, come to expression in other, still less intersecting cases. The meandering course of argument comes to an end when we have shown how things cohere that we did not even imagine were contiguous at all. If, then, I may identify what I conceive to be the Talmud's melody, it is as simple as a nursery rhyme, because in that melody people can sing of anything they wish; but as complex as a Schönberg quartet, with its seemingly unending and inexhaustible melodic lines, because people can go on singing as long as they wish, the melody never coming to an end.

The dialectical argument forms the means to an end. The distinctive character of the Talmud's particular kind of dialectical argument is dictated by the purpose for which dialectics is invoked. Specifically, the goal of all argument is to show in discrete detail the ultimate unity of the law. The hermeneutics of the Talmud—in terms of our analogy, the Talmud's melody together with the rules for forming variations on the Talmud's melody— aims at making manifest how to read the laws in such a way as to discern that many things really say one thing. The variations on the theme then take the form of detailed expositions of this and that. Then our task is to move backward from result to the reasoning process that has yielded the result: through regression from stage to stage to identify within the case not only the principles of law that produce that result but the processes of reasoning that link the principles to the case at hand. And, when we accomplish our infinite regression, we reach God in heaven, represented, on earth, by the unity of the law, the integrity of the Torah.

Dialectics is music without words, or, with so many words that in the end the words scarcely matter; they are the accidents of the case, not the occasion for the music. Now, if theology conveyed only right feelings, approved attitudes and emotions, for instance, the appropriate feelings for love of God alone ("love the Lord your God with all your heart"), we should conclude our discussion now, music sufficing. For, knowing the modes of thought and media of argument, we should adequately have defined the Talmudic melody conveyed in Judaism's theological voice. But the Talmud sets forth far more than method in thought, a doctrine of right attitude and sentiment that required no propositional formulation of any permanence. The Talmud endows holy Israel with far more substantial music than mere appreciation for sensible sound, in context, for sustained and rigorous argument. The Talmud sets forth a number of specific propositions: music to go with the words. Precisely how the words match the music forms our next, and ultimate, problem.

Six

THE MUSIC MAKES THE WORDS

*I*n the intelligent singing of the Torah, oral and written, we meet God. To say the same thing in other categories: in the rules of singing, we match words to music. That perfect match, that compelling logic—these afford the knowledge that God has manifested in the Torah. And what we learn about God is that what we dispute attests to what is beyond dispute. When we disagree, it is because of a fundamental meeting of minds; disputes are rational and coherent. And that is because the truth possesses integrity: things hold together, a logic of coherence prevails. It is our task to demonstrate the cogency of things and the coherence of logic. That is not a very protracted melodic line, and it yields only a few verses, one song. But in how many different ways, in the Talmud, are we taught to sing it!

The theology of Judaism is made up not only of music but of words sung to the music. When, in Chapter 2, we thought about "thinking music," we reached the conclusion that now defines our task: Exactly how does music define the proper words? The premise of thinking music is that there are words that fit and others that cannot be sung to these sounds at all. Sounds in our minds match, others do not match the sound of music. But then, if there are words that fit the music, it is because the music dictates thought. And that observation carries us to examine the music that provokes thought in the Torah. For the Torah is a choral symphony, music with a fitting libretto, and the sole truly precise analogy is to a cappella singing, the words forming part of the music and essential to the creation of mood and musical context. The match of word to sound is so exact that there is no knowing which came first; they meet simultaneously, at the right place, at the exact moment.

To revert to our initial analysis, when the Torah is proclaimed in the synagogue, the song carries with it specific words, imparting profound sense to those words. When the Torah is studied in the academy, all the more so do the contrapuntal melodies sung back and forth convey sense and set forth proposition. Music without words would yield, in the Torah, method without message. But that is not how things are. For method without message, like style without substance, celebrates in intellectual form nothing other than pure nihilism. To the contrary, the theology of Judaism is rich in normative statements, yielded by sound intellectual discipline. And that specific, propositional character of the theology of Judaism requires us to ask about the words that the theological voice sings and that the Talmudic melody carries.

Then how are we going to identify the words that go with the melody? It is by the admittedly subjective method of distinguishing the perfect match of words to music from the awkward fit of sound to sentiment. We have already noticed how improbable is a 4/4 march rhythm for a love song, or 3/4 time for a march. Rarely are funeral dirges played in hippity-hop jive, though it is true that it is with blaring trumpets that the *Saints Go Marching In*. In fact, there are words that go with the music in a manner we imagine to be "natural," that is, a just and exact fit between words and music. That fit comes about through repetition and attains plausibility through mere familiarity; but it then is natural, these sounds yielding these words, and no other words.

Innumerable exact "fits" between word and music illustrate that match to which I refer, cases in which, if we hear the music, we know the words that belong. Obviously, that knowledge comes by reason of repetition, the words being sung to that melody so often that we cannot imagine any other words with that music. Think of the simple phrase in the C-major key, G, E, C, E, G, high C, and try to sing any other words but "Oh say can you see." (True, the words that fit the next clause may vary, shading over into, "any bed bugs on me," but the point is clear.) Or the minor melody, A, B, C, D, E, E, F, E, A, E, and (if you are Jewish) try to think words other than "kol od balevav pe-ni-mah." Or E, E, E, G, F, D, and think other than "la donn(a) è mobile." And, to complete the ethnic key, E, D#, E, F, F, E, F, and imagine anything but "Cheer, cheer for old Notre Dame."

Now no one can possibly argue that, objectively and universally, sound matches sentiment; the fit is natural and required: these sounds must be joined to these syllables. That is self-evident nonsense. If the music dictates the words, it is because we have matured in the music that matches that particular melody with those particular sounds. It is a mark of the presence of self-evidence. Outside of our own country and its common culture, in which the *Star Spangled Banner* forms a principal part, who can insist these sounds match only these words? And, to extend our vision northward along with our hockey competition, who hears "Oh Canada" and thinks other than with reverence for the monarchs of the ice to the north.

And outside the world of Jewish sentiment (let alone the State of Israel), or outside of the universal knowledge of opera, or Midwestern college football, no one can propose that these melodic lines demand, and can sustain, only the specified words. After all, when Smetana wrote the "*Moldau,*" from which the melody for "kol od . . ." is drawn, he did not have in mind the Zionist hymn and Israeli national anthem that borrowed his tune. But to those who know the tune in the context of the Jewish polity, there are no other words that can be sung to those notes. And the same is so for the *Star Spangled Banner* and Verdi's immortal words and tune, not to mention, for high C, C, C, G, F, E, D, C, D, G, G, F#, G, A, G—try anything but "Oh-oh-Oklahoma"; for C, C, D, B, C, D— "My country tis of thee" (or, for the other world of our language and culture, "God save our gracious queen"), and so on. The point is obvious.

Now seeing how words and music in context match, we realize

that it is through the familiarity imparted by repetition that that ineluctable, that perfect match is formed in our minds. The objective facts of pure music, of course, bear no words, and that is by definition. But joining words to the music is made natural by the setting in which words and music come together. If I had to point to a single source for the recognition of the natural sound of music and the syllable of a word, it is, of course, repetition: familiarity breeds affective recognition.

And that brings us square into the middle of the Talmud, where in countless ways a few propositions are repeated. The Talmud says one thing about many things, and in that way imposes on diversity the traits of cogency. That one thing—these propositions —then defines the perfect match of words to music. The sung theology of the oral part of the Torah emerges when we say one thing about many things; then, as it happens, we scarcely have to specify what that one thing is, self-evidence forming the counterpart in the Talmud to the match of sound and syllable in music. In this sense, the method bears a message, and it is the task of the theologian of Judaism (in academic language) or the master and disciple, that is, the *talmid hakham,* disciple of a sage, in the language of the Torah, to state for the here-and-now what that message is. The Talmud leaves no doubt on that score, since its melody serves for only a few verses of a single song. All then depends on our capacity of discernment.

Stated in a phrase, the oral part of the Torah matches to its music a single abstract proposition: truth is one and coherent. The integrity of truth above all is repeatedly shown in the harmony of what is subject to dispute. How is this demonstrated? It is by finding what is rational and coherent in disagreement. Throughout the Talmud, in identifying and solving every problem of disharmony and incoherence, our goal can only be the demonstration of three propositions, everywhere meant to govern—the one thing the Talmud will say about many things:

> (1) Disputes give evidence of rationality, meaning, each party has a valid, established principle in mind; without articulated rationality no one just stands by an unexplained opinion.

(2) Disputes are subject to resolution, showing either that each party invokes a valid principle or that to begin with there is no dispute at all, each talking about a different thing.

(3) Truth wins out, every time we show not the resolution of dispute but the rationality of the law.

The first proposition, therefore, proves most important. If we can demonstrate that reasonable sages can differ about equally valid propositions, for instance, which principle governs in a particular case to which two distinct and otherwise harmonious principles pertain, then schism affords evidence of not imperfection but profound coherence. The principles are affirmed, their application subjected to conflict. So too, if disputes worked out in extended, moving arguments, covering much ground, they can be brought to resolution, as is frequently the case in either a declared decision or an agreement to disagree. Then the perfection of the Torah once more comes to detailed articulation in the wonder of dialectics.

If, therefore, I had to choose the single prevalent means for demonstrating the integrity of the truth, it would be the ubiquitous effort to show the rationality of disputes. For the Mishnah, therefore, also the Tosefta, the corpus of Tannaite statements, the very conduct and character of "our sages of blessed memory" in conveying their component of the Torah, put forth not so much rules as conflicting opinions on rules, a vast array of disputes. How do we gain by establishing that disputes are rational? When, first of all, we can show that disputes concern the application of principles, or which of two or more principles govern in a particular case, we show that, while details are subject to dispute, principles are affirmed and prevail. So the unity of truth is underscored. Second, if we find two or more sages in dispute about a given principle, one party affirming, the other party denying the same, then our task is to show that each side has a valid reason in mind. Then the principle may be subject to dispute, but for solid reason; then the law is reasonable, but the upshot is conflicted. That too yields the consequence that the law is orderly and never capricious.

The theology that comes to expression maintains the proposition of the integrity of the Torah's laws. Disputes, ubiquitous in the Mishnah and the Talmud, forming the raw materials of the writers of compositions and framers of composites, underscore the law's rationality—and, therefore, in the nature of intellect, its unity. One way or the other, therefore, the stakes for the analysis of the reasoned basis for disagreement prove high. The laws yield a law, governing principles for the social order are few and coherent, and, in the here-and-now of Israel's life, God's rule prevails—because it should, because God has revealed in the Torah the rules of life, and those rules yield a society we can understand and trust. All of this is expressed, as usual for the Judaism of the dual Torah, whether in its scriptural or oral formulations, in concrete cases. We shall now focus on examples of the several ways in which the reasonable character of disputes is systematically demonstrated, yielding the proposition that the law is possessed of order and integrity.

The first is the simplest, and my favorite, because of the clarity of the issue. We show that the range of difference is limited:

TALMUD BABA MESIA 10:6

A. Two [terraced] gardens, one above the other—

B. and vegetables between them—

C. R. Meir says, "[They belong to the garden] on top."

D. R. Judah says, "[They belong to the garden] below."

E. Said R. Meir, "If the one on top wants to take away his dirt, there will not be any vegetables there."

F. Said R. Judah, "If the one on the bottom wants to fill up his garden with dirt, there won't be any vegetables there."

G. Said R. Meir, "Since each party can stop the other, they consider from whence the vegetables derive sustenance [which is from the dirt (E)]."

H. Said R. Simeon, "Any [vegetables] which the one on top can reach out and pick—lo, these are his.

I. "And the rest belong to the one down below."

One of the urgent tasks, here scarcely articulated, is to narrow the range of difference among the positions of the Mishnah authorities. For in the end, if we want to demonstrate the unity of the law, we must confront the blatant characteristic of the Mishnah as well as of other Tannaite opinion: perpetual conflict, constant debate. And the obvious flaw is: If the sages really disagree about so many things, then what are we to do and think? And if the Torah does not give us guidance on those questions of thought and action, then of what use is it, and how can it be reliable and perfect? The Mishnah's very characteristics, therefore, precipitated the quest for limiting the range of disagreement, on the one side, and showing agreement beneath disagreement, on the other. Before us is a classic dispute, among three authorities, about a case that scarcely requires exposition. Common sense tells us that we have to elect one or the other position or the compromise. But then how much guidance can we expect in this part of the Torah, which tells us opinions but no decisions? For such writing claims of perfection are not plausibly to be made. Here we turn to the Talmud's reading of the Mishnah's dispute, which limits the range of dispute and rationalizes the grounds for dispute:

> I.1 A. *Said Raba, "As to the roots, all parties concur that they are assigned to the upper garden's owner. Where there is a dispute, it concerns the leaves. R. Meir takes the view that we assign the leaves to the roots, and R. Judah takes the view that we do not assign the leaves to the roots."*

We accomplish here two things. First, we limit the range of the dispute; second, we demonstrate its rationality by showing the principles in conflict. The dispute concerns what is superficial, not what is at the foundations; and the dispute concerns a perfectly rational matter, that is, to which side we assign the excluded middle. In fact, what is subject to dispute is not law but fact: what nourishes the leaves. A good botanist can then settle the issue. If we cannot resolve the dispute, then, we both limit its range and also establish the rationality of the issue: then reasonable folk can agree to disagree, and the flaw of confusion is removed, leaving only testimony to the Torah's range of rationality: dispute about things that, after all, may reasonably be left moot.

As is ordinarily the case, in the present instance the discussion veers off in a new direction. Our knowledge of the dialectical character of the Talmud's discourse has prepared us for that trait here, as everywhere else. But it is not unexpected for another reason besides the prevailing character of discourse; it is essential if we are to repeat the melody here too: the rationality of dispute, the coherence of truth, the consistency of sages' principles. Once we have analyzed the grounds for a disagreement and identified them as a preoccupation with the excluded middle, therefore, one absolutely required action is to ask whether we have further instances of the same disagreement, and whether the parties are consistent elsewhere with what they say here. At stake in positive answers is the proof that disputes are coherent, affecting a variety of cases— a facile way of showing the law behind the laws; sages are consistent, invoking the same principle in diverse cases—further evidence of the cogency of the law and its authorities and in the power of a few laws to cover most situations.

The somewhat wandering quality of a given Talmudic discussion, therefore, attests not to the incapacity of editors to stick to the point. Rather, it tells us that present beneath the surface are principles of reading the Mishnah and of composing the Talmud that precipitate time and again the same exercise of analysis—that is, a hermeneutics of a determinate and rather uncomplicated order. Here we ask whether the authorities, the point of whose disagreement has been identified, in fact disagree on the same matter elsewhere; if they have, it means our reading of what is at stake gains plausibility. And if they disagree on the same principle with the same results, it means that the Torah for which Meir, Judah, and Simeon stand is coherent at its deepest layers:

B. *The two are consistent with views expressed elsewhere, for it has been taught on Tannaite authority:*

C. "What grows from the trunk and roots is assigned to the land owner," the words of R. Meir.

D. *And R. Judah says, "That which grows out of the*

*trunk belongs to the tree-owner, and what grows out of the
roots belongs to the land owner."*

The upshot is that the issue does occur elsewhere, and, moreover,
the authorities are consistent in saying the same thing about many
things. But what about redundancy?

> E. [119A] *But we have learned on Tannaite authority in
> connection with produce of a tree in the first three years after
> its planting:*
>
> F. **"A tree that grows out of the trunk or the roots of a
> tree that has been chopped down is liable to the laws gov-
> erning the produce of a tree in the first three years after it
> has been planted," the words of R. Meir. R. Judah says,
> "A tree that grows out of the trunk is exempt, but if it
> grows out of the roots, it is liable" [T. Orl. 1:4A–C].**

Why do we have to be told the same thing twice? Redundancy is a
flaw in an intellectually perfect writing. We are not stupid, and the
Torah (here: the Mishnah and Tosefta) is not repetitious:

> G. *Both versions of the opinions of the two authorities are
> necessary, for had we heard only the first version, we might
> have thought that it is in the first version only that R. Judah
> takes the position that he does, because at stake is merely prop-
> erty, but with respect to the status of produce of a tree in the
> first three years after its planting, which represents a prohibi-
> tion [of the Torah], I might have taken the view that he con-
> curs with the ruling of R. Meir. And if I had in hand only the
> ruling of R. Meir, I might have maintained that it is here in
> particular that he takes the position that he does, but in the
> other case he concurs with R. Judah. That is why both ver-
> sions of the opinions of the two authorities are necessary.*

Points of differentiation may argue that in one case the identified
authorities take the position they do for considerations distinctive
to that case. Or, alternatively, we may maintain that, had the authorities not said the same thing two (or more) times, we should
have distinguished the cases and, therefore, come to an inaccurate

view of their true positions: how far each would go in pursuing his point, how each would respond to changes in the circumstance. We have to be told more than a single case, then, so that we have a full view of the range and rationality of disagreement. The Torah, by the way, is perfect, because our sages of blessed memory exhibit the traits of intellectual perfection.

We should err if we supposed that the sustained interest in limiting and ordering the extent of disputes addressed only matters of law. In fact, the Talmud's interest in demonstrating rationality of disputes extends to those about reading of scripture. And this brings us to a more complicated problem, which is that disputes rest on different modes of reading and interpreting Scripture. Scripture then does not exhibit the flaw of imperfection, as it would if it could be read every which way. Quite to the contrary, coherent principles guide the interpretation of Scripture as much as the Mishnah. Then sages may well differ on which of these principles applies to a given case. Therefore, disputes about the interpretation of Scripture also bear witness to the profound integrity of the principles of meaning of Scripture, as much as of the Mishnah and other Tannaite sentences and as much as what sages themselves say:

BABLI BABA QAMMA 10:5G

G. [If] a river swept it away, he may say to him, "Lo, there is yours before you."

I.1 A. *Our rabbis have taught on Tannaite authority:*

B. "He who steals a field from his fellow and the river swept it away is liable to provide him with a field," the words of R. Eliezer.

C. And sages say, "He may say to him, 'Lo, there is yours before you.'"

[Cf. M. B.Q. 10:5A, G: He who stole a field from his fellow, and a river swept it away, may say to him, "Lo, there is yours before you"].

D. *What is at issue between the two opinions? R. Eliezer interprets scriptural evidences of inclusionary and exclusionary usages, and sages expound the law in accord with the principle of an encompassing principle and its associated par-*

ticularization [in which case the encompassing principle is limited by what is covered by the particularization thereof.]

As we see, the difference of opinion is not subjective or capricious but entirely reasonable. Each party reads Scripture in accord with a valid principle of interpretation; at issue is only, which principle pertains to the facts of Scripture, as we are now told:

E. "*R. Eliezer interprets scriptural evidences of inclusionary and exclusionary usages, as follows:* 'and lie to his neighbor' [Lev. 5:21]—this forms an inclusionary clause. 'in a bailment of a loan'—this forms an exclusionary clause. '. . . or any thing about which he has sworn'—this forms another inclusionary clause. Thus we have an inclusionary, exclusionary, and inclusionary clause, in which case the final clause encompasses everything. *What then does it encompass? Everything. So what is excluded? Only bonds.*

F. "*Sages expound the law in accord with the principle of an encompassing principle and its associated particularization [in which case the encompassing principle is limited by what is covered by the particularization thereof]:* 'and lie to his neighbor' (Lev. 5:21)—this forms an encompassing principle. 'in a bailment of a loan'—this forms a limiting particularization. 'or any thing about which he has sworn' —this forms another encompassing principle. Thus we have an encompassing principle, limiting particularization, and an encompassing principle. You may encompass under the rule only what conforms to the traits of the limiting particularization. Just as what is covered by the particularization is certainly movable and intrinsically monetary, so whatever is movable and intrinsically monetary is included, excluding lands, which are immovable, and excluding slaves, which are treated by the law as comparable to real estate, and excluding bonds, which, though movable, are not in themselves monetary.

The dispute in law reaches into a deeper dispute about the principles of right reading of Scripture, and here the differences are reasonable and balanced.

There is a third way of dealing with disputes, and that is to show that each party has a good reason, one that is subject to generalization in many cases or, in contemporary language, "universalizable." The interest in explaining how disputes are rational and attest to the perfection, not the flawed character, of the Talmud forms so important an element in the Talmud's hermeneutics of not the Mishnah but the law that it justifies giving two further examples of how the voice of the Talmud shows the perfect rationality of disputes. What we see in the following is the presentation of a ruling followed by an explanation of the ruling; the explanation then shows us that both parties to the dispute have sound reasons behind the positions that they take.

TALMUD BABA MESIA 2:7A–D

A. [If a claimant] has described what he has lost but not specified its special marks, one should not give it to him.

B. And as to a [known] deceiver, even though he has specified its special marks, one should not give it to him,

C. as it is said, "Until your brother seeks concerning it" (Deut. 22:2)—

D. until you will examine your brother to find out whether or not he is the deceiver.

I.1 A. It has been stated: R. Judah said, "It is the lost article that one proclaims."

B. R. Nahman said, "It is the garment that one proclaims."

C. R. Judah said, "It is the lost article that one proclaims," *for if you take the view that it is the garment that one proclaims, we must take account of the possibility of deceit.*

D. R. Nahman said, "It is the garment that one proclaims," *for we do not take account of the possibility of deceit, for otherwise there is simply no end to the matter.*

It will not suffice simply to lay out the two positions and their reasons. We have invoked considerations of everyday behavior—deceit on the one side, an excess of punctiliousness on the other.

Which applies in general? The test at its foundations is one of "universalizability." Now we have to test each one against established facts, deriving from some other case altogether:

> 2. A. We have learned in the Mishnah: **[If a claimant] has described what he has lost but not specified its special marks, one should not give it to him:**
>
> B. Now if you say that one announces the lost article, *there is no problem, for thus we are taught that, even though he says that it was a garment, since he does not specify its distinguishing characteristics, the garment is not returned to him.*
>
> C. But if you maintain that one proclaims the finding of a garment, *then if the finder says it was a garment and the claimant says, "Yes, it was a garment," is it necessary to make it explicit that the object is not returned unless he specifies the distinctive traits of the garment? [Under these conditions, it is self-evident that* **if a claimant]** has described what he has lost but not specified its special marks, [one should not give it to him.]**
>
> D. *Said R. Safra, "No, what he proclaims is that it is a garment that he has found. The finder says he has found a garment, the claimant submitted information on the distinctive traits of the garment he has lost. [That is precisely the case to which the Mishnah-passage addresses itself.]*
>
> E. *"What is the sense, then, of* **but not specified its special marks?** He did not specify its most distinguished distinctive traits. [What he says are its traits can pertain to any garment.]"

The effect is to show that both sides have sound and sufficient reasons for the positions they take; and each party can furthermore reasonably sort out intersecting cases and precedents.

The imponderables may involve four distinct opinions, a kind of cubic grid of dispute, and showing how four distinct opinions cohere—not that they are the same, but that all are reasonable and each can be squared with the others, as the Talmud explores every conceivable option. Success in the venture that follows vividly underscores the simple melody set forth in so many variations.

Here, what is interesting, is the mix of principle and linguistic analysis; the four authorities explain the language of the Mishnah paragraph in such a way as to yield, as the statement of the Mishnah, the principle they espouse, respectively:

TALMUD BABA QAMMA 10:8

A. He who steals a lamb from a flock and [unbeknownst to the owner] returned it,

B. and it died or was stolen again,

C. is liable to make it up.

D. [If] the owner did not know either that it had been stolen or that it had been returned,

E. and he counted up the flock and it was complete,

F. then [the thief] is exempt.

I.1 A. Said Rab, "[If the householder] knew [that the beast had been stolen,] then [for the thief to be no longer liable] he must also know about the restoration; if he did not know about the theft, then the act of counting the herd [and finding it complete] exempts the thief [from further obligation to restore the stolen animal]. *The language,* **and he counted up the flock and it was complete, then [the thief] is exempt,** *refers only to the concluding clause.*"

B. And Samuel said, "Whether or not the householder knew of the theft, the counting of the herd would exempt the thief, and the language, **and he counted up the flock and it was complete, then [the thief] is exempt,** *refers to the entire set of cases.*"

C. And R. Yohanan said, "If the householder knew about the theft, his act of counting the herd exempts the thief, *but if he had no knowledge of the theft, even counting is not required, and the language,* **and he counted up the flock and it was complete, then [the thief] is exempt,** *refers only to the first clause.*" [Kirzner: the first clauses deals with a case in which the householder probably knew of the theft.]

D. R. Hisda said, "If the householder knew about the

theft, counting exempts the thief, if not, he would have to be informed that the beast was brought back [before the thief would be no longer liable for the fate of the beast], and the language, **and he counted up the flock and it was complete, then [the thief] is exempt,** refers only to the first clause." [Kirzner: the first clauses deals with a case in which the householder probably knew of the theft.]

The dispute is fully exposed: four opinions, showing the four possible positions on the topic at hand. The integrity of truth is revealed by the range of dispute: every conceivable combination is worked out, then shown if not the same as all others, then, at least, coherent with all others in principle. Coherence here would mean a reasonable conclusion to be drawn from a given principle, even though not the same conclusion is everywhere drawn from that same principle. That is the next task.

> 2. A. *Said Raba,* [118B] *What is the operative consideration behind the position of R. Hisda? It is because animals run out into the fields"* [Kirzner: so where the householder did not know of the theft, he should be notified about the restoration, so as to take better care of his sheep].

The dialectical argument now takes over: we challenge the assignment to Raba of the statement that he has just made, on the basis of a ruling that he made in a theoretical problem of an intersecting character.

> B. *But did Raba make such a statement? Did Raba not say, "Someone who saw another picking up a lamb in his herd and who picked up a clod to throw at him and did not see whether he put the lamb back or not, and the lamb died or was stolen by someone else—the thief nonetheless is responsible"? Does this not pertain also to a case in which the herd later on was counting* [Kirzner: thus proving that counting is not sufficient to exempt the thief where the owner knew about the theft]?
>
> C. *Not at all. It refers to a case where the householder had not yet counted the flock.*

Dialectical argument continues its challenge of what we have taken to be fact:

> **3.** A. *And did Rab really make such a statement* [that where the householder knew of the theft, he also has to know of the restoration, and where he did not, then at least counting would be required to exempt the thief from further liability (Kirzner)]? And did not Rab say, "If the thief returned the stolen sheep to a herd out in the wilderness, he thereby has carried out his duty to bring the lamb back"?
>
> B. *Said R. Hanan bar Abba, "Rab concedes in a case in which the lamb was readily recognized"* [Kirzner: that the shepherd looking after the flock in the wilderness would notice its restoration].

Now we ask whether we can demonstrate a parallel dispute on a different case; at stake then is the unity of a few principles that stand behind many cases and the disputes that concern those cases. This is an ideal way of demonstrating the integrity of truth: showing how many disputes about many cases turn out to come down to a single dispute about a single principle: a reasonable disagreement about some one thing, with two perfectly sensible positions taken in respect to that one thing:

> **4.** A. *May we say that Rab and Samuel differ along the lines of the following Tannaite statement:*
>
> B. He who steals a lamb from the fold or a *sela* from a purse must return what he has stolen to the place from which he stole it [and then is no longer responsible for what happens to the lamb or the coin]," the words of R. Ishmael.
>
> C. R. Aqiba says, "The knowledge of the owner is required [for the transaction to be complete]."
>
> D. *In the assumption that all parties concur in the position of* R. Isaac, who has said, "People keep fingering their change" [so they always know whether or not something is missed], *would the issue not be a case in which the householder knows about the loss of the coin, so both authorities*

differ as do Rab and Samuel [the householder then knows the coin is missing, the householder knows the lamb is missing; Rab stands with Aqiba, Samuel with Ishmael]?

E. *No, they refer to a case in which a lamb has been stolen and the owner does not know about it, and [Ishmael and Aqiba] differ along the lines of R. Hisda and R. Yohanan.*

Can we now reduce the range of dispute set forth at the outset? Of course, we can try:

5. A. *Said R. Zebid said Raba, "In a case in which a bailee has stolen a beast from the domain of the owner, all parties concur in the position of R. Hisda* [Kirzner: that he must invariably notify the householder, since animals wander].

Here [Ishmael and Aqiba] differ on a case in which a bailee has stolen a bailment in his own domain and then put it back there. *R. Aqiba holds that, at the moment he stole the bailment, his agency as bailee has come to an end [and the bailment must be given back to the owner], and R. Ishmael maintains that the bailment did not come to an end* [and the unannounced restoration is valid (Kirzner)]."

6. A. *May we say that at issue between the following Tannaite authorities is whether or not the householder's act of counting the herd exempts the thief from further liability?*

B. He who steals from his fellow and thereafter conceals the stolen money within the sum of money he pays over to him.

C. *One Tannaite formulation states,* "He has carried out his obligation to return the funds."

D. *And another Tannaite formulation states,* "He has not carried out his obligation to return the funds."

E. *In the assumption that all parties concur in the position of* R. Isaac, who has said, "People keep fingering their change" [so they always know whether or not something is missed], *would the issue not be that the one who maintains he has carried out his obligation holds that the act of counting exempts the thief from further responsibility, once*

the owner knows there is nothing missing, and the other party
takes the view that he has not carried out his obligation be-
cause the act of counting does not exempt the thief from fur-
ther obligation?

To underline the integrity of truth, the Talmud will frequently
give three perfectly fine replies to the same question. The massive
marshaling of answers to a single question allows us to conclude
with a systematic harmonization: we touch all bases.

> F. *Say: if both versions rest on the position of R. Isaac,*
> *then there would be no doubt at all that the act of counting*
> *exempts the thief from further responsibility. But what is at*
> *issue is the position of R. Isaac itself. One party takes the view*
> *of R. Isaac and the other party does not take the view of*
> *R. Isaac.*
>
> G. *And if you prefer, I shall say, all parties concur in the*
> *position of R. Isaac, and still there is no inexplicable contra-*
> *diction here, for one party, who holds the return is valid, as-*
> *sumes the thief has counted the money and tossed it back into*
> *the purse of the victim [who then will count it soon enough],*
> *and the other party holds that he tossed it into the hand [not*
> *the purse] of the other party* [and there may not have been
> an act of counting (Kirzner)].
>
> H. *And if you wish, I shall say that in both cases the rob-*
> *ber counted the money and tossed it into the purse of the other,*
> *but in the latter case, we suppose some money was in the*
> *purse, in the former, we imagine there was no other money in*
> *the purse.*

The upshot of these several cases may be stated in just a few words.
The perfect symmetry of reason shown here forms the counterpart to that perfect, natural union of sound and syllable that I offered as an analogy. The Talmud's conception of what we wish to
know about the Mishnah or about received statements set forth in
clarification of the rules of the Mishnah directs our attention to the
issue of what is at issue in a dispute; and that is never restricted to
the facts of the case—by definition. As soon as we ask, "What is at

issue?" in the language, "Where do they differ?" "With what principle do we deal?" and similar rhetorical formulations, we impose upon the received text—which, after all, records only the disputers—the insistence that disputes conceal agreement, on the one side, or reasonable disagreement about matters about which there can be reasonable difference on the other. So disputes underscore the rationality, that is to say, the unity, harmony, and coherence of the Torah.

The goal of all argument, therefore, remains one and the same: to show the unity of the law. But this is never shown in abstract terms; indeed, it is scarcely alleged in so many words. It is for us to identify the words through the repetition of the unstated point. The following abstract shows what it means, in concrete terms, to demonstrate the abstract conception of the unity of the law. First, we are going to prove that general point on the basis of a single case. Then we shall proceed to show how a variety of authorities, dealing with diverse cases, sustain the same principle. If we can show that many cases point to the same, single principle, we are able to make considerable progress in reaching that goal of repeating the simple phrase: the law is one, so is the Torah, and so, in hierarchical succession, is the creation formed by the Mind of the Creator. In the present instance, we mean to prove the point that if people are permitted to obstruct the public way, if damage was done by them, they are liable to pay compensation:

TALMUD BABA MESIA 10:5/O–X

O. He who brings out his manure to the public domain—

P. while one party pitches it out, the other party must be bringing it in to manure his field.

Q. They do not soak clay in the public domain,

R. and they do not make bricks.

S. And they knead clay in the public way,

T. but not bricks.

U. He who builds in the public way—

V. while one party brings stones, the builder must make use of them in

W. And if one has inflicted injury, he must pay for the
damages he has caused.

X. Rabban Simeon b. Gamaliel says, "Also: He may
prepare for doing his work [on site in the public way] for
thirty days [before the actual work of building]."

We begin with the comparison of the rule before us with another
Tannaite position on the same issue, asking whether an unattributed, therefore authoritative, rule stands for or opposes the position of a given authority; we should hope to prove that the named
authority concurs:

I.1 A. *May we say that our Mishnah-paragraph does not accord with the view of R. Judah? For it has been taught on
Tannaite authority:*

B. **R. Judah says, "At the time of fertilizing the fields,
a man may take out his manure and pile it up at the door
of his house in the public way so that it will be pulverized
by the feet of man and beast, for a period of thirty days.
For it was on that very stipulation that Joshua caused the
Israelites to inherit the land"** [T. B.M. 11:8E–H].

C. You may even maintain that he concurs with the
Mishnah's rule [that **while one party pitches it out, the
other party must be bringing it in to manure his field**].
R. Judah concedes that if one has caused damage, he is
liable to pay compensation.

If we take the position just now proposed, then Judah will turn
out to rule every which way on the same matter:

D. *But has it not been taught in the Mishnah:* **If the storekeeper had left his lamp outside the storekeeper is liable
[if the flame caused a fire]. R. Judah said, "In the case of a
lamp for Hanukkah, he is exempt"** [M. B. Q. 6:6E–F],
because he has acted under authority. *Now surely that must
mean,* under the authority of the court [and that shows
that one is not responsible for damage caused by his prop-

erty in the public domain if it was there under the authority of the court]!

E. *No, what it means is, on the authority of carrying out
one's religious obligations.*

F. *But has it not been taught on Tannaite authority:*

G. in the case of all those concerning whom they have
said, "They are permitted to obstruct the public way," if
there was damage done, one is liable to pay compensation. But R. Judah declares one exempt from having to
pay compensation.

H. *So it is better to take the view that our Mishnah-
paragraph does not concur with the position of R. Judah.*

The point of interest has been introduced: whether those permitted to obstruct the public way must pay compensation for damages
they may cause in so doing. Here is where we find a variety of cases
that yield a single principle:

2. A. *Said Abayye, "R. Judah, Rabban Simeon b. Gamaliel,
and R. Simeon all take the position that* in the case of all
those concerning whom they have said, 'They are permitted to obstruct the public way,' if there was damage done,
one is liable to pay compensation.

B. *"As to R. Judah, the matter is just as we have now
stated it.* Simeon b. Gamaliel and Simeon now draws us to
unrelated cases:

C. *"As to Rabban Simeon b. Gamaliel, we have learned
in the Mishnah:* Rabban Simeon b. Gamaliel says, 'Also:
He may prepare for doing his work [on site in the public
way] for thirty days [before the actual work of building].'

D. *"As to R. Simeon, we have learned in the Mishnah:* A
person should not set up an oven in a room unless there is
a space of four cubits above it. If he was setting it up in the
upper story, there has to be a layer of plaster under it three
handbreadths thick, and in the case of a stove, a hand-
breadth thick. And if it did damage, the owner of the
oven has to pay for the damage. R. Simeon says, 'All of

these measures have been stated only so that if the object
did damage, the owner is exempt from paying compensation if the stated measures have been observed' [M. B.B.
2:2A–F]."

We see then that the demonstration of the unity of the law and the
issue of who stands, or does not stand, behind a given rule go together. When we ask about who does or does not stand behind a
rule, we ask about the principle of a case, which leads us downward to a premise, and we forthwith point to how that same
premise underlies a different principle yielding a case—so how
can X hold the view he does, if that is his premise, since at a different case he makes a point with a principle that rests on a
contradictory premise. This brings us to our final problem of the
Talmud's hermeneutical difference: its interest in demonstrating
that reasonable people can disagree with sound reason, demonstrating the rationality that the law exposes even through disputes.

To generalize on what we have seen in these several cases: discernment consists in knowing how to generalize from the specific
case, or, more to the point, knowing *that* we must do so. Generalization takes a variety of forms, some yielding a broader framework into which to locate a case, others a proposition of
consequence. Accordingly, if I had to identify the single most important theological point that the Talmud sets forth, it is that the
laws yield law, the truth exhibits integrity, all of the parts—the
details, principles, and premises—holding together in a coherent
manner. To understand how generalizations are attained, however, we cannot deal only with generalizations. How do we investigate governing categories in the context of dealing with specific
cases? It is by identifying the single principle behind many, diverse cases.

The hermeneutics of the Talmud guides explication toward the
question, What do diverse cases have in common? Along these
same lines, that same hermeneutics wants us to show how diverse
authorities concur on the same principle, dealing with diverse
cases; how where there is a dispute, the dispute represents schism
versus consensus, with the weight of argument and evidence fa-

voring consensus; where we have a choice between interpreting an opinion as schismatic and as coherent with established rule, we try to show it is not schismatic; and so on. All of these commonplace activities pursue a single goal, which is to limit the range of schism and expand the range of consensus, both in political, personal terms of authority and, more to the point, in the framework of case and principle.

So much for the details. I claim that the music makes the words: What words? Let me state in abstract terms the specific theological consequences of these many, repetitious, often tedious, very concrete demonstrations of the rationality of disputes and the coherence of the law. The perfection of the Torah consists in its capacity to allow us to see into the heart of matters, where truth is one. The written and the oral parts of the Torah work together to encompass the entirety of created reality: nature, history, the everyday life of eternal Israel. The goal of grasping all is not otherwise accessible, except through the entire Torah, oral and written. The natural world read in its own terms cannot carry us there, and events of history interpreted in this-worldly terms of power and politics do not cohere.

The Torah is our sole guide to the plan that governs and also explains the world, natural and social alike. Without the Torah we do not know the message of nature or the meaning of history; it is the Torah that tells us that nature carries out the purpose of God ("The heavens tell the glory of God"), and that history embodies the will of God ("only you have I known . . . therefore I will visit upon you all your iniquities"). Without the Torah, all we know are facts of the world of mathematics, physics and botany, the historical events of the here and the now. It is the Torah that instructs us about the purposive character of both, the teleology of nature, the meaning of history, the consequence of the trivialities of the here and the now. All form the willful creation of one God, each testifies to the expressive action, through nature, history, or workaday reality, by that same unique God. Inert and silent facts, nature and history and the everyday world of home and village, all take on meaning and express intentionality when understood as the Torah portrays them. That is what is at stake in the theology of Judaism, identifying the single-minded purpose that all things serve.

Then the centerpiece is the unity of the components of the Torah, the rational union of its parts in all details. And that observation carries us to the penultimate step in our inquiry into the theology set forth by the oral part of the Torah: how the two Torahs work together to make one statement? In the end, if we cannot explain how the two parts of the Torah form a single, cogent Torah, we have left unanswered the central question of God's self-manifestation: why two media if it is one message? I claim Judaism speaks through a single theological voice, not two, and in that simple allegation it defines the fundamental issue at hand.

The Torah is whole and is one, and each part is required to complete the work of God's self-manifestation. Without the written part of the Torah, we do not know the origin of things: the rules of the social order; the purpose of Israel, or [therefore] the meaning of events. Without the oral part of the Torah, the written part of the Torah is incomplete and unclear. For in the Mishnah the oral part of the Torah is characterized by a consistent effort to amplify the law and make it more precise. In the Talmud it is marked by the sustained demonstration of the unity of the Mishnah and Scripture, on the one side, and the rationality of the law, on the other. Scripture, by contrast, is often too specific to its case to help us or too general to inform us.

But then why introduce singing, and why insist, as the Torah does, upon orality? Without the human component of the Torah, the person that can sing both Torahs, that is, Israel in general in the synagogue, the academy's disciples of the sage backward to Sinai, forward to the end of time, the Torah is unrealized. Without Israel, without disciples of sages, the Torah is left without incarnation. But God's self-manifestation is fully incarnate in the Torah when Israel embodies the Torah. God, Torah, and Israel are one: the harmony of well-sung notes and matching words compels the assent of the heart.

Once we have accounted for how music makes the words, we have explained the sound. What about the silence that leaves space for our voice too? Let me explain the question.

If the entire Torah, oral and written, has completed the statement of God's self-manifestation as God wishes to be known, if all we need to know about God we find in the Torah, then what place is left for us, the living, last and latest in the line of those who come to conceive the Presence that the Torah makes manifest? Why the insistence upon Israel, on the one side, and passion, on the other, in synagogue and academy, respectively? How come the Torah is set forth in the acutely present tense, which can only mean we are essential to God's self-manifestation, so that, without an Israel to whom to give the Torah, there is no giving of the Torah? These questions are validated by the facts of the lived faith of Judaism.

The premise of the re-presentation of the Torah in synagogue and yeshiva insists we are necessary, the Torah is given today, the present moment defines the critical hour. The entire rite of re-presenting the Torah means to accord to the living, in the here-and-now, the crucial place in the great chain of tradition that commences with Sinai. Should a single generation absent itself, the chain is broken. Should one moment lack its sung theology, the song is lost for all time. But to make place for us the living, there has also to be a moment of silence that we may fill with our song: our voices singing the eternal melody.

What have we then to add to the melody in the space of silence left open to us? Our wit, our discernment, our capacity to make connections and draw conclusions, which is to say, the same silences that from those who came before called forth their variations on the theme, their singing of the ancient song, of Sinai. We too possess intellect, attitude and emotion, sense and sensibility: voice for the music. Can we find occasion to take part too, to bear witness in our own behalf to God's self-manifestation in the Torah? Let us now turn from the melody to the pause, for music consists of not only sound but silence, and the power of the music derives from the pathos of silence.

Curiosity points to the silences that leave space for the voices of the living: questions without self-evident answers. There we join in, no longer only to listen to the sense and sound received from distant ages, nor compelled by self-evidence long ago discerned.

Then we ask ourselves, and answer in our own behalf. Both parts
of the Torah by their nature open up space for our mind's entry.
And that must be by definition: since the Torah demands our
engagement, the giving of the Torah morning by morning requiring also holy Israel's receiving of the Torah. But the nature of the
opening is different. So in the encounter with the Torah, ours is
the task of listening so keenly as to discern the silences as well as
the sound, and to fill silence with our sensibility and sense as well.
Then, words no longer evoked by music, ours is the work of making the match or, even, inventing the music.

That, after all, is what Moses found out in the cleft of the rock.
God did the talking. He was the One to say, "The Lord, the Lord,
a God merciful and gracious. . . ." Moses bowed and worshipped.
But then he had his say too: "If I have found favor . . . let the
Lord . . . go in the midst of us, although it is a stiff-necked people;
and pardon our iniquity and our sin, and take us for your inheri-
tance" (Ex. 34:8). Now, in the space between what God had said,
which is, that God is forgiving but also will not clear the guilty,
and what Moses then said, which is, "Go in the midst . . . and
pardon . . . ," there clearly was a question, and it was the question
that Moses asked himself and that God then had to answer. The
silence provoked Moses to participate at the moment of God's self-
manifestation in so many words: Does this mean us? And yes,
God responded, "Behold, I make a covenant. . . . " The sound at
the cleft in the rock was not God's alone. Moses too wrote some of
the notes, asking the obvious next question, that God had left for
him to ask.

Elijah, too, hearing the still small voice, responded, not sitting
still in silence himself: "He wrapped his face in his mantle and
went out and stood at the entrance of the cave" (1 Kings 19:13)—
and engaged in conversation with the Lord. God then asked
God's question, but Elijah gave Elijah's answer, directing matters
where he wished: "What are you doing here, Elijah?" That is not
the question Elijah answered. He answered the question, "So
what's going on, and why are you in trouble?" The answer ignores
the question. Elijah has his own purpose in this encounter. He
starts, "I have been very jealous for the Lord," but that, of course,

is not what God has asked; God only wanted to know, "What are you doing here?" Not, as with Adam, "Where are you?" God knowing full well where Elijah was (or where Adam was, for that matter, only wishing to engage him in conversation). God opened, Elijah entered the opening, saying what he wished to say, not what God's question may have suggested God wanted to know: "I have been very jealous for the Lord, the God of hosts, for the people of Israel have forsaken your covenant . . . and I, even I only, am left, and they seek my life to take it away." True enough, but not quite to the point. And that, of course, is the point: when God is manifest, humanity takes its own course. Nothing coerces Moses or Elijah to talk about what God wants, but both prophets raise their own concerns.

That is the way of prophets in the encounter with God's very presence. For our part, heirs of not only the prophets but also our sages of blessed memory, the Torah conveys that same presence. But conditions then are not the same; Moses and Elijah, and the others whose immediate encounters with God the Torah records for our illumination, met God on different grounds, and ours is the more secure foundation of God's self-manifestation in the Torah itself. That records God's self-disclosure, on the one side, but also sets forth the nature, the rules, and the consequences, according guidance in the conduct of conversation with God that Moses and Elijah did not have. But then, they were prophets and perhaps had no need to be told how things are done. So our meeting is a different one from theirs, and though the Presence is the same, the circumstance is not. But the upshot is the same: there is space, also, for humanity in the meeting with the self-revealing God. The Torah leaves space for our initiative, and its accounts of the rules of immediate self-disclosure leave no doubt that the silence invites our intervention. For Moses, God left off speaking, and Moses took the initiative. For Elijah, there was silence, then a question—to be sidestepped. For us, the Torah intervenes; where music matches words, the Torah makes the match; where not, we are the ones to discern the occasion for ourselves. That makes our receiving the Torah so vivid an occasion, so interesting an action —that there is space for us, if we realize the silence.

We hear the voice fall silent with our inner ear. With our mind following what is said, we perceive the space, curiosity awakened; our heart, moved by what is told, skips a beat. That is when through our own attentiveness we are invited, even we the living, to join in the receiving of the Torah. The task then is one of tense attentiveness, closely hearing the proclamation of the written Torah in the synagogue, thoughtfully following the exposition of the oral Torah in the yeshiva—the exposition of the master, the explanation, even, of the disciple. But the two parts of the Torah lay different demands upon our close attention, yielding different things for us to notice. And that is by reason of the character of each.

The question posed by the written part of the Torah, that is, the Pentateuch, finds definition in the character of that part of the Torah, so too that of the oral part. The written part of the Torah speaks of Abraham and Sarah, Moses, Aaron, and Israel, ancient Israel at one time. Surpassing that one epoch in this-worldly history, the written Torah lays claim on all ages, and to receive that part of the Torah requires the living to identify themselves with the ancient paradigms, and them with us. It is a labor of translation, of finding a voice in contemporary idiom for the words of old, so that they may speak to us in our time and place about these matters of eternity. To state matters not in the language of the Torah but in the idiom of the contemporary world, the task of theology in the encounter with the written Torah is one of translation, not of Hebrew into English but of age into age. That work, of course, is on-going and never ending. The Torah given every morning has to be received every morning: that moment. Israel, in mind, imagination, sentiment, and emotion, then makes itself present to receive the Torah, bringing with it to the synagogue, to the hearing of the Torah, the word that enfolds. The Torah then finds its entry when, in Israel's mind and heart, a space opens between word and world, to be filled by Israel's reflection.

The oral Torah, by its nature, requires no labor of mediation through cultural translation, since to begin with its idiom is one not bound by time or place or circumstance. In the passages of the oral Torah we have already examined, we look in vain for the marks of binding of thought to a particular time or circumstance.

True, the details accord with the conditions of the day, but the cloak of yesteryear hardly differs from the dollar bill or rock-concert ticket of today. More to the point, the principles in play—the giveness of fairness and equity, for instance—endure. Not only so, but the special modes of argument that the Talmud uniquely exposes require no substantial work for us to follow. We can grasp the thrust of argument. We can follow the reasoning. We can understand the issues and the stakes. That is so because the rules of logic that govern in the Talmud rule in our minds, too. Then where are the silences? Where they should be: in the spaces between one allegation and the next, in the unstated premises that impart self-evident validity to an answer, above all, in the giveness of the connections between this and that but not between that and the other thing. We can reconstruct the processes of making connections and drawing conclusions for one, a very simple reason. Our minds and the Talmud's intellects flourish in a single, timeless world of practical logic that is universal—applied reason that is ubiquitous.

The very fact that we can grasp the Talmud with only a minimum of assistance, so that a few lines in square brackets make immediately accessible to us not only the result but even the pattern of thought, settles one question but raises another. It settles the question with which we commenced, Where do we hear the silences that leave space for us? The answer to that question is, in the processes of thought to which we have access, and in the movement from point to point in challenge and response in which we share and participate, we find our place. We are there to hear the silences because our ears are perfectly able to hearing the speech. Then, our curiosity aroused, we identify space for our intervention. It is not one of mediation between age and age, but of direct and immediate participation which surpasses all special circumstance: the processes of pure thought, logic, reason, the self-evidence of one thing rather than something else.

When we consider the self-evidence of the march of sound and syllable, we were quick to concede that the union takes place, always, within a sheltering canopy of culture. We Americans hear the words "Oh say can you see," when we hear the music that goes with those words, but others, for instance, in their day the Germans, for whom those sounds at one time naturally evoked words having to do with drinking beer, for example, match different words to the same sounds. So we cannot for one minute suppose that while the specificities of culture govern the match of music and word, the immediate accessibility of the Talmud, the sense of the document's autonomy of time and circumstance, attests to its independence of a particular and distinctive culture and tradition.

A simple observation shows, to the contrary, that our immediate access in our minds to the intellect of the Talmud tells us something particular about both our minds and the Talmud's modes of thought, namely, that we share the same universe of reason. Take the same document to other worlds of thought, with other logics, other patterns of making connections and rules for drawing conclusion, and try to re-present the document as we can in our language and intellectual framework: with a few additional words to provide facts or guidance on the unfolding of an argument. I state very simply, it cannot be done. In the civilizations that rest on different and distinct intellectual structures, the Talmud requires a much more formidable labor of mediation, if, indeed, its process of thought—not only its conclusions—can be mediated at all. The Mishnah may be translated without difficulty into intelligible Australasian ("Pidgin"), so I am told; but that language (and not that language alone) would have enormous difficulty re-presenting the Talmud.

Logic on its own need not respond to particularities of circumstance. But rationality, a dimension of the social order, always does. Take the case of mathematics, for example. Mathematics forms a system of symbolic expression that rises above the specificities of circumstance because of its power of totally abstract representation; and because, when translated into the here-and-now, mathematics describes nature. But systems of expression that render into abstract language the concrete affairs of humanity— issues of justice and mercy, for example, or responsibility and blame—yield not mathematics everywhere the same and equally germane, but philosophy. And philosophy, aiming at "generalizability," reaching for universal logic, turns out through history to have its own distinctive history, to belong to one world and not to some other. Indian philosophy is not Western philosophy, for one massive example, and the rules of self-evidence that govern in Chinese philosophy mystify us, as much as ours prove curious and alien in the East. As we respond to their music, so we respond to the rationality that for them is self-evident and for us strange. So, at any rate, matters presently seem.

In the oral part of the Torah, we need no help to hear the sounds of silence because our ears are attuned to the Talmud's voice and melody by the whole of our intellectual heritage. So when speech ceases and space opens for us, we know: our curiosity, our capacity for criticism, alerts us. Our intellects naturally conform to the rationality of the Talmud because the sounds we expect everywhere conform to the scale and the harmony that dictate in the Talmud too what will be music, what cacophony, and what silence. That is not so for alien philosophies and the music of other worlds. We listen without hearing, the harmonies being alien; like the spices of India and the subtleties of Chinese cuisine, our tastes may be educated. But to begin with, we have to be taught what, in our own civilization, comes naturally.

Now to conclude: when God sings to Israel, God lives in the connections between note and note, and we sing in the silences. Ours is the song of words that match the music, by which I mean, the sense that a perfect rationality governs all creation and its rules; our minds match God's. Our sense of the right fit, the perfect match, the ineluctable connection, corresponds to how things are. There I hear the melody of the oral part of the Torah, that melodic line within the complex voice of that one whole Torah that (in secular language) constitutes the theological voice of Judaism.

But that, after all, is what God found out on the first Friday of time, when Adam was made. He asked the question and waited for the answer. The silence provoked Adam to enter into dialogue with God. Then Adam knew God would understand, so each party took for granted a shared rationality. Upon that foundation, within that premise, God's theology of humanity, matched by humanity's theology of divinity, was to be built. So in the silence between question and answer lay the future of the dialogue of Heaven and earth, God awaiting humanity's response. True, Adam drew the wrong connection; that is the human condition. But the paradigm was formed. That is, humanity and divinity meet in the silence, the moment before the answers flow when the right question is asked, beginning: "Adam, where are you?"

So let us hear how our sages of blessed memory sing the contrapuntal melody of Eden. "Adam, where are you?"—which is to say, "Where are you going and where will you be, and what road will you take from here to there?" That is a why of asking what this has to do with that, of making connections and drawing conclusions. Here we hear our sages:

> What was the order of the creation of the first Man? In the first hour [of the sixth day, on which Man was made] the dirt for making him was gathered, in the second, his form was shaped, in the third, he was turned into a mass of dough, in the fourth, his limbs were made, in the fifth, his various apertures were opened up, in the sixth, breath was put into him, in the seventh, he stood on his feet, in the eighth, Eve was made as his match, in the ninth, he was put into the Garden of Eden, in the tenth, he was given the commandment, in the eleventh, he [sinned and so] turned rotten, in the twelfth, he was driven out and went his way.
>
> This carries out the verse: *But Man does not lodge overnight in honor* (Ps. 49:13).
>
> THE FATHERS ACCORDING TO RABBI NATHAN I:XII.1.

"Where are you?" really means, "Where will you be?" And how do you get from here to there? The theology of Judaism tells the story of humanity as the whole Torah in both its oral and written parts tells that story that narrates God's changing perspective on us.

But matters do not come to rest at Eden. There is, after all, Sinai, at which Israel and God join voices. This is the story of that song of love, succeeding Eden's lament. What Adam undid, Sinai's contrapuntal song recast:

"O that you would kiss me with the kisses of your mouth"
(*Song of Songs* 1:2):

Said R. Yohanan, "An angel would carry forth the Word [the Ten Commandments] from before the Holy One, blessed be he, word by word, going about to every Israelite and saying to him, 'Do you accept upon yourself the authority of this Word? There are so and so many rules that pertain to it, so and so many penalties that pertain to it, so and so many decrees that pertain to it, and so are the religious duties, the lenient aspects, the stringent aspects, that apply to it. There also is a reward that accrues in connection with it.'

"And the Israelite would say, 'Yes.'

"And the other would go and say to him again, 'Do you accept the divinity of the Holy One, blessed be he.'

"And the Israelite would say, 'Yes, yes.'

"Then he would kiss him on his mouth.

"That is in line with this verse: *'To you it has been shown, that you might know'* (Deut. 4:25)—that is, by an angel."

Rabbis say, "It was the Word itself that made the rounds of the Israelites one by one, saying to each one, 'Do you accept me upon yourself? There are so and so many rules that pertain to me, so and so many penalties that pertain to me, so and so many decrees that pertain to me, and so are the religious duties, the lenient aspects, the stringent aspects, that apply to me. There also is a reward that accrues in connection with me.'

"And the Israelite would say, 'Yes.'

"So he taught him the Torah.

"That is in line with this verse: *'Lest you forget the things your eyes saw'* (Deut. 4:9)—how the Word spoke with you."

SONG OF SONGS RABBAH II.II.1

Yohanan and rabbis sing two variations of a single melody. When we show their harmony, the song becomes ours.

In silence let us complete our work, so shrill in praise of our capacity to think, to speak, to sing. Silence best suits our condition and our calling. For, after all, Sinai did not mark the end of the story, and the holy realm of God's rule entered the domain of history. Creation, Sinai—there is an unwritten chapter.

For we aspire to be like God. But we are not God. The regularities of that reasoned world that God made in consultation with the Torah, the compelling power of fair-minded argument about shared rules—these clash with the disorder of the world that we, humanity, endure by reason of our own responsibility. So ours is not a time for singing but for silence, in fear and awe, before the Creator of the ages; in contemplating what has become of humanity, our power to take up the melody of the Talmud fails. Here is God's judgment upon the greatest of the Torah's voices, Moses and Aqiba:

> A. Said R. Judah said Rab, "When Moses went up to the height, he found the Holy One, blessed be he, sitting and tying crowns to the letters [of the Torah]."
>
> B. "He said to him, 'Lord of the universe, why is this necessary?'
>
> C. "He said to him, 'There is a certain man who is going to come into being at the end of some generations, by the name of Aqiba b. Joseph. He is going to find expositions to attach mounds and mounds of laws to each point [of a crown].'
>
> D. "He said to him, 'Lord of the universe, show him to me.'
>
> E. "He said to him, 'Turn around.'
>
> F. "[Moses] went and took his seat at the end of eight rows, but he could not understand what the people were saying. He felt weak. When discourse came to a certain matter, one of [Aqiba's] disciples said to him, 'My lord, how do you know this?'
>
> G. "He said to him, 'It is a law revealed by God to Moses at Mount Sinai.'
>
> H. "Moses' spirits were restored.

I. "He turned back and returned to the Holy One, blessed be he. He said to him, 'Lord of the universe, now if you have such a man available, how can you give the Torah through me?'

J. "He said to him, 'Be silent. That is how I have decided matters.'

K. "He said to him, 'Lord of the universe, you have now shown me his mastery of the Torah. Now show me his reward.'

L. "He said to him, 'Turn around.'

M. "He turned around and saw people weighing out his flesh in the butcher shop.

N. "He said to him, 'Lord of the universe, such is his mastery of Torah, and such is his reward?'

O. "He said to him, 'Be silent. That is how I have decided matters.'"

BAVLI MENAHOT 29B

That is our fate and destiny, because we do not know all the answers to keep silence until the time for singing comes once more, when God will be lord of the dance. Then will come the day's turn to sing: melody and harmony. At sunrise, at sunset, comes first the silence of the spheres in their courses, then our—Israel's—song to greet the Sabbath of creation, affording a taste of what is to come in the end of days:

Lekhu neranena ladoshem
Come, let us sing to the Lord.

Then the conductor taps with his baton on the podium. Then the rabbi calls: "Colleagues, *gevirtai urabotai,* shall we open our Talmud now—and who will be the first to recite?"

Afterword

$\mathcal{T}$his book is my love letter to the Torah. A lifetime of religious experience in the Torah through encounter and reflection is distilled in its pages. What I have learned about God through the Torah I lay out here in what I offer as a statement of constructive theology. Obviously, like any postulant theologian, I aspire to accomplish not only constructive but systematic theology. But that lies long in the future, if it is possible at all; I have first to outline in my mind the systemic requirements and the criteria for system formation. Still, I have come, at least, this far. This first step of interpretation carries me long past the work of religious description and analysis, tasks that have occupied me for some years now, since the completion of the first stage of my literary-historical studies in 1981.

I owe the idea for this book—that is, for a book of constructive, not merely descriptive and historical, theology—to William Scott Green. As usual, it derived from his close reading of my work in progress. After he read the first draft of *Judaism States Its Theology: The Talmudic Re-presentation,*[1] he identified as simply extrinsic to the argument of the book, which is historical and narrowly

---

1. (Atlanta: Scholars Press for South Florida Studies in the History of Judaism, 1993).

descriptive, the final two chapters of that draft. He maintained that the last chapters took their own path and in no way continued the program of that book. He showed me how that other book described how things are, while the concluding chapters shaded over into a statement of the religious experience made accessible through the Talmud, that is to say, from description and history of theology to the formulation of a theological encounter with God: constructive theology. Indeed, as this book shows, I have moved from description to not only construction but even advocacy of how things should be.

I presently plan no further work in constructive theology, and certainly none in the direction of systematic theology. I do conceive a principal labor to require a descriptive, historical theology, worked out in the way in which the Torah as formulated by our sages of blessed memory set forth their system and structure of knowledge of God. But I cannot imagine how, out of what I take to be the authentic encounter with God afforded by the Torah's provision of the knowledge of God, a theological apologetics is to be formulated. Nor is it clear that the entire intellectual enterprise of theology can make its way, since for the larger part of the Jewish world, "Israel" stands solely for a this-worldly, secular, and political entity, and for the minority of Israel that strives for sanctification through the Torah, whether in synagogues or in yeshivas, intellect takes a very low rung on the ladder to Heaven—if, indeed, there is a step for mind at all.

It is the fact that the larger part of this world's Israel—the Jews in general—finds God, if at all, the way the gentiles do, that is, through religiosity in general, not through the Torah in particular. That religiosity may respond to nature or to Scripture as gentiles read Scripture, but it does not flow out of the Torah as Judaism presents the Torah of Sinai. Only the minority that practices the religion called "Judaism" worships God and studies the Torah, and even here it is with more intensity than reflection. For the faithful, therefore, faith calls to deed, as the authentic teachings say in so many words, but not to deliberation. So, alas, the pious take offense when told, if there is no Torah, there is no fear of Heaven. And they skip sayings in the Mishnah tractate they do study, tractate Abot, that maintains an ignorant person cannot be really pious at all. That forms the foundation of this work: how through Torah learning we discover the disciplines of piety in the encounter with God mediated through the Torah, uniquely there. Yet, it also is the fact that in synagogues and in yeshivas God takes place through encounter with the Torah, and in this world that God created as God wanted, there, and there alone, we hear God's voice. Theology is the aid to discerning the sounds. That is why it is worth the effort to try to help people to identify them; but it is also why I cannot now imagine further work of constructive theology, and also cannot at this time conceive the outer limits or simple requirements of the systematic kind that must follow.

A matter of style borders upon the issues of theology: the careful avoidance here of pronouns when speaking of God. That is for theological reasons: God is male and female, always "you," never "it," "him," or "her," "he," or "she." A lesson of contemporary feminism seems to me well worth transforming into its theological truth. Readers will note that I have avoided designating God as either masculine or feminine as well as employing awkward circumlocutions. That accounts for the occasionally jarring repetition of the word God where otherwise "Him" or "Her" might be expected. But perhaps that special way of saying things responds not only to the correct sensibilities of half the likely readers of this book. Perhaps that also is the contemporary counterpart to saying "the Lord" (adonai) when we see the four letters of God's name in Hebrew, YHWH. It proves appropriate to the task, given the wholly-other character of God—a contemporary counterpart to the use of euphemisms and circumlocutions by the Torah itself: "the All-Merciful," "the Omnipresent," "the Word," "the Presence," and the like. In our Anglo-Saxon quest for the plainest way of speaking, let God be always God, never "Him" or "Her" or "It." I also ignore the Modern Orthodox conceit of pretending that God in English stands for the "Lord" (Adonai) in Hebrew and thus do not use G-d (or D-us, or Ze-s, I suppose) when I mean God in the generic, common sense. Laundering the language can go just so far, and then we have to say what we mean plainly.

As part of the work of *Judaism States Its Theology*, I wrote the penultimate chapters of this book as Visiting Fellow at Clare Hall, Cambridge University, in the summer of 1992. I thank that splendid research center, which accorded warm hospitality to its guest colleagues: a warm shelter in the cold and forbidding world of Cambridge.

I gave a small part of the opening chapter of this book as the Bellarmine Lecture at St. Louis University and the William L. Rossner Visiting Scholar Lecture in Theology at Rockhurst College, Kansas City, and the lecture was published in *Theological Studies*. I express my thanks to both faculties for their cordial hearing of my ideas. It is not at all noteworthy, anymore, that Jesuit universities and colleges take an interest in constructive theology in Judaism. Experience in the two Missouri cities made me wish that even local rabbis—unanimously uninterested in a university lecture entitled "How, in Judaism, Do We Know God?"—asked themselves to address these same questions. But like ordinary Jews their Judaic interests are satisfied by sociology, politics, and history, all with special reference to the State of Israel and the Holocaust. If Judaism has been ethnicized, rabbis have led the ethnic cheerleading. But among them are those who seek God and find themselves called to the rabbinate in that quest and service, and still more common among ordinary Jews are those whose lives respond to God's search for them. And for those many who share my engagement with the Torah through which God's insistence comes to expression, I write this book.

A word of thanks to my editor at the University of Chicago Press, Alan Thomas, and to my faithful copyeditor, Lila Weinberg, is called for. This book owes its existence to him, and its form to her, almost as much as to William Green.

Translations of Rabbinic texts are my own. Most, though not all, quotations from the written Torah come from *Tanakh: A New Translation of the Holy Scriptures. According to the Traditional Hebrew Text* (Philadelphia: Jewish Publication Society, 1985), © 1985 by The Jewish Publication Society, and are reproduced by permission, for which I express thanks. My presentation of the Torah's mode of resolution of conflict in Chapters 3 and 4, Mishnah tractate Baba Mesia Chapter One in Chapter 3 and its corresponding Talmud in Chapter 4 is much revised from its original appearance in *The Talmud: Close Encounters* (Minneapolis: Fortress Press, 1991). The inspiration for the comparison of the way in which the written and the oral Torah make the same statement—deal with the same situation—comes from the opening chapter of Erich Auerbach's memorable *Mimesis,* though I certainly do not claim to approach his acuity. When I contemplate the shallow and truly unlearned writing that today serves as literary criticism's contribution to Talmud learning with what is to be learned from Auerbach, I gain perspective on what is enduring and what is ephemeral in scholarship. That in turn fosters in me renewed appreciation for the profound classicism of our sages of blessed memory.

No work of mine can omit an expression of gratitude for the exceptionally favorable circumstances in which I conduct my research as Distinguished Research Professor in the Florida State University System at the University of South Florida. I wrote this book as part of my labor of research scholarship, expressed through both publication and teaching at the University of South Florida, which has afforded me an ideal situation in which to conduct a scholarly life.

Jacob Neusner
Distinguished Research Professor of Religious Studies

University of South Florida
Tampa

Index